ARMS TO FIGHT
ARMS TO PROTECT

WOMEN SPEAK OUT ABOUT CONFLICT

Editors: Olivia Bennett, Jo Bexley, Kitty Warnock

Published by Panos Publications Ltd
9 White Lion Street
London N1 9PD, UK

British Library Cataloguing in Publication Data.
A catalogue record for this book is available from the British Library

Arms to Fight, Arms to Protect is published as part of Panos' women and conflict oral testimony project, which was funded by the Ministry of Foreign Affairs (Netherlands), Norwegian Church Aid, Norwegian People's Aid, Norwegian Red Cross, Oxfam (UK/I) and the United Nations Development Fund for Women (UNIFEM). Additional funding was provided by the Catholic Fund for Overseas Development (CAFOD), Christian Aid (UK), Oxfam Hong Kong and the Unitarian Universalist Service Committee (US). The project is part of Panos' wider Oral Testimony Programme, which receives funding from Novib, and which works with local communities to gather and disseminate oral testimonies on a range of development themes. For more information about the programme's aims and activities, contact Olivia Bennett.

Panos London is an independent information organisation working internationally for development that is socially, environmentally and economically sustainable. Panos also has offices in Paris and Washington DC. For more information about Panos, contact Juliet Heller.

Production and text design: Sally O'Leary
Cover illustration: Fiona Macintosh
Cover design: Sally O'Leary
Maps: Philip Davies
Picture research: Adrian Evans
Managing editor: Olivia Bennett
Printed in Great Britain by Arrowsmiths, Bristol

— CONTENTS —

Acknowledgements

This book is the result of wide collaboration, involving several hundred people throughout the world. We can't name everyone who helped in the early stages, discussing ideas, putting us in touch with potential partner organisations and so on, nor is it possible to mention all those who transcribed and translated hours of testimony, but we owe them all a great deal. Others provided invaluable comment and support for the country chapters, most notably Vanessa Vasic Janekovic (Croatia and Bosnia), Urvashi Butalia (India), María Candelaria Navas (El Salvador), Maria Holt (Lebanon), Veronica Campanile (Nicaragua), and Barbara Franklin, Tricia Parker and Corry Regnier (Vietnam). We are grateful to those who volunteered to help with the long task of getting all the testimonies typed onto computer disk: Lorna Guinness, Poonan Joshi, Sharron Mendel, Sally O'Leary, Bunny Page, Mercedes Paramio, Jacquie Webster and especially Catherine Sayers, who also did some research. Wendy Davies provided valuable additional editorial support; thanks also to Barbara Cheney, and to Heather Budge-Reid, Nigel Cross, Juliet Heller and Steve Percy for helpful comment.

Finally, none of this would have happened without the women who were willing to share their stories—it is to them that we owe the deepest thanks.

━ INTRODUCTION ━

OUR WARS, OUR WORDS

The women whose testimonies appear in this book bear witness to the experience of war in our time. Their first-hand accounts provide a perspective on warfare that no other information, however dramatic, can match. The reality is that nearly 50 years after the establishment of the United Nations (UN), with its mission to promote international peace and security, brutal conflicts between and within nations are more widespread than before and—as these women's stories vividly illustrate—it is civilians who now overwhelmingly bear the brunt of the terror and the violence.

In 1993, despite hopes that the end of the Cold War would bring more widespread peace, 42 countries were involved in 52 wars [1]. Most of these were civil wars, which is partly why the UN, whose original mandate referred only to wars between states, has been unable to fulfil its mission to prevent them.

Current estimates are that about 75% of those killed in war are civilians, a proportion which has risen steadily from around 10-15% at the beginning of the century [2]. The new "smart" weapons, designed to inflict minimum damage on non-military targets, are irrelevant to most wars. Even the most technologically sophisticated countries use weapons of indiscriminate destruction such as chemicals and mines, as well as tactics such as trade boycotts that operate almost entirely against civilians. The tendency is for war today to be conducted at close quarters—as the testimonies show, local people often get caught up in the fighting. In particular, in civil wars of insurgency and counter-insurgency, non-combatants are often, willingly and or not, involved in supporting fighters and then face retaliation from the opposing forces.

Moreover, increasing numbers of people are being driven out of their homes: in 1994, of the estimated 46 million refugees and internally displaced people scattered around the world, as many as 40 million may have fled conflict or its consequences. If the numbers of displaced and wounded are added to the estimated death figure, the total proportion of war casualties who are civilians may be as high as 90% [3]. Shocking though these figures are, it is hearing individuals describe what displacement, death and loss mean to them personally that really brings home the human cost of conflict.

"War is what happens afterwards"

War—especially civil war—brutalises society. It also destroys infrastructure, development prospects and families' ability to be economically productive. In the words of Marie from Lebanon (see page 267): "The real experience of war is not the shelling and so on, those are just moments, though they are the ones you see on TV. War is what happens afterwards, the years of suffering hopelessly with a disabled husband and no money, or struggling to rebuild when all your property has been destroyed." It is this most damaging aspect of war—the way the economic and social costs can last for generations—which comes across so powerfully through personal testimony, with its human detail and variety.

As the proportion of civilian casualties has risen, not only has women's suffering increased but so have their responsibilities. Women hold families and communities together, often playing a key role in food production and other economic activities, and caring for the children, the elderly and the sick. War distorts and disrupts these patterns and responsibilities, making them infinitely more difficult to fulfil, just when they are even more essential because of the breakdown of community structures. The pressures on women are even greater when they are forced to flee with their dependants: more than 80% of the displaced are women and children. Women are also vulnerable to rape and sexual exploitation which are common features, if not actual weapons, of war. This type of suffering can leave deep psychological wounds, which may remain hidden but can severely undermine the capacity of both women and their communities to recover.

And women are crucial to the recovery process of both their families and the wider community. Increasingly, aid and development organisations, faced with the fact that in more and more countries armed conflict is becoming the major threat to development, are seeking ways of alleviating the impact of war on women, so that they can emerge from trauma and loss, and help rebuild their societies.

The individual voice

Women have generally been under- or misrepresented in stories of war, and are most often seen as grief-stricken, powerless victims. And although development and relief agencies largely recognise the importance of women's active roles—economic and social—in helping communities survive conflict, there is still a tendency to categorise and generalise. "Women and children" are still often seen as one unit, for example. Such labels, if they are used to influence policy, can be limiting and even damaging. The term "refugees" conjures up an image of a featureless mass of people queuing to be fed, whereas time and again in the interviews Panos collected, women describe how the worst aspect of being a refugee is precisely the humiliation of losing one's identity and having all options for independent action curtailed.

Indeed, a primary motivation behind Panos' oral testimony project on women and conflict was to offset the tendency for generalisation. The aim was to contribute to the process of helping individual women speak for themselves, to gather anecdote and personal experience, to communicate perceptions as well as "facts", and so to complement more quantitative or academic studies. Thus Panos did not set out to analyse a particular aspect of women's experience, or advance a particular argument, but simply to record the individual voice. Above all, these testimonies reflect the great diversity of women's experiences and reactions: from deepened prejudice to hard-won understanding, from faith in the future to cynicism or despair, from a growing belief in one's abilities or powers of survival to a heightened sense of vulnerability and fear.

This selection makes no claim to be representative: it is a collection of personal stories from some 85 women. (Over 200 testimonies were gathered in total—for a more detailed description of the project, see page 24.) Of the conflicts in which they were involved, all but two (the communal conflicts in India) would be classified as wars, and the majority as civil wars, although in many cases there was a high level of foreign intervention. We did not seek to cover the full range of political allegiances; our aim was to cover as wide a range of personal experience as possible. The women interviewed are from varied backgrounds and experienced conflict in different ways. Some bore arms or actively participated through, for example, feeding or sheltering fighters; some supported or initiated peace actions; others were fully employed in ensuring their family's survival—at home, in hiding, or in camps. Most took on new organisational, economic or social responsibilities.

In the rest of this introduction, we have tried to pull together some common and contrasting threads in the testimonies. Many women are quoted, but the detail of their stories and the background to the conflicts in which they were involved are to be found in the chapters which follow—this overview is no substitute for reading the women's words.

OVERVIEW

Women's participation

Women's identification with and participation in war, and ability to deal with its consequences, are much influenced by the nature of the conflict. In Uganda, the women interviewed regarded the war as a senseless battle for power between men, motivated primarily by greed. They described those who caused the war as "power hungry", wishing only "to get rich by force". Women found themselves caught in the middle—looted, abducted and raped by soldiers of both sides—so that it felt as though "instead of fighting each other, [the soldiers] turned to fighting members of the community" (Culina).

In contrast, the Tigrayan women interviewed, who all participated in the struggle against the Ethiopian government, saw themselves as fighting for political justice and social progress—including equality for themselves. Moreover, they were victorious, and felt pride in their suffering and their achievements. Psychologically, they appeared to be stronger post-war than those, like the Ugandan women, who had survived a war which they viewed as pointless butchery.

Between those two extremes there are many variants. In El Salvador, many women actively supported the struggle for social and political justice and some took up arms, although within the guerrilla movement there was no clear political commitment to social progress for women. In Nicaragua, the experience of being part of a revolutionary movement left some women with a stronger sense of their own rights. "It was a wonderful fight, because those who fought and died did not die in vain, they taught us how to fight for our rights," claimed María. Others, such as the women of Somaliland, identified with the war as a justified struggle against oppression, and participated in a number of non-violent ways. The subsequent descent into more fragmented rivalries, however, is now making their sacrifices much harder to bear.

Where conflict is primarily along ethnic or religious lines, women are likely to identify with one particular side, but not necessarily to play an active role. Of course, ethnic or religious difference does not inevitably entail conflict—Muslims and Hindus in India, Tamils and Sinhalese in Sri Lanka, for example, all spoke of having lived in harmony together in the past—but escalating tension and open conflict quickly force people to declare allegiances.

For many of the women this was a deeply painful decision.

Those who belonged to two sides through intermarriage faced family splits and divided loyalties, and sometimes had to suppress part of their identity to protect children or husband. In other cases, women were reluctant to subscribe to the idea of ethnic or community identity as paramount because they held a broader view of personal identity. "Joseph and I are Catholic but we gave our children Arab names which do not show their religious identity," explained Laure (Lebanon). Many women, looking back, expressed concern that in accepting an ethnic or community identity, whether voluntarily or under pressure, they had contributed to the polarisation of their society.

Communities which have sustained a harmonious multi-ethnic existence are particularly traumatised by its disintegration and by the experience of neighbours, friends and relatives turning on each other. The closer the bonds which have been betrayed, the harder they are to rebuild. "My friends were shooting at me, at us. Do you know the feeling when your very soul hurts?" asked a Bosnian refugee. "A lot of them were my very good friends, people with whom I have shared both sadness and happiness. I lost them for ever, in the most unacceptable way...."

Joining in

Even when the women interviewed strongly identified with a community or a cause, the majority participated in conflict only when their families or homes were threatened or attacked—which may be a frequent occurrence, as the stories from Uganda show.

Women were sometimes excluded from a more active role because they were fully occupied with family responsibilities, or were expected to be so. For those who wished to contribute more, their scope for action was often defined by the roles with which they had been invested by society. During the communal riots prompted by the 1947 Partition of India, Sikh, Hindu and Muslim women clearly identified with their own communities. Representing the honour and purity of their religion, they were targets of attack by the hostile communities, and used as symbols by their own. As the testimonies show, this role was seen as more important than their individual survival and many were encouraged to take their own lives rather than suffer abduction, rape or conversion. This is an extreme example of constraints on women's active participation, one where the only act of resistance available was to turn their capacity for violent action in on themselves and commit suicide.

Women had far greater scope for action in the Tigrayan rebel movement, which encouraged, or at least allowed, them to become combatants alongside men, thus demonstrating the equality the movement professed. More often, especially in insurgency movements, women are encouraged to participate because their labour, skills and relative ability to move around unnoticed, are needed. Their roles are usually to provide support and care for male combatants and victims, but also to work as couriers and in intelligence. As Xot, a supporter of the Vietcong, put it: "There was one thing about being a woman which favoured her participation in the struggle: it was easier to get close to the enemy.... The enemy looked down on us but we infiltrated their ranks more easily than the men."

These tasks can involve as much physical courage and endurance as actual fighting, but do not overtly challenge gender stereotypes. When support includes building roads and laying mines, there is no clear line separating support from combat—but there is still an ambivalence, felt by most women as well as men, about women using violence in cold blood, or inflicting brutality. As other studies have shown, even when male-dominated fighting forces accept women as fighters, they rarely give them equal responsibility for inflicting actual physical damage on the enemy [4]. And judging from Panos' interviews, few women demand this ultimate equality.

Women as supporters and perpetrators of violence

Many of the women interviewed spoke with pride of having encouraged or incited men to acts of violence, but Kokila, a Sri Lankan Tamil, is relatively unusual in her proud acceptance of the value for women of violent action: "[Participating in the struggle] is the need of the time. Instead of dying screaming, being raped by an aggressor army, it is a relief to face the army with [your own] weapon." Women speak about bearing arms in a number of testimonies but only a few, most notably in Lebanon and Vietnam, also describe being involved in killing.

It was striking how often people claimed women combatants were more brutal than their male counterparts. This could have been due to a certain self-selection by the women who took up arms. It could be more perception than fact, stemming from a feeling that it is "unnatural" for women to use violence. In Liberia, it was said that women combatants are unwilling to talk about their experiences, except among fellow combatants, because of the feeling of shame. Agnes, a young Liberian whose own war experiences have left her deeply cynical and distrustful, said, "If I

was one of [the combatants], I would definitely be ashamed. A woman is supposed to be somebody [with a] soft spot... to be able to analyse, to love and care for little ones.... But they were very harsh and aggressive, even towards babies and children."

Clearly, no conclusions can be drawn from our testimonies, but the indications are that it is a small number of women who join men in using violence. The extent to which this is because society does not encourage them to do so, or because they have internalised a taboo, or because they are "by nature" less likely to join in premeditated brutality is unclear. "I never believe anyone who says 'I could never kill anyone'. There are times when I would have shot people if I had had a gun... I don't think women are any different from men in that way," was the view of one Lebanese interviewee (Marie).

Sexual violence and exploitation
Sexual violence and rape has always been a feature of war. Violence against women, for example, may take a specifically sexual form; a number of the women had witnessed women's breasts being cut off and the disembowelling of pregnant women. But there is now a clearer recognition that sexual violence can be an actual weapon, rather than expression, of war.

Tamil Tiger, Sri Lanka
Martin Adler/Panos Pictures

The threat and the act of rape is often used as a weapon against community identity, especially where ethnic or religious purity is at stake. Defiling women is a way of violating and demoralising men—rape is often performed in full view of family and community. In this sense it is an attack on everyone, although it is the women who suffer physically, and bear the burden of shame and social ostracism. The use of rape as a weapon of war in Bosnia has drawn the attention of the West because of its scale and organisation, all of which has strengthened the argument that rape should be regarded as a war crime. For some, well aware that rape has been similarly used in other, non-European conflicts, this recognition is somewhat belated.

More often rape is part of the general violence and suspension of normal behaviour during conflict, sometimes even seen as one of "the spoils of war". Refugee women, often living without male relatives or partners, in make-shift homes, are particularly vulnerable to rape or sexual exploitation—sometimes by the very people supposed to protect them, such as guards or police.

A different kind of sexual violence—licensed by military leaders, if not deliberately planned—is the abduction of women to supply sexual services to fighters. This was commonly practised by the rebels in northern Uganda where, since the 1980s, the spread of HIV/AIDS has added a further terrible dimension to the consequences of forced sex. Indeed, war and instability has been identified as one of the factors in the spread of AIDS, because even if forced sex is not an issue (and it often is), there is almost always disruption to family and social life, and increased movement of populations [5].

There are many other ways in which conflict distorts normal sexual relations and increases the possibilities of men sexually abusing or exploiting women. In a war-torn society, becoming a prostitute or a camp follower may be a woman's best economic option to support herself or her family. Some have no choice but to live by servicing soldiers: more than one interviewee had been rejected by her community after suffering rape.

A variant on this distortion of relationships is illustrated by the story of the young Liberian woman who has struck a bargain with a soldier of the (non-Liberian) peacekeeping forces (ECOMOG). Like most of her contemporaries, Agnes' relationships are now based entirely on economics. "We just believe in the barter system that started during the war. You get the pleasure of my body, I get the pleasure of your pocket." Her actions reflect the distorted post-conflict national economy, in which the pay packets of the ECOMOG soldiers are almost the only source of income. Liberian men—without employment or cash—are ignored, and while they see the economic rationale, are both jealous and humiliated. As Agnes points out, most deal with it by adopting a double standard: "[Liberian men] consider us prostitutes. They were helpless, they were like babies, they were not able to cater for their families any more. A wife had to sacrifice herself... to save the family. Yet the men are not grateful—they say the Liberian women will do anything for money." Such hostility and resentment between the sexes will take a long time to heal.

Rejection or devaluation by their families and wider community is one of the most far-reaching consequences for women of sexual abuse or exploitation. Even where the community acknowledges that they were victims of war and feels pity, they can be seen ever afterwards as "damaged goods". Nirmal, talking about the fate of women who were abducted and raped in the course of India's Partition, recounted how "even when they were united with their own families, brothers and fathers weren't prepared to take them back". The women were no longer seen as deserving respect. "[People] pitied these women, showed them kindness, but they thought of them as orphans, as deserted children... as if something had gone wrong with them."

Deeply traumatic are the cases where women have become pregnant by their violators and either cannot face bringing up the child, or are forced by family or community to abort or give away the child. "I will never accept that baby. If we had to live together, he would be an eternal, living witness in front of my eyes and a reminder of what I had to live through," explained Vesna, a Bosnian Croat who was raped for months by a Bosnian Serb.

The status of women

Breaking the mould

In some cases, changes in women's status are part of an agenda for social change which is being fought for, as was the case in Tigray. The determination of the Tigrayan People's Liberation Front to allow women to participate in the struggle as equals was underlined by an initial ban on sexual relations between fighters. This was later softened to allow relationships, marriage and children. "The no-marriage law had a positive role: between men and women there was talk, not sexual activity. A man would look at a woman in relation to her job, not in relation to whom she goes with," explained Mebrat. Mobilisation of non-combatant women and a programme of education and empowerment were carried on throughout the struggle, but it remains to be seen how effectively these changes in women's status will be extended into the peacetime development of Ethiopia.

In El Salvador, it seems that strict sexual discipline was adopted among liberation fighters more as a means to achieving a disciplined fighting force than as part of a commitment to a change in women's status. Once the imperative of the struggle was relaxed, the old *machista* values have tended to return. Women have regrouped as a political force to fight for their rights, although widespread economic hardship constricts their possibilities.

Consolidating the gains?

More usually, changes in the roles of women are largely unplanned, and occur as a result of the social and economic disruption, or because their work is needed by the war effort. One of the almost universal experiences of war for women is the taking on of new responsibilities—most notably economic provision for their families, but also new forms of management, decisionmaking, and administrative tasks, such as dealing with officialdom and governments.

Countless women spoke of discovering new skills, capabilities and confidence in wartime. These interviews show some of the efforts that they are making to consolidate these gains in post-war societies. Many recognise that they face another battle against entrenched attitudes and powerful pressures—social and economic —forcing them back into the domestic sphere.

In northern Uganda, where many formal employment opportunities for men have been lost—as a result both of the war and of post-war structural adjustment policies—women have risen to the challenge of earning and caring for their families single-handed. Indeed, they tend to see men as useless and irresponsible, a feeling reinforced by the years of casual brutality during the war. "Experience shows", says Rose, "most men have become hopeless while the women are very responsible and supportive to their families." But this domestic economic reality is not yet reflected in changed social and cultural attitudes: women still achieve recognised status through marriage, and single women are not respected. In this sense, these women have the worst of both worlds: responsibility without status. Whether the current government's commitment to promoting women will translate into changed attitudes remains to be seen.

In Lebanon before the war, it was considered that "the women's place is in the home only... the narrow society in which they live considers that work is shameful for a woman" (Wadad). Yet during the war, many women demonstrated their abilities to work and support families. While this did change some attitudes, it has yet to be reflected more widely—for example, by acceptance of women as political actors.

Society often works hard to keep women's expectations low. A number of Sri Lankan women—despite having shouldered the burdens of war as effectively as women elsewhere—seemed hesitant to equate this with personal abilities: "We have survived—God was good to me" was a typical comment. Many experienced a sense of isolation and remarked on the way that suspicion and gossip about women who are alone severely hampered their ability to operate independently in their communities.

The widows of Sikhs killed during the communal conflict in India following Indira Gandhi's assassination in 1984, received compensation and in many cases also took up jobs. Their economic status was transformed: women who had rarely ventured outside the home became bread-winners, and had control of a lump sum of money. But sons and in-laws, used to regarding widows' property as their own and widows as powerless dependants, could not accept this new reality and the intra-family conflicts could last for years. The local religious authorities also often viewed the widows' independence with suspicion. Again, gossip and the threat of a damaged reputation was a powerful way of constraining these women's ambitions.

Definitions and duties

Daughter, wife, mother, widow

The extent to which women are defined not as individuals, but in terms of their duties and relationships within the family (particularly towards male members) is another powerful influence on behaviour, and one which had tragic consequences for another Sikh widow. Unusually, since the rioters did not target children, her young sons were also killed in the 1984 Indian riots. Her own feeling of grief was reinforced by society's view of her as a woman who had "failed" in her primary duty to care for and protect her sons. Her sense of guilt, which her in-laws and neighbours explicitly fuelled, eventually destroyed her ability to come to terms with her loss and she committed suicide.

But forms of cultural and social observance can also be helpful, particularly in coping with death. Many women mentioned the importance of carrying out the prescribed rituals for the dead, and having the opportunity to express their grief. In circumstances where it is impossible to mourn publicly, it can be much harder to accept death. "In our culture it is common for widows to wear special clothing. But... the government committees were waiting to see if we dared mourn his death in our home. I could not do anything... for fear of being arrested. I could not mourn in the normal way," regretted Khadra (Somaliland). This is one of the reasons why it is so distressing when someone has "disappeared", but has not been declared dead—grief is compounded by uncertainty and the inability to go through the appropriate rituals. "We used to reach a point where we just wanted to know. Even if there are only remains, we want the bones, something tangible." (Wadad, Lebanon)

Even the social convention that women "need protection", while often being a means of restricting women's activities, can have its advantages. Laure, a Lebanese, describes how her status allowed her to say and do things which a man could not: "There is still in this oriental society a concept of honour, which protects women a little. I and my husband were kidnapped twice... we thought our end was approaching... but I could say to a militia man, 'I am from Beirut, Beirut is for both of us, I am your sister, your mother...' It was because I was a woman that I could have this discussion. I am sure a man would not have been able to. He couldn't touch me or push me." Several interviewees also mentioned that their society's "code of honour" meant few Lebanese women were raped. No such protection, however, was given to the many Sri Lankan domestic servants in Beirut.

Family responsibilities

Often women suppress their feelings of fear or grief because of the need to support or protect their children. While this can help women through particularly stressful times, it may also mean that they deny themselves the opportunity to deal with the psychological wounds of war: "I had made a decision not to be frightened—and I don't know what that cost me psychologically. I am still paying for it probably." (Marie, Lebanon)

Competing demands can force women to make painful decisions: the family may need her support and attention, while she feels impelled by events to be active outside the home—demonstrating for peace, participating in the struggle, organising welfare services and so on. Many women find enormous reserves of emotional and physical energy to fulfil both roles; sometimes they have instead to sacrifice one or the other, and cope with some form of guilt.

A number of Vietnamese interviewees described making agonising decisions: "There were two different thoughts in my mind.... One was love for my children. They were the dearest things I had and it was very hard to leave them.... The other thought was the desire to participate in the revolution. After a lot of consideration I decided to put aside my [family] feelings.... Nowadays, when I think about that period, I feel sorry for them.... They didn't have the love of their mother or father.... It's really painful to think of them." (Lanh)

Time and again the interviewees said their primary duty was to care for their family, which often demanded enormous skill and ingenuity. On the positive side this means that women always have a clear role: "In some ways war is easier for women. Whatever the situation, even in shelters, they are busy, looking after the children, managing the house. Men, meanwhile, have lost their role, if they cannot go out to work," commented Marie (Lebanon).

Many women said it was only the children who kept them going. One Bosnian refugee said of her son: "Without his support, I don't know if I would be alive today. He is the meaning of my life, the only bright spot in it. I have to fight for his happiness in the future."

In these situations men, whose peacetime role outside the home may have been rendered totally impossible by war, are much more adrift. This is one explanation for the common observation that women cope better than men with life in refugee camps.

Life as a refugee
Many testimonies contained descriptions of being on the run for weeks and months, hiding from attacks, desperately short of food and rest, before finding some form of safety. When a family is displaced within their own country, this may intensify the difficulty of finding food and shelter—the Ugandan women describe hiding for years in the forests around their homes, and Salvadorans spoke vividly of perpetual movement as the only means of surviving enemy attack.

But even life in the bush can seem preferable to joining a refugee camp. Loss of individuality and control over their existence, and the humiliation of dependency, is a thread that runs through almost every account of life as a refugee. Mita, talking of her own experience in India as a relief worker, mentioned her unease at the tendency to treat refugees like children who will only be rewarded for good behaviour. "You know, it is like [relief workers are] saying, 'If you are good deserving poor—then we will help, otherwise we won't'."

Over 80% of the displaced are women and their dependants

Sarah Errington/Panos Pictures

Of the women forced to leave their countries, many said that nothing could prepare them for the shock of their new status. One Bosnian woman, a professor of chemistry, describes how the reality of her position suddenly hit her: "We received an official document for refugees. They explained to us our status, rights and how to get help. That's the moment when I became aware of my loss. I lost my homeland and my personality."

As well as dealing with the problems of overcrowding, shortages of food and health facilities, and tensions with the host community, refugees in camps often experience intense boredom. "Most nights we are woken from sleep because of the noise; in the morning we face a blank world," said Felicia (Sri Lanka). Looking after children in these circumstances can be particularly hard, especially when displacement means relocation in another, possibly hostile, culture. "Our children, just for being Nicaraguan, were marginalised. They were mistreated in the schools. They told the little girl that 'the Nica' shouldn't open her mouth." (Nicaraguan refugee in Costa Rica)

Where attempts were made to provide education and training for women, as for the Salvadoran refugees, camp life had its positive aspects. Similarly, in Liberian refugee camps in Nigeria, women not only appreciated that their children were being better educated than those left behind in war-torn Liberia, but also spoke of how they themselves had learned by exposure to other ways of life. They spoke admiringly of the entrepreneurial spirit of Nigerian and Ghanaian women, vowing to emulate them instead of returning to their previously passive domestic existence. The experience also prompted them to question their previous identification with America, rather than other West African countries.

For most refugees, going home—even when they know devastation awaits them—remains a driving force; but for some the events which forced them to flee were so terrible that going home is not an option. Vesna, a victim of ethnic cleansing, said: "I can't ever imagine going back [to Bosnia]. I want to be far away from the place where I suffered."

Coping with the aftermath

The collapse of the formal economy is an almost inevitable companion to war. Producing food from the land may still be possible: the women in northern Uganda, for instance, carved new food plots out of the bush and sometimes were able to visit their own farms to harvest. Those women who found themselves living away from their land, or unable to take up their previous jobs, often survived by petty trading. Even women who had never done such work before seemed adaptable and prepared to take up tiny opportunities, often more so than men. "The men want substantial work, not all these little chances that the women are willing to put up with," commented Amina (Somaliland).

Compensation

In contrast, women are often disadvantaged when it comes to claiming compensation and other forms of support. Land titles, for example, are often given to men as recognised "heads of household". Carmen from El Salvador contested this: "I said you must include me, because he might be here today but not tomorrow, and I'll always be here with the children." Moreover, gaining access to the compensation often requires knowledge of rights and entitlements—which many testimonies suggest women lack. Often they have no experience of dealing with bureaucracy, or have to look after children, which makes time-consuming visits to offices, standing in queues and so on, all but impossible.

Women also spoke of their distress at their powerlessness, their frustration at not being unable to get what was due to them. Some women's groups in Sri Lanka, recognising this, made it a priority to inform women of their rights and facilitate their access to compensation and support.

Education

A consistent concern among the women interviewed was the effect on their children of disrupted schooling, and of growing up witnessing brutality and the breakdown of social and moral structures. In an impoverished post-war society, it can be even harder to find school fees, but education was almost always seen as essential—the passport to a better future.

Many women also expressed the need for "education for peace"—learning how to deal with conflict without resorting to violence, and how to live with neighbours of different religions or ethnic groups, as well as, importantly, learning the history of the conflict itself. "For the coming generations it is important they understand what we've been through, so that they don't repeat what has taken place.... If we forget history, we forget everything," said Esmeralda (El Salvador).

Responsibility and reconciliation

Many women perceived conflict as something entirely outside their control, a struggle for power at a level beyond their reach. But they recognised the effort that has to be made by every individual to rebuild society after conflict: how do you accept a son or daughter who may have tortured or killed? How do you deal with going back to your village when your neighbour fought on the side that killed your husband or raped your daughter? "I almost didn't want to talk to [the mothers of the other side] because at times you feel afraid or remember your sons. I sometimes thought it could be this woman's son who killed my boy and I'd feel bad." (Rosaura, Nicaragua)

A significant number said they could never forgive. Eva, a Bosnian refugee, admitted: "I don't know how to forget. I simply cannot forgive and forget." For them, some other way of building the future has to found.

For others still, forgiveness would only be possible when they felt justice had been done. "Those who killed our people, they too should suffer; our hearts will be at rest when there has been some justice, some revenge." (Shanti, India)

Other women said revenge and punishment would only perpetuate the cycle of violence, but felt that the solution did not lie in simply ignoring what had happened. "Our children must learn so they can benefit. Human nature is forgetful. I will tell my son what happened. We will live with [Christians] but the new generation should know what happened, so that it doesn't happen again. They had planned to kick us out of our homes and we will not forget." (Ahlam, Lebanon)

The view that an understanding—personal and public—of the causes of conflict, and an acknowledgement of responsibility, are essential to the rebuilding of society came out particularly clearly in the testimonies from Lebanon. Women expressed a strong sense of the futility of a conflict which produced no victors and no gains. Responsibility for the conflict—and therefore for rebuilding society—is seen to lie not just with political leaders and combatants, but also with all those individuals who allowed themselves to be pushed into supporting one group or another, and thus fuelled the conditions for national disintegration.

Some women spoke at length of their belief that individuals cannot be expected to overcome inter-sectarian suspicion and personal grief unless politicians take the lead in acknowledging the wounds inflicted and re-establishing standards of humanity and justice in national life. And when governments or political parties deliberately suppress parts of the truth and rewrite history this can create profound difficulties for individuals, especially in dealing with grief and anger. Personal loss is much more difficult to deal with when your government does not even acknowledge your experience.

Depression and disillusion

It is recognised that demobilisation can bring ex-combatants a period of depression and purposelessness, often made worse by having to rebuild lives in a shattered economy. It is less often acknowledged that for non-combatants there may be a similarly difficult transition. Here Marie talks about Lebanon's civil war: "Sometimes it was very exciting, to tell you the truth. Living through the shelling and surviving, not being killed, living with life and death—you had a great rush of adrenalin. I think you collapse with exhaustion after the excitement... I was depressed for nine months after the war ended."

Disillusionment with the outcome of the war, even when it was an apparent victory, can make peacetime even more difficult. Sabaah of Somaliland described how she fears that her husband's death may have been in vain. "Some people want us to rejoin Somalia.... We told ourselves that if Somaliland came into being, that would help us to accept the loss [of our men]. [To rejoin Somalia]—for us this is a second death."

A different kind of depression, but one which is gender-specific, is that suffered by women whose chances of marriage and motherhood have been destroyed by war. In some cases this was because of rape and subsequent social rejection, but often it was because the women were seen as too old by the end of hostilities and the return to normal life. Men had no such problems. This was often mentioned in the Vietnamese testimonies, where women also spoke of the difficulties for women who had been disabled and were in need of care. Thom, now in her 40s, was badly wounded in the Vietnam war. She expressed her sorrow at how the war had deprived her "of hope—the hope of having a family.... Men who are wounded like me are still able to marry, and when they get ill their wives and children can help. I am still single."

Psychological wounds

On a personal level, a prerequisite for achieving forgiveness and reconciliation is to find ways of dealing with the trauma inflicted by conflict. One interviewee in particular (Mita, India) reflects at length on rehabilitation work and the real difficulties of understanding the wide variety of individual responses, not least because of class and cultural gaps between relief workers and refugees.

The sudden appearance of psychiatrists in refugee camps can be undermining and even threatening to people's own coping mechanisms. As a woman displaced from Vukovar, Croatia, commented, "It hurts that no one comes to the camp for a year, and then they come to look at our psychological problems and symptoms. We have lost everything, but not our dignity. We are not crazy." While for many women sharing their experiences with others was in itself part of a healing process, this view was by no means universal. Others clearly felt that recollection only deepened the wounds.

Although post-conflict psychological support is now generally recognised as important, it has tended to be dominated by Western concepts, which are not always appropriate. A doctor in Mozambique described a traditional method of healing for families and communities: "As soon as a *madjiba* (soldier) arrives in a village, he is received by the elders—who do not let him contact his family because he is full of innocent souls who he killed and who are protesting. They take him to a place of worship near a river or well. Here they call the ancestors, seeking their assistance... so that the spirits of people he killed may not persecute him. They bathe him, and his clothes and belongings are treated with medication to free him of spirits. The ceremony is not so much for the benefit of the young man as for the benefit of the community [but] it frees the individual who feels accepted and re-integrated [6]."

Relief and rehabilitation

A number of women spoke of the role of NGOs in rehabilitation. Zamzam of Somaliland was particularly critical of their tendency to impose their own agendas and development models. She also felt they were too quick to make assumptions, prejudging which members of society to consult, for example, and thus reinforcing unhelpful social structures. "The agencies for the most part, they didn't listen. They look at what they have been told is the 'culture'. Their conclusion is 'In this country you must listen to the men'. They go for two men who have been pointed out to them as elders, bypassing a hundred needy women on the way. These men they consult are unaware and indifferent to the needs of women."

In Uganda, however, it was a different picture. Women said their task of supporting their families had been greatly assisted by an international NGO's methods of promoting shared learning and economic activities. "Women have found strength in working in groups. Now we are carrying [out] many collective activities, digging, different ways of generating income and [having] constant discussion and meetings among ourselves," explained Olga. And in many countries, women mentioned the social and emotional as well as practical value of working collectively.

Women in South Sudan tend their crops during a lull in the fighting
Betty Press/Panos Pictures

Actions for peace

It is sometimes assumed that women have an innate tendency to be peace-makers, and that if women had more political power, fewer wars would be fought. But as Laure, a founder of Lebanon's Movement for Non-Violence, pointed out, "[women] were not among those who decided on the war. If they had been in the centres of power, what would they have decided? One mustn't make optimistic assumptions."

The fact that women are so often the ones putting life back together, during and after conflict, perhaps gives them a greater appreciation of the real consequences. The testimonies contain many vivid descriptions of women reconstructing homes, caring for the wounded and disabled, coping with traumatised children, finding a livelihood, and sometimes literally picking up the pieces: "They'd thrown the grenades and ran away, the local authorities ran away. There were just women collecting the wounded and the dead." (Ban, Vietnam)

At the same time, there is little doubt that it is harder for many men to adopt the caring and nurturing roles which society expects of women. Men are more vulnerable to psychological pressures—often exerted by women—to fight. Even those who feel uneasy about active participation may find it hard to escape conscription or mobilisation; some mothers spoke of sending their sons away to avoid this danger.

The women's stories also show that where the conflict is seen as a struggle for some perceived justice or liberation involving the mass of society, or as a legitimate defence of home and community, women tend to be just as much in favour of the war as men—or at least to feel that peace is not an option. "We were in our homes and we were attacked. Where is there any room to avoid war? There was no room, no choice, we did not choose war, war came to us," commented Ahlam (Lebanon).

On the other hand, those women who saw war as a struggle between men over things to which they do not in any case have access (political power or economic resources), were rarely supporters of the conflict. But in these cases, neither did they feel they had much influence to bring about peace. They are likely instead to feel a sort of world-weary cynicism about men's greed for power: "Power is a prostitute. Power cannot stay in one place, it's something that is supposed to circulate. So if one person wants to hang on to it, definitely there will be problems." (Shirley, Liberia)

Women became activists for peace where they could see an alternative way of resolving the issues being fought over, or where

they felt that an impasse had been reached and that violence could achieve nothing more. One Nicaraguan described her concern that "Nicaraguan society had reached a point where we believed everything could be solved solely through arms." She and other women followed their own conviction that reconciliation must begin at home and worked "to convince the man of the house... the son, the uncle, the cousin, that [war] was not the solution."

Yet it cannot be assumed that women are by nature more likely to work for non-violence or peace than men. In these testimonies, where the participants of such initiatives are mainly women, this is sometimes for a variety of cultural and practical reasons, including the fact that it could be dangerous for men to move around the streets for fear of being targeted by the opposition. It was not necessarily the case that fewer men subscribed to the same views.

Talking about a movement for peace in Lebanon, Laure, an activist, observed that "it was very largely women... perhaps because women were more able to move about, they dared give their opinion. We were less watched perhaps, but in this particular case we certainly showed more courage."

WOMEN'S POWER

From the jigsaw of individual stories, one important general picture does emerge. Despite powerful words of grief and disillusionment, and harrowing tales of brutality and betrayal, the dominant impression given by the women is one of great resilience and self-reliance. Although they were victims of war in many ways, the women were not helpless, but active and resourceful, calling on reserves of strength and ingenuity to support and protect their families and resist despair.

Where they do present themselves as helpless, there is usually an external reason for this: cultural norms which have taught them to view themselves as weak, or to blame; social rules that limit their ability to act; or situations such as refugee camps where the very real lack of scope is often exacerbated by being treated as passive "recipients".

In the aftermath of war, too, women's potential for positive activity seems limited more by social convention and the grinding necessities of daily survival than by any lack of will or ideas. Yet it is at these times, when all creativity and commitment are needed for the task of rebuilding and recovery, that the benefits to the whole community of empowering women should be particularly clear.

Development or community organisations working in war-torn areas need to recognise that people will be affected by war in all sorts of hidden or unquantifiable ways—traditional relationships of trust and support may have irretrievably broken down, for example, between different groups or generations. As Zamzam of Somaliland pointed out, NGOs have to learn to listen. Gathering oral testimony is one way of gaining insight into the experiences women have had, experiences which will affect their current perceptions and future priorities.

Psychological support and understanding for women who have suffered the trauma of war—and particularly experiences such as rape which may lead to them being devalued in their own culture—could enable them to regain confidence and self-respect, without which they can hardly carry on their normal lives or support others. Where women have become the family breadwinner, empowering them could mean giving them training, tools, capital and credit. It might also include working with communities to break down prejudice against women alone and gain greater acceptance for those women now operating outside their traditional economic and social roles. These are the needs most often and articulately voiced, and one area in which many development agencies and women's organisations are seeing a role for themselves.

At the community level, women speak of wishing to participate in the formal and informal organisations that can help heal and rebuild society. Empowering them could mean easing the burden of their domestic tasks so that they have more time available, as well as strengthening the social fora through which they can act. And finally, enabling women to participate in political decisionmaking at every level including national—an experiment which has not been tried in most countries—would meet a well articulated need, and test the extent to which it is true that women are less likely to wage war than men.

1. Using the definition of war as open armed conflict between organised military forces, at least one of which is a government's, causing at least 25 deaths per year. See Smith, D, *War, Peace and Third World Development*, Occasional Paper 16, Human Development Report Office, UNDP, New York, 1994.
2. Figures quoted in Smith, D, *War, Peace and Third World Development*, op.cit.
3. Ibid.
4. Smith, D, "Women, War and Peace", briefing paper for Human Development Report Office, UNDP (read in manuscript, 1995). For further reading and useful bibliographies, see Vickers, J, *Women and War*, Zed, London, 1993; El Bushra, J and Piza Lopez, E, "Development in conflict: the gender dimension", workshop report, Oxfam UK/I-ACORD, 1993: and Walker, B (ed), "Women and Emergencies", *Focus on Gender*, Vol 2, No 1, Oxfam UK/I, Oxford, February 1994.
5. See *The Hidden Cost of Aids: The challenge of HIV to development*, Panos, London, 1992, p13.
6. Panos had to abandon testimony collection in Mozambique; pressure of work forced our partners to cancel at too late a stage to set up another project.

THE PROJECT

Altogether, the "women and conflict" project gathered over 200 testimonies, in 12 countries and as many languages. Usually we worked with an existing women's group; sometimes the local coordinator put together a group of interviewers representing different organisations and interests; more rarely we worked with one or two individuals.

We sought partners interested not only in the information, but also in gaining from the process of collection. Few interviewers had prior experience of gathering testimony, but were chosen for their relationship to the women they would interview—they were usually from the same area, spoke the same language and had had similar experiences. This meant they were able to identify the areas of concern and interest. In most cases we ran a workshop, primarily discussing and developing the themes on which the women would wish to focus, but also exploring the techniques and value of oral testimony collection [1]. This training included collecting, transcribing and analysing practice interviews.

Interviews were recorded on tape, transcribed word for word in the language of the interview, and then translated into English. The process was not trouble-free. The interviewing required considerable skill (and personal qualities): interviewers were not working from a questionnaire, and the emphasis was on flexibility and open-ended questions, so that the interviewee could follow her own train of thought. However, collectors could not adopt a completely random approach either, since they did have certain themes they wished to explore. And of course the subject matter involved memories and experiences which were extremely painful. Our emphasis, however, was less on cataloguing events (as a human rights project might), more on documenting women's perceptions and understanding of their experiences. In some cases, a longer training period would have helped the interviewers. Moreover, and not surprisingly, it was easier to do this kind of testimony collection in some cultures than others.

Practical difficulties included the fact that transcribing is time-consuming and tiring work—all those who did this cannot be thanked enough. For some women, simply getting time to do the interviews was difficult; for others, shortage of batteries and typewriters, or stolen tape recorders all added to the burden. In many cases, projects took 18 months to come to fruition. Testimonies were collected in El Salvador, Sri Lanka, Uganda and Tigray in 1993; the remainder during 1994. Translation proved as fraught with problems as we anticipated; the standard was variable. All these factors mean that the quality and character of the testimonies vary, and that the English translations often fail to reflect the rich language of the originals.

Moreover, the testimonies in this book are a small proportion of the whole collection. Extracts were chosen on the basis of their individual interest, and in order to best illustrate the range of themes and experiences. Panos has the original full-length testimonies in translation (and the Central American collections also in Spanish), each one summarised and indexed. Those selected for the book, however, sometimes had to be substantially cut; their length varied enormously but many testimonies were over 10,000 words. Yet the more times one read the women's words, the more difficult it became to leave some out—we are well aware this selection does insufficient justice to the articulate and powerful originals or to the full range of individual stories.

The testimonies in the book have also been lightly edited, mainly to remove repetition or confusion (and the questions). Square brackets indicate inserted or "relocated" text for clarification; round brackets are translations/interpretations; and three dots indicate speech patterns rather than gaps in text—many transcribers used these to indicate where people tailed off, left sentences incomplete, or jumped from one phrase to another. References which are glossed (see page 274) are in bold the first time they appear in each testimony. The numbering of the testimonies (eg SOM 1; SRI 18) relates to the overall collection, hence the inconsistencies and "gaps" in the book. All interviewers are acknowledged, not just those whose interviews are reproduced here.

It is not Panos' intention that work with the testimonies stops with this publication. The local groups or coordinators kept the recording equipment, tapes and transcriptions. Their ideas for "feeding back" the experience and the collected information into their communities include local publication in the original language of the collection; using the testimonies as the foundation for a bigger documentation project; using the transcripts in radio programmes; and taking them as the basis for discussion in women's literacy and awareness-raising activities, as well as in conflict resolution work, in some cases between refugees and host communities.

1. For more on the ideas and practice of using oral testimony in development, see Slim, H and Thompson, P, *Listening for a Change: oral testimony and development*, Panos, London, 1993.

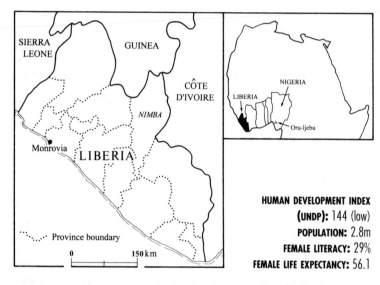

**HUMAN DEVELOPMENT INDEX
(UNDP):** 144 (low)
POPULATION: 2.8m
FEMALE LITERACY: 29%
FEMALE LIFE EXPECTANCY: 56.1

1800 Slave revolt in America **1821-2** Foundation of Liberia by freed slaves from America **1847** Independence **1847-1980** First Republic; oppressive rule of native Africans by Americo-Liberians **1904** Citizenship granted to native African Liberians **1944-71** Development under President Tubman **1980** President Tolbert overthrown by Samuel Doe **1985** Unsuccessful coup against Doe, brutally punished **1988** Second unsuccessful coup **1989** Charles Taylor's NPFL invade; civil war begins **1990** Deployment of West African peacekeeping forces (ECOMOG) **1991** Taylor's forces join with Sierra Leonian rebels to invade Sierra Leone, starting civil war **1992** "Second war" - Taylor's forces attack ECOMOG in Monrovia **1993** Ceasefire and UN Observer Mission; Monrovia under ECOMOG control, but fighting continues sporadically elsewhere

➤ LIBERIA ➤

Founded by freed slaves from America in 1821, Liberia gained independence in 1847. However, the settlers, known as the Americo-Liberians, inflicted many injustices on the native Africans: only after having adopted Christianity and a "western lifestyle" for at least three years could native Africans become Liberian citizens and win the right to stand for public office. The result was that indigenous Liberians were seriously underrepresented in the governing structures and the provinces where they lived were badly neglected.

Between 1944 and 1971, President Tubman undertook a gradual process of unifying Liberians, building roads and hospitals, and increasing educational and employment opportunities for all Liberians. When President Tolbert took over in 1971, he failed to continue this process and conflicts surfaced between the government and opposition groups. His government was overthrown in a military coup led by Samuel Doe in April 1980.

Despite the brutal execution of Tolbert and his aides, Doe was at first welcomed by most Liberians, optimistic that a government led for the first time by a native Liberian would benefit all 16 ethnic groups. But Doe gradually surrounded himself with members of his own (Krahn) ethnic group and a smaller number of Mandingos, seen as the Krahn's traditional allies.

Doe promised to return Liberia to multi-party democracy by 1985 but proceeded to suppress all opposition; he won a clear majority in elections amid widespread allegations of rigging. Doe then maintained power by intimidating, jailing or killing opponents, his main instrument of repression being the Krahn-dominated Armed Forces of Liberia (AFL).

Civil war began in December 1989, when Charles Taylor's National Patriotic Front of Liberia (NPFL) invaded from the Ivoirian border. An Americo-Liberian by descent, Taylor had been a member of Doe's administration until 1983 when he fled to the US after allegations of embezzlement.

It was the conduct of Doe's army which created initial success for the rebels. The AFL slaughtered and looted the people of Nimba (the province from which the NFPL had launched its attack), and men, women and children from this region joined the rebels. The conflict quickly degenerated into a brutal inter-ethnic war.

Differences between Taylor and one of his commanders, Prince Johnson, led the latter to form a breakaway faction: the

Independent National Patriotic Front of Liberia (INPFL). With the war now waged by three factions, the situation became even more difficult to resolve. To the continuing shock of many Liberians, the US failed to mediate: Liberia's strategic importance had been greatly reduced with the end of the cold war, and events in the Gulf were beginning to dominate the international arena.

After a number of unsuccessful attempts by the Economic Community of West African States (ECOWAS) to bring about a negotiated solution, a peacekeeping force—the ECOWAS Cease-fire Monitoring Group (ECOMOG)—was deployed in August 1990. The intervention helped put an end to the carnage, but the force came under vicious attack from the NPFL which, unlike the other two factions, had opposed its deployment. ECOMOG succeeded in driving the NPFL out of the devastated capital, Monrovia, but suffered a setback when Doe was captured and later died at the hands of the INPFL.

Since November 1990, a series of ceasefire agreements has foundered. In June 1991, another faction, the United Movement for Democracy in Liberia (ULIMO) joined the conflict, ostensibly to force the NPFL to accept a peaceful solution.

The delicate stalemate between ECOMOG and the NPFL was broken in October 1992 when NPFL rebels, who had been regrouping, attacked ECOMOG and Monrovia. This operation, usually referred to as the second war, resulted in enormous loss of life. A ceasefire was agreed in July 1993 and a UN Observer Mission in Liberia was deployed. Since then, although Monrovia has been firmly under ECOMOG control, fighting has continued in other areas between NPFL, ULIMO, and other factions which have since emerged.

The brutality and bitterness of the conflict has undoubtedly caused immeasurable suffering to Liberian women, but it has also changed their perceptions and expectations about Liberian society. Pre-war, the vast majority played no significant political or administrative roles. Even in business, women featured very little, unlike their counterparts in other West African countries. During the war, some women took up arms, and many became the sole providers for their families. A new determination to participate actively in their country's political and business affairs strongly characterises many interviews, while changed attitudes to men range from a straightforward desire to be independent to a deep cynicism and loss of respect, especially among those who stayed in Monrovia, where social structures all but collapsed.

These interviews were gathered by Funmi Olonisakin, research student at the War Studies department, Kings College, London University, and coordinator of the London-based NGO, African Women in Conflict and Security Studies.

Shirley   **LIB 1**

A large proportion of Liberian refugees live at Oru-Ijebu camp in Nigeria. Many have been there since 1990. Shirley, leader of a newly formed women's group in the camp, speaks here, along with other members.

To be a refugee in Africa, our own continent, is bad. No husband. Kids. Nobody to assist. The men are suffering. Some of our boys here are wearing women's blouses - not because they are being funny, but because they don't have [shirts]. And all over the camp, you see some guy coming to your room saying, "Oh girl, please let me have [some] toothpaste", or "Please give me bath soap". We have to help our brothers [because] this is "no man's land".

There are people who come into the camp and say they want boys to go out there and work. But when it's time for payment, the police have to step in. The [employers] don't want to pay them. Refugees don't have the money to go to court, so what do you do?

The [local] people speak their dialect, so we cannot understand one another. There are some cultural problems. [Most] don't bother us, but you know, in every society some people are nuisances. So, the nuisances among them sometimes throw words at us - that the federal government is paying us salaries, right down to the babies. But we don't listen to that because we know it is [ignorance]. The educated ones among them know that we are suffering.

Before, a typical Liberian man would like to take care of his girlfriend the best he can. [Now, since the war,] some men cannot afford it. Some receive money from [family in] the States and they can help their girlfriends. But those of them without any means of income are pimps. We cannot blame them for that. The love is there, the mind is there to do something, but the hand is not there (the will is there but their hands are tied). There's just a silent understanding [between us].

If I had money, I could start a nice business here in the camp and be saving my few **kobo**. One cannot leave without savings. If I had a good bit of money, I could make arrangements with those shoe manufacturers in the east [of Nigeria] and bring shoes here to the camp to sell, at a reasonable price.

Camp life

We have [experienced] a whole lot of changes. You know, we are all human beings, but we are not equal. Like some of us who had been living a very good life before, [now] because of the war, we are mixed up with some illiterates. [This is] very hard. An illiterate person is narrow-minded. They think in one way. But if you are educated, you will always have a second thought.

We have diseases here and we are just packed together. We have TB in this camp now, a highly contagious disease. [I know] the person [with TB] did not go to the store to purchase the disease, but only an illiterate will see somebody sick and [stay close to them]. Avoiding a person who is sick doesn't mean you are selfish or that the person is not a human being. My point is that these [sick] people are not supposed to be kept amongst us.

As for the girls, some of them are getting a little money from outside, doing business, to help their partners. Some are on the streets. The ones you see in the camp here are fine. But some of them cannot stand it, so they go out, and stay in Lagos. In every country where they fight a war, you must expect some impatient people.

Mothers and children

We the mothers, it's not easy for us. If you are single and you don't have food today or the UN has given you your [quota] and it's finished before the month ends, you can meet a friend [who is] eating and join them to eat. You can even buy bread out there, minerals and drink. But tell me, will you take your child from house to house [just] to eat? It's impossible. Definitely, people will start to gossip. Human beings must talk.

The way you bring up your child, that's how they will grow up. Some people don't [want] to talk to the kids, and some are really hard on them. Just because there is war [should] we leave them to go astray? No. We still restrict them. Some have already gone astray. The teenagers coming up don't have any respect [for anyone]. But we are very united here. Suppose I have a kid, a teenager, who doesn't want to stay at home and wash clothes or help with domestic work, you will see other friends of mine start to put mouth on this child (tell the child off). Everybody will talk to the child. We will embarrass you, talk to you, make you know that you don't live like that with your parents.

[Being a single mother] has made me very very strong. It has *Wars open* made me have the faith that I can make it without a man. [In *everybody's* future] you are not going to pet the man. You feel you can go out *eyes* there and get it [for yourself]. Liberian men have more respect for women [as a result of the strength women have found]. We are precious jewellery to them. That is the only thing I like about the Liberian men. Many of our boys have been insulted in buses and so on. When they see an older woman getting in a bus and they try to give her their seat, people say "Ha! my friend, you dey craze (are you crazy)? Who be woman (what is a woman)?" A Liberian man would never say that. That is why we stick up for them.

War, power struggles and tribalism

African leaders nowadays are very greedy for power. Doe came to power by the gun. But power is a "prostitute", it cannot stay in one place, it's supposed to circulate. If one person wants to hang on to it, definitely there will be problems. So we expected [war] when [Doe] won the elections—everybody knew how he won. But we didn't expect the crisis to be so bad—slaughtering one another like goats [although] we are all one Liberia. It became a tribal war. Right now, the crisis in Liberia is senseless to most of us in exile. We don't have any crisis here in the camp. We are from the 16 tribes of Liberia and we are united. We feel that we are not politicians. We are only here for shelter.

"Women are on the move"

Wars open everybody's eyes. Even the babies being born are aware. Liberian men don't like to do business, but the war has made them learn. Before the crisis, you would see the Lebanese all over with stores here and there. But I promise them that tomorrow, it is going to be very serious competition between the Liberians and the foreigners.

We [women] are going to speak out for our rights. Before, we would sit at home and [the men] would do everything. Even if you had a master's degree, sometimes your husband would tell you not to work. But I am very sure that tomorrow women are going to sit in some of the ministries, heading the ministries.

[Children] are not going to be eager for [material] things because in exile you know your parents don't have these, and if they don't have, you cannot force it. Tomorrow, when they get back home, they won't be bothered about these things, they won't be that materialistic.

VIOLA: After staying in exile for almost three years, we realised that women have an important role to play in the country back home. We should organise ourselves and cry for peace. When we look at it nationally, we have achieved nothing. That is why you see the women all gathering here today.

You know, when you realise you had a key and that that key could have been used for five years, you regret not using it. Our country was a very sweet one. In Africa, they used to call Liberia small America. Now we realise that [our country] is not even developed at all.

One thing I like in this country, and also in Ghana, is that people are self-reliant. I was in Ghana last year when a ladies' organisation built a stadium. I was moved. They did it like taxation, give what you can. Can you imagine that—a football stadium!

Women are on the move. We have learnt that it is not only government that brings development to the country. It is the citizens themselves. Two, three, women can gather together and make a big difference.

SHIRLEY: Liberia is still sweet. Friends write to us [from there] that they are living fine, things are going smoothly with them. We who are in exile, where there is no war, we are suffering. [But there], their eyes are open wide to business.

SIA: I think they are going by the rules of the jungle where only the fittest survive. Those making it are in a circle—the UN, ECOMOG, the Lebanese and Indian traders. ECOMOG brings food —*garri* (cassava grain), pepper, you name it. If you have the money, you buy from them and you make your own business, then you are in the circle.

Something that has encouraged me is this. Liberian women before, I must admit we were very lazy. Their attitude was, "Me, go to the market and sell?!" When I saw women—well-educated women, some with masters degrees—on the move, I said, "When I get back to Liberia, I will take off this lipstick and these high-heeled shoes!"

Anonymous   LIB 5

This leader of a woman's group at Oru-Ijebu camp is a Krahn, married to an adviser to one of the president's brothers.

When the war started, they were searching for us from house to house. I managed to escape. When [the rebels] crossed the border they started with the Mandingos. From there, they started looking for the president's tribe. They said the Krahn were ruling—so it was mainly jealousy. They started slaughtering people and we were afraid. I managed to escape because I speak so many dialects besides [the language of] my tribe. That's what saved me. But [whenever] you came across some reasonable rebels, they were not concerned with tribe and things.

It came to a crucial point when they were looking for government workers. They were just killing and killing. My husband was working with the government. I have been here three years now and I don't know whether he is living.

They seemed to be like mad men. They had been training in the bush for a long time, so when they met women they were hot. If they saw that you were looking fine and they didn't want to kill you, they would keep you whether you liked it or not. If you said no, they would kill you.

I thought the war was just for a short time. Like in 1985, November 12th, the coup was just for one week. I don't want to go back now. When there is complete peace, when there is no fighting in any part of Liberia, I will go back. I don't know where I am going to stay if I go back. The house in which I was living has been burnt down. I've got nobody to depend on that I can go back to stay with.

Plenty of women joined the war [as combatants] but they are not in this camp, they are back home. If [the rebels] killed your husband, you could go out of your mind. What is the next thing [to do]? You are going to take up arms. If they kill your husband, kill all your children, loot your whole house or end up burning your house, what is the next thing? You go crazy. So, most of these women took up arms.

Gossip

No woman wants to expose herself [about traumas suffered during the war] because some of us don't keep our mouths shut. Like if I explain my problem to you, as soon as I leave, you will tell the other person, "She did so and so, go see her." The other person will say, "Missus here, the rebels did so and so to her." There are some that act mature and some that don't—they think that because of the war they can act in a foolish way. But we are all affected by the war. We have to control ourselves.

"To keep my mind from thinking"

My dear, if you sit down and you are doing nothing, you will be thinking [too much]. This month, I ended up teaching in the kindergarten. The money is nothing, but it's to keep my mind from thinking. By the time I come home, half of the day is gone. When you are doing nothing, you sit down and think about everything. I don't even want to talk to anybody.

Lack of resources

SIA: We have a home economics school here but there are no materials. You go to a dressmaking class and you don't even have a yard of cloth to cut anything. They've just got us sitting down. It's not that we are lazy but there is no help. We want to do a lot of things but we need help.

SHIRLEY: I learnt that they may improve the clinic we have here. We don't have a lab. We don't even have an examination bed in the clinic. You go to complain of headache and they just give you chloroquine (an anti-malaria drug). It is not always malaria that causes headaches. It is not always malaria that causes colds. So, last time [at the meeting of the women's organisation] we stressed this.

"Africa is sweet"

If we go back home with grudges against one another from exile, definitely another civil war will break out.

There are some people who are not planning to go back home now. I would prefer to go out of Africa, [to somewhere] where I can work, save money, and [then come] back to enjoy myself. I feel that Africa is sweet. Other people would like to stay. We have some that are willing to stay in Nigeria. If you are strong, you can make it. You just have to work hard. That's all.

I feel let down [by the US]. I don't know about other people.

SIA: I do not feel that way. If no one goes to [help] you, that's the time you gather more strength and momentum to do something for yourself. But if every time you clap your hands or cry wolf, somebody comes, that is nothing. So, I don't feel hurt at all. The only reason we say "America, America" is because of our foundation, when they carried our forefathers away and brought them back again. Other than that, there is nothing. Liberia has never been colonised. They say we are Americo-Liberians. We are not Americans. We are Africans.

Attitudes towards international agencies

WATA: [The UN] are telling us they will give us **8,000 *naira***. Tell me, what do you do with *naira* in Liberia? I thought they would give us dollars so that we can at least buy a few items [here], then take the balance to Monrovia to spend. If the UN gave people even 100 or 250 dollars [US], this camp would be empty now.

SHIRLEY: I am sure that the money [from Geneva] comes in dollars but [the people here] are changing it to get their profit. We Africans should try to help one another. I feel that there are certain things we are entitled to that we are not getting. If you look through some of the refugee books, you'll see that each person is supposed to have a tent. We don't get these things.

WATA: And we are not supposed to get this rotten local oil. We are supposed to get something decent.

SHIRLEY: In Guinea, they get vegetable oil. It is only here that we get local oil and local soap. They are not providing clothes, kerosene, toothpaste. I feel sure it's because of this local oil that the children are always sick.

[The international agencies] are all one and the same. "You chop, I chop (eat)"—it's a closed door thing. At first they used to give each person two cans of *Geisha* (brand of canned fish). They stopped that abruptly. Even the babies' food—they didn't bring any last month. I feel sure that Geneva is providing the money for these things.

The Red Cross are the ones distributing this food. We have warned them. I am sure the cash is given to them to go and purchase these things and they [use] it, and buy local oil and local things for us.

Agnes   LIB 2

Agnes, who lives in Monrovia, was a high school student when the war began.

During the heat of the war, there was no food and there was massive killing. It was a real traumatic period. So I fled to Nigeria to try to relax my mind. When things got so bad, I was so offhand, free. What I saw in Liberia made me live an "I don't care life".

I had a sister who was married to a Lebanese national. She fled with one of her kids, who is an American citizen. [The Americans] evacuated her with the baby but refused to evacuate the other three [children], who were then killed by NPFL rebels. They were beheaded right there in the house. She hasn't gotten over it yet. She is in psychiatric care in the United States.

Atrocities under the AFL

It might sound strange but the worst moment for me was before the rebels came. The [AFL] were very brutal—looting, raping, killing, beating. They had a curfew. If you were found outside at one minute after six, you were shot down. Only the Krahn people and close associates of Doe were well treated. At that time churches even used to pray for the rebels to come.

People were not allowed even to be together. If they saw four people sitting together, they would say you were discussing about

These days, the relationship between men and women is strictly financial

the rebels coming. Even in the churches, they had spies. The AFL sometimes carried their guns into the churches, to hear what the pastor had to say or what the congregation was whispering. There were no safe havens. I regret that the rebels came, but I prayed at that time for them to come.

Violence and vendettas

[The rebels] flushed the AFL out and retaliated on behalf of the civilians. But some people started passing information on the rebels. Then the rebels became very brutal because they didn't trust anybody.

The INPFL rebels were not so bad. The killing was massive among themselves but not so much against civilians. But with the NPFL side, everybody was their own boss, so they did anything that pleased them. They killed a lot of civilians, even more than soldiers.

It was stress and the fighting that caused [the AFL] to be so brutal. But the NPFL were under no kind of stress because they already had half the country. I just call them naturally wicked. They came with some grudge, like we were the cause of the war.

[Atrocities happened because] you could easily convince your colleague to do something evil. I could say, "This person did something to me during normal times, so let's get rid of him." That's how most of the atrocities were carried on. People were convincing their friends to take revenge on their enemies.

Exchanging bodies for food

Women were treated like geese that were battered. I would say that our bodies were exchanged for food. The rebels were in charge of all the food in the country at that time. Some women that had pride, high esteem, they would rather die from hunger. But if you wanted to live, you had to have some connection with a rebel.

These days, the relationship between men and women is strictly financial. We just believe in the barter system that started during the war. You get the pleasure of my body and I get the pleasure of your pocket. I trust no man. In Monrovia now, you don't trust nobody. If I say I have any true love for anybody, I'll be lying. If you tell me you love me, I'll tell you I love you, but I am at your pocket.

[War] made me kind of independent. I did not depend on my parents for food, they depended on me. It makes me live an "I don't care life". I don't care any more what people think about me. I care about what I do, and please myself. [Generally] it has changed people's behaviour. I'm sorry to say it has made the girls very loose. They don't care what their parents or anybody thinks about them.

We [women] talk about [what happened]. You sit and tell me your experience and I'll sit and tell you my experience—without shame, because everybody knows it was done. It was not done willingly. Nearly everybody passed through the same process.

Men think of me as trash... I think of them as animals

Men blame women, women blame men

Men feel the women are responsible for what happened, that we did it wilfully. They consider us prostitutes. During that period, they were helpless. They were like babies. They were not able to look after their families any more. A wife had to sacrifice herself, the marital contract, everything, to save the family, yet the men are not grateful. They say Liberian women are prostitutes and will do anything for money—[as if] we could have sat back and prayed to God for some miracle to sustain our families!

We sacrificed ourselves, our image in society, our integrity, everything, to save their lives and the children. So, my reaction to Liberian men is equal. Just as they think of me as trash, a prostitute, I think of them as animals because they are not thinking rationally. They don't want to be rational and say, "She was under stress", or "She thought maybe she might die if she refused". They have forgotten all the suffering we went through for them.

I feel it was the men who brought the war. They knew this war was coming. The Liberian woman didn't even know what a rebel was. People started looking it up in dictionaries. But the men knew. They just thought that the war [would be] finished within a week. [I feel hostile towards them] because I feel that everything that was done to me during the war was because of them. The guys that knew were the big guys up there, like some of the ministers, people who owned agencies and companies in Liberia, people connected with the government, people working in Doe's administration.

Before the war, Liberian women liked to be faithful to their husbands, they helped to uplift their husbands and were proud of them. Now the wives are not faithful to their husbands any more. They blame them for what happened. Children don't care any more because they feel their fathers cannot cater for them. They please themselves. Some of them were even combatants in the war.

[My personal behaviour has changed]—like, number one, my drinking habit—I drank only occasionally before the war. But now I drink any kind of alcohol, in any form, without anybody to tell me what to do. It's a habit that developed during the war because we saw all sorts of things going on. You had to drink alcohol to be able to sleep, so that you won't suffer nightmares or see terrible

People were more afraid of the female soldiers things, even day visions. You would drink alcohol and smoke a lot of cigarettes because of the smell of the bodies in the streets. There was mass hunger in the city. If I smoked cigarettes and drank a bottle of beer or stout or any alcoholic beverage, I didn't feel the hunger. Now, it's very hard to quit.

"Our African brothers"

ECOMOG are truly our African brothers. They came here for our wellbeing, and they are human. I wouldn't expect them to be out here for so long without having affairs. ECOMOG has handsome guys and Liberia has pretty girls, so I expect there to be attraction. [Liberian] men are jealous. [ECOMOG men] treat women with respect. They make you feel like a woman. They care.

Most of [the young men who return from the war] become rogues. When they come back, they don't even see the same girl waiting for them. She knows she was only there [with him] for the time being, to survive. She knows he is not her type. With married men, their wives would have been gone long since, with their children. So, they become frustrated and turn into thieves and armed robbers and looters because they believe they have no place in society. The children are even ashamed that their father was a combatant.

Female combatants

Girls [who trained to be combatants] went away for months. People didn't know, until they came back with arms and everybody was shocked. [The female combatants] were very aggressive. If you were approaching the checkpoints... the way they would react, if you were not strong, you would collapse. They would command you to take off your jewellery, your shoes. Anything nice on you they would take away, and give you the ragged clothes they were wearing. And they were very quick to kill. The least mistake you made, you were down.

Their aggression was mainly against women. They would [strip you] naked. They would shove the grenade somewhere up in your private parts. They would put their hands all where they're not supposed to go, saying they were looking for grenades. People were more afraid of them than the men, because the female combatants' temper was very quick.

If I was one of them, I would definitely be ashamed because nobody expected Liberian women to be so brutal to her fellow Liberians. A woman is supposed to be somebody [with a] soft spot. Even if a man is not thinking rationally, she is supposed to be able to analyse, to love and care for little ones, older girls, men and so on. But the [female combatants] were very harsh and aggressive

even towards babies and children.
   I have friends who fought in the war and they are living normal
lives. Everybody knows the sort of atrocities that went on in the
war. Carnage. But they don't feel ashamed. They sit and talk about
it naturally, like it's some kind of memory they are trying to recall.
[Other women] feel normally [about them]. Recently, ECOMOG
said people shouldn't call their friends rebels or think back to what
they did to you. They shouldn't have vengeance in their minds, or
else there will be no peace.

Women would rather suffer in silence

   Some women [took up arms] to feed their families. They saw it
as the only way their family could survive. [But as far as] most of
the men are concerned, when you [a female combatant] come
back, you are out. They feel you will have an effect on the children
in society. They hardly want you to come near the children.

Rehabilitation

I know some [organisations] that deal with former combatant boys.
They help to rehabilitate them, send them to school, help them to
be engineers, teachers, whatever you want to be. They provide
food, clothing, medical facilities. But I don't know of any kind of
rehabilitation centres for women. Most of the women only tell their
friends [that they were combatants]. You hardly find women
combatants saying that the government should try to help them.
   [Women who were] raped during the war tell their close
friends. You hardly hear of women coming out in public to talk
about all those things that happened to them. They would rather
suffer in silence until they can get over it. They try to live with it
or live with the idea that it didn't happen to them alone. If
hundreds of other girls can live with it, you can also live with it
and, gradually, it vanishes away.
   If I was raped, I may not want to disclose that particular secret
to a friend. But if she tells me something more terrible that
happened to her in the war, it would give me more courage, more
confidence in my friend, so that I will be able to relay my story to
her. But most of the raping was done in the open. A particular
rebel may like your daughter, and right in front of you—the mum,
the dad, the other sisters and brothers—it will be done openly. So
that was how many girls got to know that their friends were raped.

The growth of dictatorship

At the beginning, people welcomed the coup [that deposed Doe].
Everybody thought it would be over with [quickly]. Everybody
wanted [Doe] down. But unfortunately it was just the beginning.
We are in more than a dictatorship now. If dictatorship was

Orphans, especially the girls, take on responsibilities at a young age
Jeremy Hartley/Panos Pictures

something like in mathematics where you have square roots, I would say we are in dictatorship squared. Everything is even getting so much worse in Liberia that people are even regretting the death of Doe. It was better to live with the devil you know than the angel that you don't know.

Fears about the future

The only thing I will advise a Liberian girl to do is to go to school and learn enough that you won't have [to listen] to anybody telling you garbage, because after this war we are going to receive a lot of garbage. My fear is that maybe I won't be able to pursue my education and that my [future] kids won't be able to either. My fears are for my sisters and brothers who are young. I don't want them to turn out to be criminals. And [I fear] that we won't have good future leaders because it will be the same old people coming back in to office.

We [should] appeal to the UN and NGOs to open more nursing schools, orphans' homes, home economics and paediatrician schools for women, so that women will be involved in helping reduce the high rate of prostitution. Most of the young girls and women have kids and they have to support their kids through school. There is no money, so definitely the prostitution rate will be high. It is highest within a certain age group, let's say 18 to 25.

Most of the women above 25 were already married before the war and already working, so they don't find it [so] hard to cope. But women from 18 to 25 were kids before the war. They were not married, or they were still at school. They were not responsible for themselves. Now the parents are not making money. Most of the younger folks have older sisters who try to chip in [and] help their family.

Rose   LIB 3

Rose is the secretary-general of Liberia's National Women's Commission (NAWOCO) in Monrovia.

The National Women's Commission was established out of the war, [out of] need. We had fragments of women's activities here and there, without any coordination. We decided to get together and establish the commission as an NGO. We ourselves have been running it and making the decisions. It consists of about 41 women's groups now.

We encourage structures where women at the grassroot level form working groups, [so that] projects and activities can be channelled to them. It could be home economics. It could be a community-based backyard garden project where women get together and clear a piece of land to grow vegetables. It could be a community-based clinic. Or it could be just peer counselling.

About 85% of our membership cannot read or write. We have women leaders who are not educated, but they have their own wisdom in tribal customs and tribal norms. We have to respect that leadership, and develop it.

The Abused Women and Girls programme

The idea for the Abused Women and Girls (AWAG) programme came right after the ceasefire in 1990. A group of women including myself attended a workshop run by Save the Children Fund, UK. The lecturer [asked us to return] on Sunday. We talked about the Ugandan experience where women were raped and molested, and he brought literature which we read. We were moved because we knew that these things had happened [in Liberia] and were still happening in other areas of the country where fighting was still going on. We decided to form an association called the Association for Women in Crisis. Its aim is the rehabilitation of victimised women, abused women and girls, through trauma counselling by professionals, or peer counselling, group therapy. A female doctor

She thinks she caused the rape herself, even though it was a war situation

does a medical assessment on the impact [of trauma].

We have health education, talks about family planning, nutrition, hygiene, sanitation and general things. Besides that, we have preventive education and counselling about HIV/AIDS. We did one or two periods of HIV testing but we had to discontinue because in Liberia we don't have the right equipment to do secondary testing to verify the primary result. With primary testing the probability of errors is high. So, in order not to frustrate the sisters, and not give them the wrong hope or wrong impression, we discontinued it until the health authorities here can improve on testing methods. We have increased awareness about HIV/AIDS, but we are short of films and [other] educational materials.

The HIV counsellors have meetings with women's groups, in the schools, in the churches. In one month they see about 2,000 or 3,000 people, distribute [information] materials as well as condoms. We also talk about [taking] care of a victim, and about the psychological effects on a victim's family. All the myths about AIDS are cleared away.

Legal rights and income generation

Our centre has a legal affairs unit that explains to women what their rights are. If you've been molested, or battered by your husband, abused physically and mentally tortured, you're distressed, you don't know what is out there for you. How can you get redress? The legal aid [programme] is being run by a female counsellor. We avoid that extra anxiety and trauma to the victims [that would be] caused by having men deal with them.

Our traditional laws are different [from Liberian state laws]. [The woman] is considered to be property. If she is raped, her husband doesn't appreciate her any more. If she has children, he is not going to support her like he would his other wives. If he is sympathetic, he might give her [support] but she would still feel unwanted and bad. She thinks she caused the rape herself, even though it was a war situation. Some women were pregnant when they were raped. Some had miscarriages on the road while [fleeing the interior for Monrovia]. Some have never had the opportunity to see a doctor. For two, three years, they have carried the pain.

[The counsellor] teaches a course for paralegals—they do not go to court, but they know the basic laws and tell these women. She also does basic research, to see which laws are appropriate for women's advancement and development. And we now have an association of female lawyers.

The legal counsellor is also going to [investigate] the rights of abused women. In Liberia, women cannot come out and say "I was raped", or "My husband batters me". It's like a taboo. But in developed countries, women can go on television and they can go to court. They can sue, and it becomes a big story. So we would like to look at other people's experiences and see how they moved from where we are now to get to where they are, and see what we can borrow from that experience that will benefit us [in the framework of] our culture and way of life.

The women who took up arms...they've disappeared... it's like they never existed

The [AWAG] programme is also tied in with an income-generation component. You meet this woman, she is dejected, she feels no one loves her and she wants maybe to commit suicide. You talk to her, calm her down, get her to the point where she trusts you. Then you tell her her rights, take her to a point where she starts to look after herself and feel like a person again. Then what next? You don't want to send her out there when she cannot earn an income.

So we do practical things. Since this is a period of national crisis, we cannot use sophisticated methods. So we do food processing. We teach the women so that when they get to their village, they can make vinegar and preserve their food. We also teach them baking—how to make pastry, cookies, tasty doughnuts that they can sell. But we lack basic materials and supplies. Women raise their own funds. This is wartime, and we try to help each other the best way we can.

Tied in with income generation is marketing. How do you price the materials you are going to use? How do you buy at the lowest cost? Because you have to make a profit. These women cannot read or write, so it's [not] sophisticated big book things we do here.

Assisting female combatants

Women took up arms and they've disappeared. You can't find them, it's like they never existed. How do we trace them? How do we motivate them not to look at the negative aspect of coming out, but to look at it positively so they can be helped? We are trying to develop a programme to identify these girls, [help them find] their productive capacity, rehabilitate them through counselling and training.

Mothers of combatants

[Some] parents believed in the cause. They called themselves freedom fighters. If you were brainwashed and sent your son to [fight], that parent would believe he was going for a good cause. Now that they realise the cause was a selfish one, they feel bad.

Survival That son may have been involved in a lot of atrocities, especially
comes first against civilians. How does he come back into the community? You
as a parent, how will you look to your neighbours? And so for
parents, it's like wanting your child, loving your child, but not
wanting that child around you in the community.

For instance, a female combatant was in the rehabilitation centre
and her mother used to visit her. She completed her rehabilitation
training but the mother did not want her back in the community.
We had to talk to the mother. She had her own trauma, knowing
that her daughter took up arms, maybe killed, and got involved in
a lot of evil. She did not want this stigma on her in the community.
We had to talk to her, [encourage her] to pay more attention to the
girl and see the positive side of this child that had come back,
forgetting the negative things. We have a parable: "There is no bad
bush to throw a bad child" (your child is your child).

"Healing the wound"

In the urban area, women have to hussle and bussle. They won't
have time to think on whether they were raped or not. They have
to feed the family; survival comes first. The desire to survive is
healing the wound. It may not be healed but it's covered. And they
don't want to go back, they are moving ahead. But in the rural area,
where families were so close, the war has disrupted family ties. You
find old folks missing, children missing, husbands and wives
separated. So the programme is even more necessary there because
that traditional structure is broken down and the hurt is great.

"Women have proved themselves"

Women are becoming independent of men. We love the men, we
need them—they are our husbands, brothers, fathers, uncles—but
we are not waiting for them like before to be the only providers.
Men have come to appreciate this role and they talk about it with
admiration. They [also] fear it, but they are willing to go an extra
mile with the women. It is now common to hear a man say, "We
wish to have a woman president." That's how far the women have
gone. In Liberia, women have proved themselves. But somehow, the
suppression is there. It's camouflaged. You don't see it but it's there.

In the refugee camps outside of Liberia, the women are learning
masonry and carpentry and about building their own homes. Just
imagine that woman coming home. She can open her own
masonry firm. Right now, women are bus drivers, drivers for
international agencies. You could not find that before. They had to
have a secretarial or office job. Another good thing is that Liberian
women saw how women in Nigeria hussle to make a living, how

enterprising they are... women in Ghana, women in Gambia, how self-sufficient they are. The first thing [those women] say now is "How can I get money to start on my own?"

Right now, women don't like to go to Europe like before. Before, we knew more about Europe or America than we knew about Nigeria or Sierra Leone or Ghana. Now, a Liberian woman [will say], "I am going to Sierra-Leone", "I am going to Guinea", "I've got a business partner there", "I'm going to get my goods". These are the positive things.

All is not rosy, because our government has to back us, and we have to have a unified country. The government has been sensitised now to plan for gender issues.

Anna   LIB 4

Anna is president of the Slipway Women Development Association, in one of the poorest neighbourhoods of Monrovia.

Before the war, I was employed full-time at Libtraco (Liberia Tractor Equipment Company). In 1992, most of our customers were behind rebel lines and we couldn't get to them. So the proprietor of the business said they had to let some of us go, by paying us off.

I was home, with nothing to do, but then you know, I can sew. So then I said, why should I just sit around all day? I went out and got in contact with some people who were opening offices and told them that I could sew curtains. I started getting customers. I got one of my former office mates and we joined up to open a small company. We started purchasing materials, doing curtains, and that is how I started making my livelihood.

"Let's go and do something"

One day, one of my neighbours said that she had the chance to go to one of the UN meetings. They were trying to organise women in different communities. She turned to me: "Let's go and do something, think about something." She called another friend and the three of us decided we would go from house to house and tell women we should get together as one force and form some club and see how we could better our condition.

Some of the women responded. Others were reluctant. We came back and listed things that we thought would be necessary to start up with. Then they asked me to be their leader but I said I didn't want to be in the foreground. We gathered about 15 ladies who were excited about the idea. That was how we started our little association—Slipway Women Development Association.

The women are hard to get together. I must be frank. At times [when we need] to sit around a table and discuss things concerning ourselves, they won't come to meetings on time. Some of them won't come at all except when they hear we are having little refreshments, then they come running and all that.

But we started thinking about where we can open a sewing school for young girls. Then we talked about getting together and trying to get some money to buy fish, which we can season with salt and pepper, then dry it and smoke it. That would go very fast on the market and [the profits] would sustain us a lot. We have been having fundraising rallies and other things, to get some money to put us on our feet—but we haven't been able to do that yet. We are still trying. Just the other day we had a little programme and made about 2,500 dollars (US$55). But then we had to pay off some of our dues to our parent organisation, NAWOCO (National Women's Commission). We go to meetings with NAWOCO every Thursday, to discuss our problems.

One day I heard some children making a noise. I saw these girls outside and I called them in. These four promising young ladies, I said to them, "Why are you in the streets making a noise when you

Families find ways to scrape a living in the war-torn city of Monrovia

Martin Adler/Panos Pictures

could be doing something [useful]?" So I took them to my husband's factory, cleaned up one little area and had them there for three days a week, sewing. The money I earned from [selling] curtains, I took some of that and bought some real cotton materials, needles, thread and an extra pair of scissors. I got them interested. But there came a time when I couldn't afford it any more.

Struggling for funds

I started looking out for who could help me. One friend suggested [an official] at the Liberian Council of Churches, so I went and saw him. After some time, he gave me some money. But we didn't get any help from anywhere else. Most of the people that we got in touch with do not deal with small groups. In Slipway, we started late. We didn't get the know-how as early as the other communities. But anyway, we are trying to grab hold of their skirts!

We have been doing a lot of writing [applications] and all that. I personally was tired. We had sat in the office there for almost two months—every week, every week, every week—and nothing came out of it. [Each time] I left the file there, when I went back they said, "Oh, you have to bring another file." That's how they carried on, so I got fed up. But then, surprisingly, this guest came [to NAWOCO] to look through the files and ours came up first. She sent word to me this week to come to the office.

Reluctance to talk about abuse

You very seldom find somebody [who admits having been raped]. I called my women and asked them to please be open, because we are all women and trying to seek one another's wellbeing. So, one girl, only one girl, after the meeting called me and said she had stayed behind because something like this had happened to her sister. She said that in their tribe [Mandingo], they could easily be put out of the family for that sort of thing. Then I tried to explain to her that the little girl was not responsible.

So she went and told the girl and convinced her. The girl received treatment. But most people don't want to talk about it. They don't want their friends or relatives to know.

"We can step on women"

The fighters had a common saying, "What is a woman? A woman is nothing. We can step on women". I feel that that is how they were taught and that it was the effect of the drug on them, because most of the time they were on cloud 52. They had no regard for women or womanhood.

You just couldn't reason with the rebels. It looked like they

For some women it was heartbreaking for their children to carry guns had a list of things they would charge you with and they would [find] one thing that you couldn't get away with. I just kept out of their way. When the soldiers started burning [homes] and doing all kinds of things we had to leave. I had to go from village to village to look for green plantains and green bananas and make soup or roast them for my family to eat and survive. If you didn't do that, you'd just perish. Women were the breadwinners for the family.

[Before the war] a woman would call a taxi [to go a short distance]. But during those days [wartime], there were no taxis, no vehicles. We had to walk sometimes for 30, 40 or 50 miles, looking for food. After struggling for three years on their own, certainly women are stronger. I should say some men are finding it difficult and others appreciate it.

Combatants come home

[Some young fighters] came and turned their arms in. Some of them said they were tired of fighting, others that they were hungry. They go to this rehabilitation centre and, after that, to the Children's Assistance Programme. Most of the mothers or guardians received their sons heartily when they saw them, because for two or three years they hadn't seen them.

Originally some of the women encouraged their sons to take up arms, because for them it was the new way of life. With the gun, they could go anywhere and harass the people for food or money. But for some, it was heartbreaking for their children to go out and carry guns.

[Women fighters treated civilians] the same way as the men. They killed women as well as men, just like their men did. Somebody said that some of the women were more aggressive than the men.

I still tell God "thankyou" that none of [my children] were interested in leaving home and joining [the rebels]. I was so afraid. I was afraid, not for the girls so much, but for my one son. Many other young boys were leaving, to have money and, you know, all these material things. But he said no and he stuck with us.

But most of the young boys joined these people, which is very sad. Some of them were compelled to because in the areas where they were working, you either had to join or they killed you. So they took up guns and as soon as they found a way of running away, they came back to join the society. But others deliberately joined and are still there. As for girls, some of them joined because they were looking for food, others because they were looking for husbands, others because they had no choice.

No news of husband

It was during **Octopus** that the rebels took [my husband away]. Since 1992, I haven't laid eyes on him. He was hale and hearty when he walked down these steps that morning.

One lady said she saw him in the market [in a town in rebel-held territory]. But they say it is difficult for people to come from that side. People are coming, but you have to have money, nobody can come free. [The money] is not the problem [for us]. The problem is to locate him.

Before he left we were running our own business, but when the war came, everything just went downhill. People stole machine parts, sealers, you name it.

The risk of AIDS

The women, especially the young girls, are with ECOMOG men. Most of them don't want to go back to school. I think that this is not right and [a risk to] their health. I'm sure that two years from now this dreadful disease, AIDS, will be at a peak in our country because they are not taking any precautions.

Some of the older women try to talk to the young girls, but they have just taken this to be the new way of life. They want to dress up and look their best, but they don't want to go to school to learn to support themselves or do something so that respectable men can take them as wives one day.

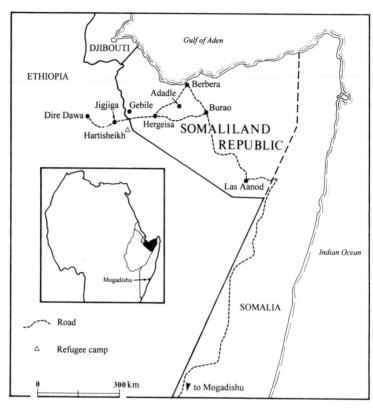

Road

△   Refugee camp

0   300 km   ▼ to Mogadishu

HUMAN DEVELOPMENT INDEX (UNDP): (Somalia pre-1991) 165 (low)
POPULATION: (Somalia pre-1991) 9.3m of which Somaliland is about 3m
FEMALE LIFE EXPECTANCY: (Somalia pre-1991) 48 years
FEMALE LITERACY: (Somalia pre-1991) 14%

1886 Northern Somalia becomes British protectorate **Early 20th century** Opposition to colonial rule from Sayyid Mohammed **1941** Italian colony of Somalia and British protectorate of Somaliland united under British military administration **1950** Somalia under Italian/UN trusteeship **1960** Independence; Somalia and Somaliland united **1969** Barre becomes president **1973-4** Mass literacy campaigns **1977-8** War with Ethiopia **1981** Launch of SNM armed resistance to government **1988** SNM offensive in northern province; government bombardment of Hargeisa; most of population flees **1991** Jan: collapse of Siad Barre government in Mogadishu; civil war breaks out in Somalia. May: Somaliland declares itself independent **1991-2** Famine in Somalia **1992** Dec: start of US/UN intervention in Somalia - Operation Restore Hope **1994** March: US withdrawal **1995** March: UN withdrawal

⟶ SOMALILAND ⟵

Somalis are one ethnic group sharing one language and one religion, Islam. They number around 5 million. Much of their region is arid and unsuitable for settled agriculture, and life is based on traditions of nomadic pastoralism. In the past there was no central political power but a clan structure, with six main clans divided into sub-clans, each ruled by its adult males. British, Italian, French and Ethiopian colonial interests in the late 19th and early 20th centuries led to the five-way division of the nation between Somalia, an Italian colony; Somaliland, a British protectorate; Djibouti; eastern Ethiopia; and northeastern Kenya. At independence, the British and Italian colonies voted to unite, to form the Somali Republic.

The Republic's elected but autocratic and nepotistic government was ousted by a (widely welcomed) military coup in 1969, and General Mohamed Siad Barre became president. The next two decades saw oppressive one-party rule, corruption and decay of state institutions, and the growth of presidential powers (often serving the interests of Barre and his clan allies). But there was also progress in education.

During Somalia's 1978 war with Ethiopia (the Ogaden war), the former USSR, hitherto a supporter of Barre, changed sides, and the US and Western powers became Barre's main backers. Defeat in this war (and the influx of Somali refugees from Ethiopia, on top of a devastating drought in 1974) seriously weakened the government. Somali national solidarity was disintegrating and armed opposition movements arose along clan lines; clannism had not died despite the rhetorical commitment of successive governments to suppress it in favour of a nation-state identity.

Barre targeted particularly severe economic and political repression at the powerful Isaaq clan in the north. Harsh military rule was imposed on the whole population, who were assumed to be supporters of the armed opposition, the Somali National Movement (SNM).

The government's peace treaty with Ethiopia, formalising the end of the Ogaden war, precipitated a crisis for the SNM: with Ethiopian support cut off, the SNM attacked Hargeisa in an attempt to seize control of the northern province. The ensuing fighting and heavy bombardment by government forces drove the inhabitants of the northern towns to flee: about 400,000 were displaced into rural areas, and another 400,000 or more became refugees in

Ethiopia or Djibouti, leaving devastated ghost towns behind them. By 1990 the SNM had gained control of most of the northern region. In January 1991, Barre was driven out of Mogadishu by another rebel movement led by General Aideed: the clan divisions Barre had encouraged in an attempt to maintain his position, spiralled out of control and toppled him from power.

Freed from Barre's oppressive rule, the people of the north—Isaaqs and most non-Isaaqs—declared Somaliland an independent state, and elected a government to set about the task of reconstruction. The economy and infrastructure are in ruins and the government penniless. The self-declared republic has not been recognised internationally, and has received little aid. But despite banditry and occasional outbreaks of inter-clan warfare, progress has been made towards demobilisation, and restoring law and order. Meanwhile in Somalia, the clan warlords are still locked in a murderous power struggle.

The economic and social life of most Somalis is shaped by the nomadic pastoral economy and patrilineal clan system. Even urban professionals are likely to retain their sense of extended family/clan identity and obligations. For women this traditionally meant a subordinate, though active, position, usually without education or independent economic possibilities. Women were traditionally exchanged in marriage to form alliances between clans—an important social role which often created divided attachments for women when their clans were at war. Though pastoral women have a significant economic role in tending small livestock, they do not share in the more valuable rearing of camels, nor do they participate formally in family and clan decisionmaking. On the other hand, Somali women are by reputation forceful and outspoken.

These interviews are with women in Hargeisa, whose husbands died fighting in the SNM. Conservative elements in Somali society were antagonised by reforms Barre introduced to improve women's legal status and access to education and jobs: these interviewees, however, probably benefited from them. Mostly educated and in employment even before the loss of their husbands forced them to be self-reliant, they are not in this sense typical of the majority of Somali women. The SNM did not have a progressive social/political agenda, and never seems to have attempted to empower women or encouraged them to be other than reactive and domestically focused in their contribution to the struggle. In the post-war period, emancipation of women has not emerged as an issue for the Somaliland leaders.

These interviews were collected by Rakiya Omaar. Originally from Hargeisa, Rakiya is now based in London and is co-founder of African Rights, a human rights organisation.

Sabaah   SOM 1

Sabaah's husband was a lecturer at the National University in Mogadishu. Active in the SNM, he crossed into Ethiopia in 1982. Two years later, Sabaah joined him and stayed in Ethiopia until Somaliland was liberated.

I [came back to Hargeisa] once, because I wanted news of my family. I experienced a lot of problems when I came. I found my own family could not hide me. [They] told me about the **tabeleh** committees which noted the number of people living in each household. Guests were reported to the authorities, and a visitor from the SNM would be killed and [the family] too. So they told me to go.

For 17 days, I [hid in] another house, then I decided to return to Ethiopia. [But there] was a curfew in Hargeisa, and I was forced to remain for two months. The curfew made transport difficult and I could not leave on foot. It was also very difficult to find a place where I could be hidden.

The rise of clan identity

Before [liberation], people were fighting for something bigger, for their independence and their identity as Isaaqs. But when that was achieved, it was replaced by sub-clan identity. A lot of people have forgotten the obligations they should have towards themselves and us, the SNM and the war, because of their attachment to their clans.

Most of the fighters who went through the tough times, who know us personally, who appreciate the bonds of brotherhood and who are blind to clan distinctions, they have died.

The SNM included all clans. We were a movement and we widows still consider ourselves as such. What has disunited the people is politics. People are used by politicians in pursuit of power. A politician tells some *deydey* (bandit) to cause havoc, so that the government will send a delegation to soothe their feelings. He doesn't care about the general welfare, only his personal interest. As far as our group is concerned, we do not see either politicians or clan elders as furthering our interests. We do not think in terms of

Our men died...we haven't tasted the fruits of their sacrifice

clans, but identify ourselves as SNM. We are used to a different way of thinking.

"The bridge of blood"

Before [we returned to Somaliland], everyone was fighting for an objective. This helped to console you, even if you had lost a loved one. We considered ourselves as the ones who had made the sacrifice, the bridge of blood that made it possible to liberate the country. We told ourselves that when we went home, we would get appreciation [and] the opportunity to rest. But since coming back, we have not had any rest whatsoever. The **"brothers' wars"** broke out. You hear bullets. You are always tense. It is a particularly depressing situation for us war widows. Our men died; the widows and their children should have a chance to rest. Well, we haven't tasted the fruits of their sacrifice, or anything like it.

We can't even ask [for appreciation yet]. People are not settled. They are not asking themselves, "What did we do? What did we achieve? Who deserves the credit for it?" The ones who are shooting are young men who took up the gun after the country was liberated. They don't know the war orphans from others, they don't know who fought, or how this country came into being. If they don't even appreciate how this country was won, they are not in a position to understand our needs or thank us.

[My husband died fighting in the SNM.] It touches me with a pain beyond imagination [to see these *deydey* now labelled SNM, put in the same category with him]. These boys have nothing to do with the SNM. But I tell myself to be patient: we will realise the fruits of his sacrifice, people who know us will come along, the country will settle down and eventually good will triumph.

These bandits don't know the price that was paid for their freedom. Yesterday the bandit was tending his family's herds—that is his background. Many people jumped on the SNM bandwagon when it came into the country, joining it from Ethiopia at the last minute or right here in Hargeisa. What [the young bandit] sees is that he can ride these "technicals" (cars) without anyone telling him to get down. So he gets into the "technical", grabs some *qat* at one checkpoint, some money at another. He has no appreciation of what people like me went through. He doesn't realise the sadness that is within us. For him, shooting his gun, getting hold of some *qat*—it's all the same to him. Other people are invisible to him.

Many of the bandits have now been sent to Mandera rehabilitation camp [set up by the government for demobilised militias]. At the end of their training, their mind will have been

Picking up the pieces: Fosiya returns home and opens up a kiosk
Martin Adler/Panos Pictures

cleansed of all that is associated with banditry and clannism, of all the rubbish that accumulated there. [Gradually] the problem of banditry will end. I am always full of hope. I am one of those whose loss even includes death, whose husbands set their hearts on clearing the country of an enemy from without. This internal problem is bound to finish. I tell myself to be patient. So me—I live always with hope, joyful hope.

"A second death"

Some people want us to rejoin Somalia. Therefore, they are against the idea of Somaliland standing on its own feet. When a foreign delegation comes to visit, and hears gunfire, of course the news they will broadcast to the outside world is that there is no peace here, no stability. So some people make it their business to find out [when a delegation is arriving] and then tell the gunmen what to do. [These are obviously] people with a political objective.

We war widows have become both mothers and fathers   Seeing people who want us to rejoin Somalia is even sadder for us than the death of our husbands, because it is a rejection of what they died for. Our husbands fought and died for one thing—that we could be free and independent as Somaliland. We told ourselves that if Somaliland came into being, that would help us to accept [their] loss. These guys want to make sure we don't get what we fought for. For us, this is a second death.

Women and the fight for peace

We face obstacles that have overwhelmed us. We have organised demonstrations, distributed written appeals, done what we could. But we war widows, those who the problems have really touched, we are always very busy. We are always worried about how to feed our children and look after them, for we have become both mothers and fathers. We feel crushed by personal problems that appear to us bigger than those of Somaliland.

Economic survival

I have a little kiosk and sell cigarettes, tea, milk. Whatever I can make out of that, I use to look after my seven-year-old son, and my 12-year-old brother who is an orphan. That is how the three of us manage to survive.

When people first came back to Somaliland, women [who set up little kiosks] had a lot of problems from bandits. Sometimes the bandits got drunk and smashed the kiosks, and raped the women. We cannot afford to have homes or kiosks made of cement, so they were corrugated iron, which made it easy for the bandits. But since the police were established and Mandera camp was set up, the situation has improved.

The future

The most important priority is to ensure the education of our children. I am only responsible for two—but imagine the widow with five children. How can she pay [their fees]? It would be an enormous help if school fees could be waived in our case. Then there are the women like myself, who have prior education. But we lost a lot of that during 10 years in the bush with the SNM. Now, we can barely read or write. We need to be re-educated so that we can cope with the world.

Given my responsibilities, I cannot opt for education. I have no choice but to work, so that the children can go to school. What we would appreciate—me and other women in my position—is financial assistance that gives a group of five or six of us the chance to have a small business venture.

To show respect and appreciation to our men who died, we should create a public garden in their name. Books should be written to record their history, and their photos published. All this should be housed somewhere public that everyone can visit and say the *faataha*. The world does not stand still; there will be waves of future generations and we want them to know that there was once a movement called the SNM that fought the Siad Barre regime.

The most important priority is to ensure the education of our children

Khadra   SOM 2

Khadra and her husband were teachers. In 1982, he was accused of encouraging students to protest against the Barre government and was forced to escape to Ethiopia to join the SNM.

I knew the serious problems [my husband] was facing in Hargeisa, and could see that he could not stay. The children were young, I was a working woman and he had to run to save his skin. He did not tell me of his plans. He reckoned that if he told me, seeing that I was a woman, somebody would hear of it. So he did not consult me. When he did not come home at his usual time, I knew then that he had left.

I had to ensure the welfare of the children and not betray the fact that he had gone, because any family whose men were known to have left were liable to be arrested and badly treated. I continued to work [as a teacher], and hired a maid to look after the children. But the ministry learned that he had left.

They came and asked me, "Where is your husband?" I told them, "My husband was around until one day I could not find him. I have no idea where he has gone. I don't know what made him leave. But whatever the reason, you can see that I am here, taking care of my children and working at my job." Some of them said, "She's only a woman—what more can she say?" So that is how they came to leave me [alone].

As you can imagine, I had my fill of difficulties—with five children under seven. I received my first letter from my husband two years after he left. It came through a cousin of mine, a nomad. It was carefully hidden and she brought it to my house in utter secrecy. Of course, I knew where he had gone and that he was generally okay, but it was through this letter, written in his own hand two years later, that we were able to establish direct contact. I read the letter, tore it up and threw it down the toilet. If the house was searched and the letter found, tracks might be established. The *tabeleh* committees kept a special eye on us, compared to other houses. I did not respond with a written letter. I told the woman, "You can be a letter for me. On your return, tell him that we are okay."

I went once to Ethiopia, in 1986, leaving my mother in charge of the house. Some nomad women brought me to the SNM base in Jigjiga and I saw my husband there. I only stayed a week, for fear of being found out by the *tabeleh* committee.

Unfortunately, we heard of his death on 31 May 1987. He died in a military confrontation in Jigjiga. May God give him peace.

Unable to mourn

In our culture, widows usually wear special clothing. But the government committees in our midst were waiting to see if I would dare mourn his death in our home. So I could not mourn him in the normal way. I telephoned his family who were living in Djibouti and asked his brothers to organise the mourning rituals there. I couldn't do anything in Hargeisa for fear of being arrested.

Worse for me was going to school. One of the teachers asked me if I was unwell. He had obviously heard of my husband's death. I replied, "No, I'm fine," and asked if I looked different. He replied, "Yes, you look very different."

The next day, I flew to Mogadishu. Luckily the holidays were beginning. This gave me the chance to escape the surveillance at home. I could mourn my husband, wearing the special clothes for the prescribed four months and 10 days.

I stayed nearly five months and then returned to my children. When I went back to the school, wearing my normal clothes, they said, "We heard that your husband died and you were hiding the truth." But I was lucky: they left me alone, though they could have fired me.

But we experienced many difficulties at home from the *tabeleh* committee. They would question the children, asking if their father had come back. "Have any men been to visit you?" The children learned to understand the questions and answer no. So when they were asked, "Who was the person entering your home?" they would say, "Nobody." They understood the pressures, when they saw so many visitors asking us questions, while our neighbour was spared these things. They asked my eldest daughter if it was true that her father had been killed. She said she did not know. She did know, of course, but she also knew that if she told them that, we would be in trouble.

Women and the liberation movement

Women often sold their gold to raise money, which was pooled and discreetly channelled to the SNM. If their men have gone off to fight a war, women of course want the effort to succeed and bear fruit. So some sold their gold, some contributed money they earned, others borrowed money. Not even the people next door knew what we were up to.

I am an educated person, and I was aware how much our people were suffering. There was no respite for the Isaaqs—not for the one who came to visit, nor the one who occupied a senior post, nor the one in a lowly position. The government made no bones even about killing people. They used to paint the slogan, "Breaking the back of the Isaaqs", on the trees. You understood why our men could not tolerate life here. They left to join the SNM—colonels, academics, doctors. Even those who were not directly touched left in order to end these problems.

When women discussed these things together, some who had not been personally affected would say, "These men who left are the cause of the detentions and problems." I always replied that they left on account of the repression and enslavement of Isaaqs. "You may escape the problem now, but if they take away your next door neighbour, you can be sure they will come for you soon." And that's what happened: the women who used to blame the SNM were eventually victims too.

Flight into Ethiopia

The day the SNM attacked Hargeisa, I was alone at home with the five children. We stayed put for six days, with shelling and so many bullets flying you couldn't count. I finally had no choice but to escape with the children. I tore one of the cotton curtains, and wrapped some clothes in it, strapping the bundle to my oldest girl. I gave the next child a tin of dried milk to carry, and the next a jar of water. Then I bundled up some blankets and strapped the youngest girl to my back, on top of the bundle. Early in the morning, I told the fourth child to hold onto my dress, and we set off walking, following the crowd.

We came across a small group of SNM fighters. I did not want to tell them that we were an SNM widow and orphans because I did not want to give them more sadness by saying, "Look, here are your families, your orphans, running away in the opposite direction."

They reached one of the refugee camps in Ethiopia. Khadra's mother joined them from Mogadishu, and they stayed there until Somaliland was liberated in January 1991.

Life in a refugee camp

When we were living in Hargeisa, we were at least settled in our hearts. But when we became homeless, we were unable to put our hands on any of the things we needed. There is no one nearby who can assist you. It was a very cold and dusty place. When you go out to look for a little help to survive, the dusty wind nearly blinds you—and the cold could be unbearable. There were also a lot of bugs. The children were consumed by them. But we had no alternative. Life forces you to bear the hardship as best you can.

It was so dusty. It was as if the soil was taking deep breaths, blowing clouds of dust. You had to queue for water, sometimes for four hours. And the children were always covered in dust, and needed to be bathed. It was a very hard life. Queuing for rations took all day. Luckily, I had my mother to leave the children with.

The agencies helping the refugees gave us gas and little stoves. But we could not use them. The gas was very expensive for us. The agencies seemed unable to calculate how much gas a family needs. Besides cooking three times a day, we also need fuel for paraffin lamps at night. Culturally, we have always used charcoal, so we bought charcoal from the nomads. Like others, I gradually sold the gold I fled with, so that the family could survive.

Life back in Hargeisa

We came back about four months after Barre was overthrown. When the schools re-opened, I went back to my old job. My small salary, that covers the basic necessities, comes from the fees paid by schoolchildren. Life is a struggle. But at least all the children are in school. I am confident that things will improve. The children whose fathers fought [in the SNM] are treated like any other orphans. Many of the pupils who have lost a father cannot pay their school fees. We do not ask them to pay. But the teachers are careful not to single them out, so as not to give them a complex.

Busaad   SOM 3

Busaad is the widow of a prominent SNM fighter, and has five children.

My husband—God rest his soul—was a colonel in the army, but he crossed into Ethiopia to join the SNM in 1982. I stayed behind; I was eight months pregnant at the time. As soon as it became known that he had crossed, the authorities visited me at home and gave me hell. "When did he leave? Who went with him?"

I was bounced from one interrogator to another. Every time a car stopped outside, I would wonder if I would be arrested. The truth is that he had not told me anything about his decision to leave. He just left, so I told the truth that I did not know anything.

The sadness in my heart ...I could not afford to show it

The day my husband died, we heard the news from the *qat* trucks [that come daily from Ethiopia]. Of course you feel the sadness in your heart, but I could not afford to show it. For a whole day, the government was boasting about his death on the radio, and I knew that the surveillance on me would be tightened. I could not observe the traditional ritual for mourning my husband in my own home.

Flight from Hargeisa

When we heard that the SNM had come, we were very happy. In our childish fantasy, we thought the whole thing would last a day and a night; but the fighting raged for seven days, during which we did not dare leave the house. The house next door collapsed, killing a lot of adults and children. The whole world seemed to have gone up in flames.

Some neighbours told us that they wanted to flee. At first, I refused to go. Let the house collapse on our heads, we would die sometime anyway. Where was I going to go? Where would I find water for the children? We might as well die in our home. Finally, the last remaining neighbours came to see me. They had organised donkeys to evacuate their children that night and insisted we join them. We left that night, clutching the children by the hand. Artillery shells were falling in every direction. We reached Biyaha Shinaha—it was an amazing sight, like a massive football stadium full of people. Everyone just squatted next to somebody else.

After a while [living in the camp], there was nothing to eat. So we decided to come back to Hargeisa—the SNM was in control then—to collect the food we had left in our homes. A group of women left together, carrying plates on our heads to collect food for the children. As we set out, the bomber planes came. We had heard that they can see peoples' eyes and that it was best to stand absolutely still like a piece of wood. So that is what we did, hugging the plates to our sides so that the plane did not see their whiteness. During the day, the plane came back and forth. When we eventually got back to the children, we found them crying under the trees where we had left them. Whatever food we might have brought, it would have been nothing when everyone was so needy.

It took us a month to get to Ethiopia. We were columns following each other's footsteps. One group arrives, sets up a little

Before, there was a certain shame attached to a working woman

hut for the night, they leave, then it is your turn. We had to move very slowly because the children had difficulty walking that distance. Of course, we were not on the road the whole time. We began to walk in earnest towards Ethiopia only after we had given up hope of being able to return to Hargeisa.

When we arrived in Ethiopia, we registered at Hartisheikh. After three months, we moved to Debile. I chose Debile because there were some small reservoirs nearby and it was less dusty. The men who owned the reservoirs knew my husband's name and gave us the water free of charge. The water was the chief attraction. When I had to go to collect our rations from Hartisheikh camp, I left the children in the care of an old woman living nearby. It was about five hours' walk, but there were often delays, especially in the early days. Sometimes you would be told that the food had not arrived. Then you had to stay away for two or three days, to avoid all that walking back and forth, and because you couldn't face your family without bringing any food.

The rise of clan divisions

Two months after Barre fell I came back to the country for which my husband had died. Initially the SNM was one man, united. They succeeded because they were united. But when the survivors who should be shouldering the country's responsibilities together are eyeing each other, dividing themselves into clan X and clan Y, who is going to remember the widows and orphans?

The bandits include all the former criminals who were in prisons. They include the men who used to rob us of food when we were refugees in Ethiopia. When the war was raging here, there were many young men unaware of the existence of Hargeisa. Instead, they had their chests hanging over the fence, eyeing the distribution of rations to the refugees. Some were themselves refugees, and others were nomads living in the area. Some carried sticks and would ambush the women as they went back to their families with their rations. They took the food from them, loading their cars. When the country was liberated, these young men came running back, grabbing weapons from the depots. I remember at least a hundred who had been there at Debile and who had never fought in the war, but who grabbed a gun when they entered Hargeisa. They are now claiming to be part of the SNM.

Economic survival

Because of economic pressures, I am now forced to sell vegetables in the marketplace. My oldest daughter, who is 18, cannot go to school because she is looking after the younger ones. While she does that, I sit in the marketplace, selling vegetables. Some of the women who bring vegetables from the Ethiopian border also have warehouses. You take the vegetables from them as a loan and spread them out on the ground. It is a gamble. By the time you include what your family needs, forget about a profit. Most likely, you will end up in debt. If you don't pay back, she will try to embarrass you. It is up to each woman how she pays back her debts. Some women group together to contribute to a revolving fund, but that is only for those who have money in the first place, or single women working for themselves. If they have money it is theirs. But a woman who has a family dependent on her, and who has no other source of income, cannot save money.

Nowadays, women seem to be better at work than men

Amina   SOM 4

In 1988, Amina fled Hargeisa to escape government retaliation against the opposition. She returned after liberation and is now part-owner of a warehouse.

The wars have changed women's lives profoundly. Before, the number of women who worked was limited. There was a certain shame attached to a working woman, with the exception of some older women who worked as traders, going to places like Aden, Jeddah and Abu Dhabi, or some well-educated women who worked in offices. It was rare to see younger women like myself in employment. Our husbands worked and we stayed at home. But since the troubles started, it is rare to find a woman sitting at home. Circumstances have forced them out of their homes. The one who has children is working for them, and the one who has none has to work for herself.

Lost bearings

Nowadays, women seem to be better at work than men. They are all on the move, bustling about to make ends meet. Men seem to have lost their bearings about their family concerns, lost confidence in their abilities to maintain their families. If men were working as hard as women, I think Somaliland would have made enormous progress by now.

Life has become very expensive, and employment opportunities for men are very scarce. Women are forced to resort to petty trade, but men want substantial work, not all these little chances that women are willing to put up with. One woman brings a few clothes from Djibouti, another sits on a street corner selling a little

"Little chances" for survival

Hamish Wilson/Panos Pictures

bit of flour. Men do not want to engage in this kind of trade, they do not seem to be able to cope with it.

Women are very motivated, eager to work and see their country settle down, but the experience of living in Ethiopia has had serious negative consequences for men. They have gone through new experiences and new problems, and they have indulged in diversions far in excess of what was considered normal before. Sometimes, it seems that they have forgotten about the existence of their families. Plenty of men drink or chew far too much *qat*. A man who spends what he gets on *qat* and spends most of his waking hours eating *qat*, when is he going to remember that he has a wife and children, let alone look after their economic needs?

Working together

Women support each other by pooling their resources and their strengths. There are many women with some education, and they give what guidance they can to the economically active but illiterate women, to help them keep what they have worked for. Women get together to establish a store or set up some business, usually in groups of five or six, sometimes just two. There is a division of labour. It is always the woman who can read and write who does the travelling and who keeps the accounts, and decides on prices. The illiterate one does the selling, the counting and balancing of the cash.

Men take advantage of women's lack of experience

Sometimes women are cheated by men who take advantage of their lack of experience. Women have to hire men to look after their stores, often men related to them. Somebody has to sleep in the warehouse, and a woman cannot do that herself. It is also unthinkable for a woman to stand guard outside a store. But this has to be done, especially with the presence of so many armed young men. Some women go abroad to buy things and then hire a man to sell them. One may want a rest, another may feel that as a woman she should not spend all day in a warehouse. Perhaps she has to see to the exchange of her money, or she feels she is needed at home. So they look for a man within the extended family to be a business partner.

Exploitation

Our own warehouse is an example of what can happen. A group of us built up the business, each contributing what she could. Some got their contribution from their husbands, others sold their gold. We used to stay in the warehouse until after our mid-day prayers and then go home for lunch. The young man we hired to be our partner would remain behind to mind the store, sleep there and look after it. He was somebody we all knew, related to one of us. So we did not worry or have any suspicion that he might cheat us.

But when he realised that we had more or less placed everything in his hands, he cheated us. He stole more than 10 million **shillings**. Up to this day, none of it has been paid back. We feel we cannot take action against him, because he is a relative. But also, the chances of getting some of the money back are greater if we negotiate with the elders of his family.

Why aren't women politically active?

Mainly, I think, because the majority are uneducated. This is a big obstacle to their participation in political life. Most cannot read or write. So they prefer to concentrate on their children, their families and their homes. They tell themselves that it is better to look after their immediate, concrete interests rather than indulging in the noise of politics. But of course there are educated women who are politically aware. They are running around, making plans and trying to do what they can. Let's wait and see what they achieve.

A lot of women see that men seem to have failed at politics, and they get demoralised. They say, if the men cannot succeed, forget about women—and this of course demoralises them even more.

Zamzam   SOM 5

Zamzam did her teacher training in Mogadishu, as there were no educational facilities beyond secondary school in Hargeisa.

When I completed my training in Mogadishu, I came directly to teach in Hargeisa—against the advice of many people who told me that in Hargeisa there would be no career prospects. I knew that schools in Mogadishu and in the north were not equal, but I was only conscious of the need for teachers in the north.

There were constant confrontations between students and the government. There was always someone in the classroom from the Security Service or the [ruling] Party. You cannot teach properly when you know every word you say is being monitored, and the students were of course ill at ease as long as these spies were in the classroom. So these kinds of pressures drove teachers away.

"A sort of hell"

By 1981, people had realised that they could expect nothing from the government, and they began to organise themselves. A group of young professionals decided to provide the services that the government had failed to provide, starting with the Hargeisa Hospital. The government interpreted this as an attempt to bring about a confrontation, so some of the group were arrested—the others escaped. That was it for the people of Hargeisa.

Women and children in particular began a sustained stone-throwing campaign [against government offices and so on]. The government responded by deploying heavy weapons and imposing a curfew. There was a sharp decline in the economy when they closed the road from Djibouti, shutting off imports. That was when I began to see men leaving Hargeisa to join the SNM in Ethiopia.

There was a constant air of suspicion—questions as to your movements, whom you associated with, your political affiliations. Schools were in political turmoil, and women had to keep a constant watch over their children. Most [Isaaq] families had men in the SNM, and there were transfers of money, the clandestine return of men in search of clothes and so on. A family whose father is in Ethiopia is not going to cut off links to him. The *tabelehs* were very intrusive. So life became a sort of hell. Soldiers would search people's homes in the middle of the night. Well, you can imagine the behaviour of soldiers given license over people. They were told to look for SNM men hiding in the houses. Instead, they looked for gold and money, taking whatever they found.

But you had the impression that women coped with such

difficulties better than men. Every [Isaaq] woman and her *The conflict*
daughters had to attend events like the October celebrations *became a*
[commemorating Barre's accession to power]. If her husband or *kind of ritual*
son was known to have joined the SNM and she refused to attend,
this would be interpreted as hatred of the government. So these
women's time was divided between trying to assure their
childrens' survival, especially given the declining economy—in
many cases, the father who used to have this responsibility had left
the country—and staying involved in activities related to the
government.

So many men had crossed into Ethiopia, that the people left in
the region were mostly women and children. It became
embarrassing for the government to fill the prisons with women
and children. So the conflict became a kind of ritual anticipated by
both sides. The government knew that people hated the regime
more and more; and people knew that the government had the
power to make their life more and more miserable. The authorities
came up with a lot of new and baffling regulations: for example,
forbidding people to build houses.

But what could we do? Who could we complain to? There was
no TV or [international] telephone lines. It just became a matter of
the people and the government hunting each other. The security
agencies were of course competing with each other, for there was
the reckoning to be done later with the government. "Security
police, what have you done?" "We have arrested X number of
people and called this number of women to meetings."

People came to regard these practices as "normal", and told
themselves that worse was to come. So nothing shocked them or
reduced them to despair. By the time the SNM attacked the north
in 1988, people knew the hardships war would bring. Still, the
opportunity to escape governmental repression was a relief.

Being a refugee

We had to flee. We stayed in Ethiopia for a while, then I went to
Djibouti. The experience of becoming a refugee is awful, truly
wrenching. It is impossible to convey the misery of it. It was very
difficult to stay in the refugee camps where you saw so many
problems, but lacked the power to improve anything. Refugee
camps are the biggest source of depression.

So I came to London, out of desperation. I felt like somebody
who had been taken by the scruff of the neck and yanked out of
the town where she was born. Imagine, you are in your own
home, your belongings are all over the place, there are matters that

I felt like a human being with half of her missing

need your attention. You go to bed thinking of all you must do the next day. Suddenly, somebody walks in, takes you by the neck and throws you out of your home. It is something that you can never understand unless it happens to you.

I felt completely disoriented in London. I used to get lost on the train all the time. I had no sense of direction. I would remain in the train and go right past my destination. This happened to me all the time. I felt like a human being with half of her missing.

Eventually, after a period of feeling as if I was in a slumber, I got a job with the Somali Relief Association and went back to Hargeisa in August 1991.

Misgivings about NGOs

Often NGOs do things because they want to raise funds. But they are indifferent to the suffering of the people. How can they do their work if they don't actually care if the people live or die? I came to see that many foreign NGOs arrive with their own agendas and ideas which have nothing to do with the needs of Somaliland.

They seemed uninterested in building up governmental institutions. The experienced professional people were taken by the foreign NGOs, who offered them a few hundred dollars. Why don't they keep the person at the ministry of education, for example, and pay him the same money there? The effect is to cripple governmental institutions.

You get the impression that all international NGOs take themselves for anthropologists. Most of their questions to a Somali concern clans: "What clan is strong here? Which clans fight each other?" They hold meetings with two men who have been pointed out to them as elders, bypassing a hundred needy women on the way. These men they consult are unaware and indifferent to the needs of women.

Once we were talking to UNICEF about the installation of piped water. It is the women's job to collect water for the family, so UNICEF should have consulted the women. But they didn't. They went straight to the men, the ones they called the elders. The elders wanted the pipes installed near the mosques. So women were forced to collect their water in front of the mosque where the men go to pray. They have to watch their modesty in front of a mosque full of men preparing for their prayers, while dealing with the problem of collecting the water.

Agencies look at what they have been told is the "culture" and conclude, "In this country, we must listen to the men." No matter if the man eats too much *qat*, sits on a street corner and has no idea how his wife and children are doing. He is the one who will be allowed to make the decisions.

No matter how active women are economically, it will not last, because they are locked out of the larger decision-making process. They have no role to play in national affairs. When there is a war between two clans, they can demonstrate against the fighting. But they are not the ones who will sit under a tree deciding if there should be war or peace. They are the primary victims of this fighting, but they just have to wait for the decision.

Women are not fully aware of what they lack, of the rights they do not have. I understand their reluctance to go against the culture and religion. But they are thinking human beings who know that the absence of their rights will create problems for them, and it seems to me that the responsible thing to do is to speak up about this.

Even when they establish women's organisations, they allow the NGOs to dictate their needs. I watched NGOs tell groups of highly motivated traders and businesswomen about sewing machines and projects that they do not need or want. The NGOs tell them about some programme they tried out in Nicaragua or Bosnia or I don't know where. "This project works in other places, take it." They don't find out what this country needs, given its circumstances. It's not their problem. The minute there is a problem, there is a plane waiting for the expatriates.

I think the women's groups in Somaliland are stuck in grooves of what women's groups used to be. They haven't looked around and taken a proper survey of what the country needs now. They are all running parallel, competing, instead of coordinating their activities and priorities. They are very needy, and it is easier for them to take whatever they are offered than to refuse and wait for what they really want. Women woke up rather late in the day, and having woken up, they took their mindset and ideas from the men. All the time I have been in Somaliland, I cannot point to a women's organisation which has really responded to the needs of the women of Somaliland. If the women's organisations are not looking after the needs of women, who else will fill the gap?

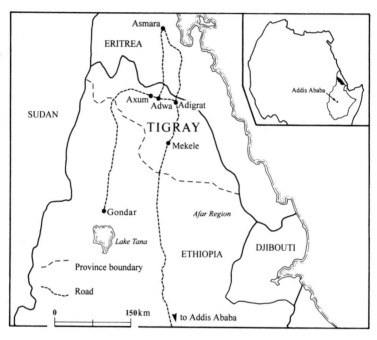

HUMAN DEVELOPMENT INDEX (UNDP): (Ethiopia) 161 (low)
POPULATION: (Ethiopia) 55m of which Tigray is 5m
FEMALE LIFE EXPECTANCY: (Ethiopia) 48.1 years
FEMALES WITHOUT SCHOOL EDUCATION: (Ethiopia) 73%

1875 Defeat of invading Egyptian forces **1889-1913** Menelik consolidates the Ethiopian Empire **1889** Italian colonisation of Eritrea **1896** Defeat of Italians invading Ethiopia **1916-74** Haile Selassie is Regent until **1930**, then Emperor **1935** Invasion and occupation by Fascist Italian forces; Haile Selassie flees **1941-54** Defeat of Italians; British occupation of Ethiopia; return of Haile Selassie **1943** First Tigrayan uprising **1961** Start of Eritrean struggle for independence **1962** Ethiopia annexes Eritrea **1960s and 70s** Growth of opposition against Haile Selassie **1972-4** Severe famine **1974** Overthrow of Haile Selassie; Derg takes power **1975** Start of TPLF armed struggle **1977-8** Red Terror - Derg campaign against opposition groups; war with Somalia; Ethiopia supported by USSR **1984-5** Severe famine **1989** TPLF gains control of all Tigray **1991** Mengistu flees, EPRDF forms Transitional Government **1993** Eritrean independence **1995** Adoption of new Ethiopian constitution; elections

— TIGRAY —

Ethiopia contains more than 70 distinct ethnic/linguistic groups, and has existed as a state within its present borders only since the late 19th century. The Amhara nationality has held power for most of the years since then, although the largest ethnic group is the Oromo, spread over the southern half of the country.

The majority of Ethiopia's people have always been poor peasant farmers, oppressively ruled by a "feudal" land-holding and military aristocracy. The 1,600-year-old Orthodox Church was also an economically burdensome and conservative power. Although the warlordism prevalent in the 19th century gave way to greater internal stability under Emperors Menelik (1884-1913) and Haile Selassie (1916-1974), most farmers remained in poverty, barely subsisting from tiny plots and heavily taxed.

Agriculture is still a struggle, especially in the highlands of Tigray and the central provinces, where overcultivation, deforestation and soil erosion combine with unpredictable rainfall to produce the regular droughts and famines for which Ethiopia is known. In 1974 Tigray, one of the least developed provinces, had schooling for only 8% of the population, no modern health services in rural areas, and only two all-weather roads.

Tigrayans first rebelled, unsuccessfully, against neglect and discrimination in 1943. There was briefly hope of a better future in 1974 when the government of Haile Selassie was overthrown by a military coup. But the regime of Mengistu Haile Mariam—known as the Derg ("Committee")—soon became equally oppressive, imposing its version of socialism through a system of enforced neighbourhood and peasant associations, villagisation and collectivisation. Not only was this system economically inefficient, but national resources were increasingly consumed by wars—in 1978 against Somalia, from 1961 against the Eritrean People's Liberation Front (EPLF), and from 1975 against the Tigrayan People's Liberation Front (TPLF). The regime was armed by the Soviet Union but also received development and massive emergency support, to mitigate its failed policies, from the West.

The TPLF's armed struggle was launched in 1975 by a handful of poorly-armed students, and over the next few years, along with its neighbour and ally the EPLF, it became the strongest of several opposition movements facing the government. Unlike the EPLF, which was fighting for independence from Ethiopia (achieved in 1993), the TPLF's goal was to establish a democratic government within Ethiopia. Based on a Marxist ideology, it mobilised Tigray's rural population in support of its agenda for social and political change, and in the areas under its control, carried out administrative and land tenure reform, and provided education and welfare services, in very difficult circumstances and with almost no international support. Derg attacks on civilians, including destruction of crops and frequent aerial bombardment, encouraged support for the rebels; and the 1984-5 famine merely intensified Tigrayans' determination.

By June 1989 the TPLF was in control of the whole province including the capital, Mekele, and had linked with other opposition movements to form the Ethiopian Peoples' Revolutionary Democratic Front (EPRDF). By this time the government was economically and militarily exhausted, and Mengistu fled in May 1991. A Transitional Government was formed in Addis Ababa, with the EPRDF predominant but most of the country's other nationalities also represented. The new government immediately set about a programme of reform, decentralising power to elected governments in Ethiopia's regions and dismantling the Derg's state-controlled economic system. Elections to establish a democratic government are due to take place in May 1995.

It was the TPLF's commitment to improving the lives of ordinary people, including women, that attracted so many Tigrayans to support the struggle. Traditionally the status of women in Ethiopian society was extremely low. They were often married at 12 or 13, and had little education, and few economic or political rights. The TPLF introduced new rules on marriage and divorce, education including consciousness-raising targeted at women, improved health and welfare provision. It gave women an active role in grass-roots and higher level politics, access to land and to hitherto exclusively male productive activities such as ploughing. In 1982, women formed 25% of TPLF "fighters", by which is meant being involved in actual combat, underground work, political mobilisation, education or welfare provision.

The TPLF created a spirit of determination and unity, promoting a habit of self-discipline and a willingness to put community needs before personal concerns. This is clearly evident in the interviews carried out for this project, and it reinforced a reticence about personal affairs and opinions which is general in Ethiopian culture. All the women quoted here were active supporters of the TPLF, and retain the strong commitment to the movement's goals and methods that brought them victory.

The interviewers, Woyni Bisirat, Abeba Shiferaw, Worknesh Bekele, Yibralem Yibegin, Haregeweini Gebreselassie and Yeshi Gezai, are all members of the Democratic Association of Tigrayan Women. The interview with Herity and Mebrat was carried out by Fiona Meehan of the Relief Society of Tigray (REST).

Herity and Mebrat   TIG G1/2

Herity joined the TPLF in 1976 and is now Deputy General Secretary of the Democratic Association of Tigrayan Women. Mebrat was also a fighter and senior figure in the TPLF women's movement.

HERITY: I and my brother were fighters [based in TPLF-controlled areas], and our father was killed by the Derg, so our house [in Derg-controlled Mekele] was a suspected *woyane* (rebel) house. Every month an auditing committee came to look at the books and receipts [of the family business, which mother continued to run].

Surveillance by the Derg

My mother had no contact with us and didn't know where we were. Psychologically she was damaged—and is even now—by [this], and [because of what] the Derg was doing to the house. She was like a prisoner, [and they kept] taking things from the house, again and again.

From 1976, when we joined the **Front**, until 1980, she had to pay money to [the Derg] because they said we were in prison. [The] money [was] for food, soap and clothes they said they were supplying us with. Finally, my mother sent people to search in Addis and they told her we were not there. [My brother and I] were at the front but my father had [in fact] been killed in 1976. She asked [the authorities] repeatedly and [at last she and other families in the same situation] were given a letter saying the men were supporters of the Front and that "revolutionary action" had been taken against them, meaning that they had been killed. You were not allowed to cry. It was considered a crime. And they asked again: "Where are their bodies?" [and were told:] "You can't ask us that."

[The authorities kept saying my brother and I had been killed]— it was propaganda. They would say to people: "The fighters from around here—we have imprisoned them, we have killed them."

The village women used to say: "How can you be fighters?" They terrorised people. [When we returned] our mother was... shocked. She had no idea we were alive.

I know some women who still don't believe their chldren have died. The TPLF has declared: "From now on, if your children don't come, you have to assume they are martyrs." But even [now] they don't accept that. Last year [1993], during the celebration of the TPLF's anniversary, the TPLF told the fighters: "Whether you are in the west or the east [of Tigray], you must write a letter to your families." They told the people: "The fighters who have not written letters to you [should be assumed dead]."

Attitudes towards female fighters

HERITY: [Village people] used to ask us: "How can you go alone into the field? Don't you feel afraid?" They asked so many questions and wanted to know all about us. They asked about some personal things: "How do you sleep (what are the sleeping arrangements)?", "What do you eat?", "Men eat fast, so how do you eat with them?" They wanted to know [whether there was] rape, and [about] sexual things. Some young women asked about [how we managed when we had] our periods.

MEBRAT: At the beginning most of us [fighters] were women from urban areas. The [village] women used to say: "How can you be fighters? How can you go into the field with men?" You would try and explain and then they'd say: "It's because you're educated. We couldn't do that." And on the other hand the men would say: "Oh, they're not educated, they're nothing. They can't do what you do." They tried [to stop] the women coming. It was obvious that they felt threatened.

HERITY: There was a saying "women have no veins", meaning she is physically weak. Another saying was "she has a brain like a donkey". There were jokes to undermine women. They used to say that if a woman built a house it would fall down the next day, because she had no idea how to do it. Or if a woman touches a plough, the plough has to be broken, because she takes the strength out of it.

[In those days] you couldn't just call a meeting for women. You had to attend the cultural occasions: church, birth [celebrations], weddings, religious holidays, [when] women gathered in large numbers in one house or another. Of course, in that kind of group the agenda is different and you shift it. When they talk about their holidays or their problems, you divert this to other agendas like health, the Ethiopian struggle [or] the economic situation. So they started to see us as members of the group.

[In time], women decided they needed meetings to discuss political issues. Men took this badly. "What are women doing?" they wondered. At that time the **EPRP** was spreading the unhelpful message that equality meant men doing women's tasks—carrying babies, baking *injera*. This was untimely. So people asked us: "What does equality mean?" We taught that the main issue was to participate in all aspects of society, and to own land. Sharing [responsibility] in all things was [good], not bad, but we should get there gradually. [Men] were convinced and accepted [what we said], but [many] still obstructed us. So we taught women that they had to struggle themselves, After a while, women became organised at neighbourhood and district levels.

MEBRAT: The approach of the male fighters was one of the things that attracted women to the TPLF. Before that, the only men with guns that women in Tigray knew were either bandits or army, who threatened their dignity.

Mobilising people through song

HERITY: Songs were a very important instrument of mobilisation. In the past there were just [professional] singers for [festivals] and marriages. But in wartime everyone was singing together. All the time there were cultural shows. When you teach people you don't just lecture, you use drama, song, dance. Cultural groups went to other areas to share their experiences. Even now, they create songs for every occasion. Songs are created according to needs. For example, on one training course, some women were not interested in learning theory. They said: "The training is in cutting cloth [and making clothes]. Why should we waste time on theoretical stuff? If we have to learn all these things on paper we'll be here for six months or a year..." So they created plays [to help them] learn the importance of theory.

There was a song in the Baito (people's council) elections about evaluating—you can't allow someone to join a work [team] without evaluating him [or her]. People might be opposed, and say: "We know him. He talks too much in meetings and he doesn't practise [what he preaches]."

"We know her, this Hariya.
She grew up in our village.
She talks too much
But she doesn't practise it.
We have to elect people who share our problems
And participate in our solutions....

She puts herself above the people.
She is not like us.
Leave her, leave her,
Don't elect her.
We are electing people who share our problems."

The development of the Women's Associations

The structure and aims of the TPLF's women's organisations, and the regulation of sexual relations and marriage between fighters, were constantly discussed and developed from 1977 to 1988.

We [women fighters] came together [in 1977] and discussed whether there was a need for a [women's] organisation inside the TPLF. Among us there were women who, because they were physically strong and doing activities [like men], did not see the point of organising the women alone. They thought equality meant physically doing every activity that men do. This is not what we call equality in reality—whether we carry the same bag or whether we have differences in physique.

MEBRAT: We knew that just because we were fighters, it didn't mean we were free. Women's oppression could be reflected in many ways.

HERITY: We [also] realised that [merely] by being combatants we would not solve women's problems, and that to address the problems of rural civilian women we needed to change the culture. Discussions were almost our entire life. You would write an agenda and sit there for hours and discuss it. It could be on class, the class struggle—you were working, or teaching the people, in different ways.

MEBRAT: The [Women's] Committee's main task was to politicise women. By 1981 the TPLF had many women fighters, because from 1979 onwards, women from the villages joined the organisation in their thousands. So the Committee was going to many districts, to mobilise women in the villages. Schools for women were opened, for midwives...

The Women's Committee also worked on women's consciousness. Health was very much stressed, because there was this attitude in women fighters of "I don't need any special treatment". We always got two tablets of soap a month, and for men it was one. Even this, there were fighters who rejected it. They said, "We are equal, there is no difference [between us]." Because of this there had been problems with women's health.

For some years, we never thought we needed a women's organisation within the TPLF. We knew that women [outside] needed an organisation but [the question was] "Does that include us?" Almost unanimously we decided: we are no different from other women, we have to get organised, [along] with all the women in the villages. It was only for convenience that we had our own [association], because our way of life was different. You are here today, and tomorrow somewhere else. So we couldn't be organised with women in the villages. The first conference dealt mainly with the chauvinistic attitude in the organisation, because I think every woman [present] felt that deeply.

We needed to change the culture

Sexual relations

HERITY: For almost 10 years we had a no-marriage law in the Front. Marriage was thought to be unimportant. People thought first of the struggle.

MEBRAT: Nothing official [in the way of sexual relations was allowed]. It wouldn't have been possible—in the early period—for women who participated in the struggle. There was no means of buying birth control [and] no culture of using [contraceptives]. Even for those who did have this culture, it was not convenient. One day you're here, tomorrow you're somewhere else. Today you're near a river, tomorrow you may not get water. It's difficult.

The no-marriage law was tough but it wasn't [fully] implemented—never. [When there was an infringement], if the punishment [had been] very harsh, it would have created conflict. It was very pragmatic. It wasn't the law that was strong... I think it was the attitude towards it that prevented marriage, otherwise it wouldn't have been possible to go 10 years without marriage. It became like a taboo, so you were afraid not of the law but the attitude.

[The no-marriage law] had a positive role. Between men and women there was talk, not sexual activity. A man would look at a woman in relation to her job, not in relation to whom she goes with and what she does. Had there been marriage it would have been a problem for the women, it would have been the continuation of the [old] society, the way it looks at women. In previous wars women participated by bringing food, maybe for the leaders. Maybe society would have continued [to expect] women to serve those who are in the struggle.

Of course there were negative attitudes too. Sometimes [men] wanted women to hide their bodies. They looked at the way women dressed, the way they walked and laughed, and they sometimes criticised. But compared to the [positive] contribution I think this is much less—the negative influence.

Between men
and women
there was
talk, not
sexual
activity

Changing views on marriage

It was in 1985 that [marriage] was allowed. There were discussions before the [1985] conference, and there were [views expressed] for and against marriage. Especially among women, there were many who disagreed—[because] babies would arrive and we would not be able to work. There were discussions about whether it was possible [in war circumstances] to allow marriage, and about how many children, how to bring children up, things like that. [For] some, [there was] a feeling of insecurity, but this was not raised [publicly]. Because we were few women, there was a concern [that] you would have problems... [Women felt that the men] might all want a woman and... trouble.

Most people wanted it but, you know, they didn't even want to talk about it. After the conference, marriage [happened] very fast—because people were [already] thinking about it.

HERITY: [Certain rules were introduced:] a married person was given annual leave of one month with their wife or husband. If a woman fighter became pregnant, after three months she would come out of the army and work in a safe area. A month before she was due to have the baby, she would rest—maternity leave [was] three months.

There being so many babies was a big problem for us. At the grassroots it was thought that contraceptives [caused] deformed children. The TPLF brought condoms, everything for family planning, but there was no acceptance. Although people wanted to have just one child, they didn't use contraceptives, and there were so many abortions.

"I freely choose"

MEBRAT: [After the marriage laws changed] it didn't make a very big difference, but the relationship was very free and open. There were a few women who, instead of sticking to their job, were tending to give unnecessary time to... But I think because there was no question of property among us... I freely choose my friend and I freely divorce, and that was it.

In our marriage law there are certain [rules], like if [people] marry and the woman gets pregnant, and then they divorce, he cannot marry [again] until the baby is a year old. And for everybody, if they get divorced they cannot marry [again] before six months have passed. The purpose was not to force them to come together, but for them to think about it. It was good. It was not long [enough] to be a punishment, it was really an honourable time for reconsidering your relationship. Because, you know, there was nobody [mediating] between us, it was only me and him to think about it. It's not like in normal society where the parents come and tell her [what to do]... his parents, the priest and the judge...

I think there were six months of transition, so if you formed a friendship with a certain guy you told someone in your department, and they would know you were friends. [This was important] because we lived [crowded] together, so he or she could provide possibilities for [a couple] to be together, and to some extent protection also—because if, formally, people didn't know who your friend was, then problems would arise. There would be friendship and then marriage. In fact, all these formalities didn't work as far as the fighters [were concerned]. Once you got together you were considered married. There were no ceremonies either, [not] even tea, special dress... nobody cared about it.

I think most people who are together don't think about [not having legal married status]. We have no certificate, we have nothing, [but] somehow we don't face any problems. But there are a few problems, especially for some women... like [if] they have a child and then get divorced. Our rules were built on our life, and our life was just [that] you eat what the organisation provides... our rules had nothing to do with property, salary or anything. Now there are [new] rules and regulations about obligations, especially now she has a salary and he has a salary. Some [female] fighters have two children by different [male] fighters, and [the men] don't care to help them. The women think their pride would be affected if they asked him to help. Even the one who has been hurt by the fact that she is the only one caring for the baby, she doesn't raise [the problem]. But they really have problems, so I think there have to be rules for such cases.

Care of children

There was a second conference about this marriage [question], and do you know [in] the discussion about children, they said one is enough, because of this and that. But anyway, we [were] not going to have two in such a situation—from our experience it was very difficult. The organisation gave priority to children and provided us [with] so many things—lemon, sugar, clothes and shoes—but still there were problems. Before [having a child] we were very relaxed when planes came, we never thought about it. I never thought for myself: what will happen to me? But, after that, you think about the baby, so you are always [feeling] tension.

HERITY: In the first conference, it was arranged that women should stay with their children until they were three and, while bringing

them up, they should study. [The TPLF] opened schools for them.
MEBRAT: Many women opposed it. They said, "We must leave [the babies] and go to our battalions. That's it, let somebody [else] take care of them." But it wasn't true when you had the baby. I don't know... other women are a bit careless about their children. Among fighters it was different... [there was] attachment. I think life was too hard—you had to take the baby everywhere with you, to meetings... you know, in meetings you hear the voice of the baby as well as the chairman and others one cries, another laughs... You had to cook, and if there is malaria threatening you every day... It was very difficult. The problem was not food and clothes, [it] was circumstances.

[The role of fathers] depended [on circumstances]. There were very few [instances] where the man and the woman were together. One might be in the east and one in the west. Even to see each other... there were laws about when to see each other, 40 days a year, every six months, but in reality who would go from the east to the west every six months, or [even] every year? Usually you would see each other at big meetings, every two years. Also it wasn't convenient for two [parents] to take [on the] care. For those who were together, it depended on their attitudes. Some of them helped each other. [Some women had this kind of relationship:] I was one.

There was discussion about whether women should leave the children after three or six months and let centres take care of them. But we thought it should be the mother or the father who takes care of the child. Considering the life we had, [the children] were very healthy. Almost everyone had only one baby but they all grew up, except for very rare cases. Our health department had set their priorities for children. They gave [so much care] to them.

Abrehet   TIG D3

Abrehet, 30, was a fighter in the TPLF.

In the past, during the time of Derg, I entered school when I was a child. But when I saw the oppressor government and its cadres kidnapping girls by force, forcing people to walk on their knees, I left school and stayed at home.

The Derg told us that the TPLF was full of lice and with very big ears. Since we were children, we were very scared. But later on, in 1979, we saw them. They had their own songs. They took us to the forest and talked to us there. Although we didn't know much about what they did, I realised that they were kind and that they stood for the people and for peace [and] I knew that the Derg's sayings were total lies. Later, they came to our area and started to teach us. I was only 13. Although I was young and had no idea about the aims of the struggle, I really had the national feelings. I also used to be friendly with the fighters. I tried to join them many times but I wasn't allowed because I was too young. However, eventually, when they understood my feelings and interests, they took me [in]. I joined them in 1982 and in 1984 became a member of the Cultural Artists (the **Front's** musicians).

They used to say that a woman was a handicapped creature

When I compare what I knew in the past with what I know today, I am amazed. I now know a lot and have a clear idea about the struggle. In the past a woman had no right to decide on her own. When a woman got married to someone she didn't like, and if she refused to live with the person, she was kicked and beaten. What's more, people used to say that she was caught by *Tebib* (evil-eyed person) and they used to give her unnecessary medicine. In the past there was no chance of expressing yourself in a group, of getting proper treatment or of learning as you liked. They used to say that a woman was a handicapped creature. This is not totally solved even now. We were being considered as weak individuals.

During the struggle the Front has allowed me to learn up to grade five. I have even started grade six. I appreciate this very much.

Akeza   TIG F3

Akeza stayed with her child while her husband fought.

My parents were very poor. My mother lost her son and brought me here. She sold wood and *injera* to pay for our needs. I used to help by collecting wood and fetching water. I would take [the *injera*] to market and sell it. I used to buy and sell little things and give the profit—5 or 10 cents—to my mother. I had no idea about how people led their lives. All I did was eat and play.

Suffering under the Derg

My family were all displaced [during the war]. I wanted to go with them but my mother made me stay. I was left behind crying, with all the problems I had. After that, my father died and I buried him myself.

[One day I was arrested] and remanded in custody. Some powermongers who wanted to join the Derg's political party saw me **wearing trousers** and accused me of being a member of the

TPLF. They took me and beat me on my back for about six hours. [The next day] they beat me from six in the morning until noon. I was on the verge of death. But I decided I would rather die than tell a lie, and expose myself and others.

Many people from our area were dying because of the war. We were afraid we would be killed by one of two bullets—the TPLF's or the Derg's. We had no idea about the TPLF and knew nothing about its aims and objectives. But when the fighters who were at Machare told us the aims of the struggle, we wanted to join it. But because of the beating I had suffered, I had a problem walking up and down hills, and I couldn't walk on stones and weeds. So I didn't go, but I had a deep-rooted desire to join the struggle.

When the TPLF first came to our area, we secretly gave them food and water. Then, when the Derg [soldiers] came searching for them, we would hide them under a piece of cloth or even carry them around as [if they were] sick people. Their rifles were hidden underground. When the enemy left, they would take their rifles again and preach their cause.

Separation and survival

My husband took part in the struggle. When he left, I asked to go with him, but he said no. He said I should take care of our child and when our son grew up I could join the struggle. He said he would rather die himself than see our people dying, that he wouldn't break his resolve and that **February's light** would not be darkened.

[He joined the struggle] because he understood its purpose. [He] was an educated person, he organised meetings day and night to [speak] about democracy to his people. He compared the past with the present, and spoke about a better future. He understood his past oppression and remembered that one day when he was going to trade goods he had been hit by 15 bullets. I was happy [that he went] when I realised [it was to fight] the oppression we had both suffered.

I was always hopeful that one day things would change. The changes could come either through education or [improved] farming. So I told my husband to struggle and free Tigray. Only then could we help ourselves. With this belief I didn't suffer much.

It was through my own efforts that I survived; I knew that [my husband] could only help me in the future. I bought and sold beans and *siwa* (local beer) and made 5 or 10 cents' profit. I used to trade things and feed myself, eating one [small loaf of] bread for lunch and one for dinner. But when I fell sick the trade stopped and I was left with an empty stomach. I had to save money, and when I had collected a good sum I was able to buy clothes. I used to buy cereals at a low price and sell them when the price was high.

My husband has come back now. He worked [as a member of] the district administration committee. I felt happy [when he came back] because I had got what I wished for. When he left to join the struggle he knew there would be death and life, losing a hand and gaining honey (suffering and reward). This was his belief.

If a tree is propped up with a piece of wood it will soon fall down

Justice for all

I faced poverty before, but during the struggle I realised what we were striving for. In the past, even trade licences were given only to the rich or to those who paid bribes. But today is the time of democracy and human rights. As one of the oppressed people, I have the right to work and eat. Nowadays, even if a seven-year-old child wants to be a merchant she has the right. Things have improved: [there is] democracy and business [is easier]. The rights of women are also respected. We can argue, accuse [people who wrong us], claim back what we lost, do what we feel like—anywhere and at any time.

If someone has problems he or she can go to court and get justice. There is no difference between male and female, oppressed and oppressor: justice is available to all. Land is shared equally between men and women. In the past, only bureaucrats had [much] land—up to 10 large plots—but now, oppressed women are getting their share without discrimination. An adolescent of 15 can have his share of land and use it. The grain which used to be sold by the previous government, in order to buy rifles and bullets to kill the oppressed, is now owned by the oppressed themselves.

I don't expect anything from the government or the TPLF. If the government follows a democratic path, these are all gifts to me. I can do a lot in business. If a tree is propped up with another piece of wood it will soon fall down. I want to be self-reliant, I don't want to be dependent.

I don't want [to claim back what we have lost]. You can't bring back someone who has died, or if someone loses an eye you can't bring the eye back. What we really want is to work hard and make up for our losses. For this we need to struggle to make our state prosperous. I have a bright hope [that my children will receive education] so that they can lead a good life.

In the future I [feel we] need electricity and big industries. This can be achieved if we all struggle to bring development to the state. Our ruined state will develop and, with trucks able to move from place to place, trade will be facilitated and the state will prosper. [This will mean] women have the opportunity to work.

Fetyen   TIG F4

Fetyen, who is nearly 50, became a local coordinator of support to the TPLF. Her account is notable for the almost mythical way she describes her part in the conflict.

I was born when Italy was defeated. I am an orphan. I grew up with my aunt. I used to fetch water, collect wood, shake the milk to make butter, grind grain—I was short so I stood on a stone to grind the grain. I would go with my friend to fetch water from far away, without saying that I was tired.

Derg propaganda

At the beginning [of the war] we heard that the TPLF fighters had wide mouths and very big ears, so we were warned to keep clear of them. We heard that they ate human beings, that they opened their mouths and chewed you [up], that they were not human. This was the propaganda used by the Derg cadres. [Then] we had a series of meetings with them and we saw that they were human beings like us. We realised that [the stories] were just lies on the part of the criminal government. We accepted [the TPLF] as our children, and with happiness.

At first we felt that when two governments fight with each other we would be the victims, we would be in the dark. We were covered by a dark curtain. [The TPLF] taught us that they had come to free us from the oppression of the criminal government. When we realised that they were our brothers and sisters we became free from the fear we had felt. [Then] the people elected me as a coordinator, and I willingly accepted because I wanted to follow the guidelines of the TPLF.

Helping the TPLF

When they left for a campaign, we met and discussed what we could do. First we collected 36 wooden mortars. We dried *injera* and crushed it with a pestle. We assigned about eight people to watch it so that the enemy couldn't put poison in it. While doing this we sang and danced. We sent all the food we prepared to the war front. We didn't stop there. We discussed how to welcome them [when they returned]. We each agreed to contribute three or four cups of sorghum and barley to prepare *siwa* (local beer). We gathered the people and they all agreed with our idea. Both subdistricts, Boyen and Gararsa, prepared about 84 big pots of *siwa*, and then waited for our fighters to come. We had about 5 **quintals** of dried *injera* left.

Then the Derg came and burnt Abdera. All the people fled. I decided not to run, leaving my possessions behind. I was even prepared to die. I buried 3 *quintals* of dried *injera* and the *siwa* underground. Then I left the place and slept in a church. When I returned to keep an eye on my possessions, I met 35 fighters and another 10 people waiting for food. I uncovered the hole [where the food was hidden] and gave them 30 big cups of the crushed food and one pot of *siwa*. I told them to carry the food to the war front.

We felt that when two governments fight with each other we would be the victims

There were about 30 other fighters who were seriously in need of food. I baked about 45 *injera* and divided them among the fighters. I was not afraid. I also sent food to the fighters at a place called Hirika. After this, without the knowledge of the Derg [soldiers], I sent the remaining food and *siwa* to the fighters. The Derg [soldiers] left our area without getting it. After this I left to see the fighters who were in Afar area. I met fighters carrying flour and they asked me to bake them bread. They asked some other women, who refused. On the way, they fought with Derg [soldiers], who took half of the bread I had given them.

All our sons

When I fled with my son, we had 16 radios, nine bombs and 30,000 bullets in a sack. I carried them on my back and reached a place called Magale. I gave [the ammunition] to [a fighter named] Kidane and he asked: "Why did you bring this? If you'd been found by the Derg you would have been killed. Why didn't you leave it there?" I replied: "You have made a lot of sacrifices and I am no better than any one of you".

When [our fighters] fought at Hirika, we joined the fighting and provided them with six or seven plastic [containers] of water, seven or eight plates of *injera*, and bullets. I had no fear at all. I am not boasting. If you want, you can ask the people of Boyegararsa. They will tell you the truth. My sons argued that it was [their role] to struggle and die, and that I should go home. But I told them: "It's not just an old lady like me, but even you young boys are struggling and making sacrifices." So I said I wouldn't go back.

One day they fought with Derg [soldiers] and I carried bullets under my dress and gave them these while the fighting was going on. Even in the war area I carried milk, water and *injera*, and helped the wounded. I did all I could for my **Front**. I gave them roasted beans, sorghum flour and eggs. I went to Magale and helped the wounded for about 32 days instead of attending to my home, my son, my brother and my husband. I understood that all the fighters were our sons and that they were fighting to free us all.

My son hasn't returned. I am not grieving; instead I feel happy

When [the fighters] returned from Korem and Alamata I organised members of the Women's Association and welcomed them by giving 75 *injera* and four plastic [containers] of *siwa*. As a result, I was praised as the star of the Women's Association.

"Mother of Heroes"

After that I returned home. I brought an ox to plough my plot of land. [The next day] at about 9 o'clock in the morning, 8,000 Derg soldiers moved towards [our village]. I had heard the firing of bullets during the night. As I was preparing breakfast we found ourselves surrounded by Derg soldiers. They ordered [my son] to surrender, insulting him and saying, "You son of a bitch," but he managed to escape. My ox was hit by a bullet and died. Then the militia and the fighters gave me 64 **birr**. They praised me and called me: "Mother of Heroes."

[My son] hasn't returned. [I am not grieving;] instead I feel happy because I know he is one hundred times better than those who are stealing and being punished.

Our main reason [for struggling] was to eliminate the fascist government and establish a just order. Although [in the old days] we sang a song and praised him a lot, the past Emperor had cast us aside. Here in Burika our fathers had large plots of land, but they were taken by the feudal landlords. They even took bread, *siwa* and honey from us. They became the owners and we became their donkeys. They filled their containers and underground holes with our grain. We couldn't talk because our mouths were zipped shut. So until we become totally free, we will continue to struggle and will never go back again.

"The sky and the earth"

[Life] is improving tremendously. We must stand by our Front. We must avoid evil thoughts. We must also be able to teach the realities to those who are not [politically] conscious.

Now [there is peace]. Before, when we [moved around] we were afraid we would be hit by a jet fighter and we used to hide underground or in the jungle. Even when we saw a crow we thought it was a jet fighter and were terrified. We went to the market at night like bandits. [In the dark] we used to turn the mouths of our grain containers upside down, unknowingly, and all the contents would be spilt. We would hold the legs of a child, thinking they were his hands. Later, we even told our people not to go to the market and, as a result, grass grew in the marketplace.

But now we can walk around in the daytime freely and do whatever work we want to do. In the past, outlaws used to

"We thank our Front, it gave the poor *teff*, sorghum, beans"

Neil Cooper/Panos Pictures

threaten us, pointing long sticks at us and pretending they were rifles. We had a cobra-like government which was not satisfied even if it ate too much. How can you compare that with [the conditions] of today? It is like the sky and the earth.

The TPLF has rescued our people from being taken to the

We have come out from behind the dark curtain rehabilitation areas in big trucks. It took our people to the Sudan for some time and saved the lives of many. We thank our Front, for it has saved us from poverty and death. It also shared the land equally among men and women. A man of 25 or a girl of 15 can take his or her share. It gave the poor *teff* (the staple grain), sorghum, beans—free, for sowing on our plots of land.

Now our land is free. I also thank God for sparing my daughter. We have come out from behind the dark curtain. Our house is open, [no enemy] enters. Our cattle go and come in peace. I would like to live in peace, without any ups or downs. I refuse to say that the Front hasn't given us this or that. The TPLF means us, the people—so we have to discuss things with each other and solve our problems.

But I have one grievance against my Front. We sent our children to fight and die, but we haven't been told whether they have died or not. Why doesn't it tell us whether they are alive or dead?

Saedia   TIG C4

Saedia is a 40-year-old Muslim woman.

I was married at the age of nine. The son of my uncle arranged my marriage according to the Muslim religion. I was in a dilemma whether to escape or not. I was a very little girl. We women were especially oppressed in the Muslim religion. We had no right over the property we owned with our husbands. The husband gave only 30 **birr** and the wife barely left the house. The main cause was the feudal system of Emperor Haile Selassie. Women had no right to say even a single word. We had no right to go out of our houses to visit relatives and friends. There was no way out.

My son and brother joined the TPLF [because] they were oppressed and we women were oppressed, especially in sex. My brother didn't come back. Many people died and were wounded and people's property was destroyed. All this was expected. Unless you sacrificed, you wouldn't be successful. I didn't feel [anything] —this was normal.

The TPLF gave the best answer to the question of women. There is justice and women are treated equally. Whatever the husband and wife own, [they] have the right to share equally. All our rights are reserved. The Muslim men are already convinced, and they treat us equally.

Ghidey   **TIG B6**

Ghidey is a teacher in Axum.

The military government put me in prison when my husband and sons took off. They asked me over and over where they had gone. While I was bringing up young children, I did all the assignments given to me from the TPLF underground. Once I was to be assigned chairman of the Women's Association of the Derg, but I refused to accept it, because all my feelings and senses are with the TPLF.

My eldest son, Mulugeta, joined the TPLF on 16 March 1976. All Mulugeta's friends were in prison and I was very much afraid for my son. I locked him up for six days in my bedroom. I did not want to see him dead [at the hands of the Derg] so I sent him out through the window at night and he went and joined the TPLF.

After the bitter struggle my husband and younger son returned, but my elder son didn't come home. It was understood that someone had to give his life for the oppressed masses. I felt proud of my son.

"The bright future"

Long live the TPLF! Conditions are improving. You see people working, going here and there. We go to church at any time, day or night. We sleep at night without any disturbance. We have the right to speak what we feel at meetings. We can move anywhere and lead our lives smoothly and peacefully. We have ceased the armed struggle, but the struggle will continue in the economic reconstruction. We should not be idle. Everyone young or old should work cooperatively according to his or her ability and this will lead us to the bright future.

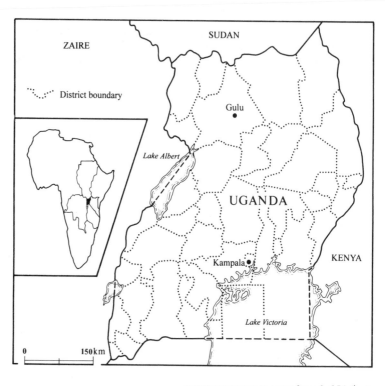

HUMAN DEVELOPMENT INDEX (UNDP): 154 (low)
POPULATION: 18.7m
FEMALE LITERACY: 35%
FEMALE LIFE EXPECTANCY: 43.9 years

1877 Arrival of first European missionaries to Kingdom of Buganda; Muslim influence already established **1884-5** Berlin Conference divided Africa into "spheres of influence" for European powers **1888-93** Imperial British East Africa Company administration in Uganda **1893** Buganda becomes British protectorate **1962** Independence **1966** Obote suspends constitution and declares himself president **1971** Army Chief General Idi Amin seizes power **1979** Invasion by Tanzanian army and Obote supporters **1980** Obote elected; clandestine National Resistance Army established to fight Obote **1985** Obote overthrown; regime of Tito Okello **1986** Jan: NRA enter Kampala; Yoweri Museveni becomes president **1987** Two main rebel armies in North defeated by NRA, including the Holy Spirit movement **1994** Elected assembly starts to debate new constitution

～ UGANDA ～

Uganda's boundaries—established by the British during the 19th century—contain at least 28 ethnic groups. These fall into three main divisions: Bantu-speakers in the south and west of the country (including the Baganda, from whom modern Uganda derives its name and its capital city); Nilotic speakers in the northwest and east (including the Acholi, the group to which the interviewees belong); and Central Sudanic speakers in northern West Nile region. At independence the future looked bright, but Uganda suffered instead two decades of turbulence and economic collapse. A contributory factor was rivalry between ethnic groups, and underdevelopment of the north compared with the south of the country.

In 1966 the elected Prime Minister Obote, from the northern Langi people, suspended the constitution and declared himself president. Opposition was violently suppressed by Obote's army chief Idi Amin, who himself seized power in 1971. Years of murderous repression followed, particularly aimed at Obote's people, the Acholi and Langi. Up to 500,000 people may have died before the Tanzanian army helped Obote overthrow Amin. Elections (widely suspected not to have been free and fair) returned Obote to power in 1980, but one group of his supporters, led by Yoweri Museveni, soon broke away and formed the clandestine National Resistance Army (NRA).

Obote's second period of rule saw more violence against the NRA, other rebel groups and civilians, with another estimated 500,000 deaths. An Acholi faction in the army overthrew Obote but were themselves ousted by the NRA, who took control of Kampala. Museveni became president.

Peace was restored to most of the country within months, but in the north resistance continued. These interviews come from the northern district of Gulu, and relate to the period 1986—1991. The various rebel groups, including Alice Lakwena's Holy Spirit Movement, were not united, and did not generally have coherent political or social programmes. Most civilians did not actively support either the government or the rebels, but were caught between them, suffering the looting, brutality and scorched earth policies of both sides. By 1990 the government—the National Resistance Movement (NRM)—controlled most of the region, but in 1994 there were still pockets of banditry and revolt.

Museveni's declared priorities have been to restore the

conditions for the economy to function, and to establish a representative political system which avoids the ethnic rivalries of the past. Popular representation is through a hierarchy of Resistance Councils from village up to parliamentary level, and a new constitution is being adopted.

Uganda's economy is largely agricultural; soil and rainfall are fairly favourable and in general there is no shortage of land. But from relative prosperity in 1962, with exports of coffee, tea and cotton, and relatively good education and health care services, the years of war saw a collapse of infrastructure and the formal economy. The government's negotiations with aid donors have inevitably entailed a stiff structural adjustment programme (SAP), which adds its bitter effect to the difficult aftermath of the war.

The Acholi traditionally lived in family groups farming around a homestead, and cattle were an important part of their wealth. Cotton production was significant; and many Acholi men had jobs in the army and civil service. But cotton marketing collapsed during the Amin years, and cattle were almost entirely wiped out during the fighting of 1985-90. Now, when people need income more than ever to pay for education and health services, non-agricultural jobs—especially for men—have fallen victim to SAP-imposed "retrenchment" in government services.

In traditional Acholi society, women were a subordinate but protected part of a polygynous extended-family social system, farming their husbands' land. After two decades of war, gender relations are in confusion. Faced with the absence of men and the demands of survival, women took on new responsibilities and gained strength and independence. At the same time, the brutalisation caused by violence and the collapse of social institutions and morality left them vulnerable to sexual and economic exploitation. Men are finding it hard to re-establish their place in post-war society, undermined by the loss of their cattle and the absence of off-farm employment; and social expectations and legal rights as regards land, marriage and women's role are in a state of flux. The government is committed to inclusion of women and recognition of their concerns in the political process at all levels—Uganda has five women ministers as of 1994—but at village level a new order will take time to emerge.

Interviews were gathered by Lucy (Kidaga) Larubi, Florence Okwera, Emmeline Orach, Aneko Florence Aroma, Beatrice Adiko and Betty Ocan, all from the NGO ACORD (Agency for Cooperation and Research in Development). The collection was coordinated by Rosalba Oywa.

Edisa   UGA B2

Edisa, an orphan, received no education. She has brought up her 10 children and nine of one of her husband's six wives. When government troops killed a man in her village, people became scared and talked of leaving....

I was firm and had not thought of leaving my home, although the situation was really bad with rampant killings and the older children had run off to town. This was mainly because my crops were ready for harvest in the fields and I knew that wherever I would go, I would have the problem of feeding my children—so I persisted and remained here with my two youngest. After some time my husband came back to take us where he and the other children had settled. I was still against the idea of leaving our home, where we have plenty of cultivable land, and told him my fears of how to feed them. This annoyed him very much and he asked, "Why do you want to die because of food?"

After a long heated discussion and with other people's advice, I eventually went to my sister. She didn't [resent] us but her husband wasn't happy because I had six children with me and this meant a lot of food. Their perception of us was not good. One could feel that we were being despised, though not openly.

[I couldn't acquire any land there] because I had no money. My brother-in-law lent me one acre. I managed to grow sorghum on half of it and in the other half I planted millet intercropped with pigeon peas. This harvest was fair, but the next season the crop completely failed. Life became so difficult that I thought I would not bear it. I had to work in people's gardens for both food and cash. When I remembered how much food I left at home—and here I had no food for my children—it made me very sad. And worse still, my husband seemed not to care. In fact, we would quarrel most of the time and he ended up deserting us.

Women and girls turned into "camp followers" to avoid being raped

The return home

I finally came back [home] in 1992, but during the whole of 1991, I used to come on and off to cultivate my land.

I personally had no interest in returning to this home as all that I had was destroyed. You would not call it a home [that we came back to]. In the days when I used to come home to fetch some more food, [when] I recalled how I was nearly killed by one of those three government soldiers, I would fear to enter the compound. The first time I returned and saw the destruction, I felt like crying but there were no tears in my eye. Then I realised I was in deep sorrow. Even the water pots were beaten and broken, so you can imagine what would have happened to a person. The huts and granaries were completely looted, then burnt down. In fact, on our return, we feared to live in this compound; we settled half a mile away. The village was completely deserted.

Some of the [village] people who didn't flee turned around to loot homes of those who had fled. And the rebels also looted homes. Even the government soldiers, who were brought to protect people's lives and properties, destroyed granaries [and] huts by burning them down or they would remove the roofing poles and use them for firewood.

Parents blamed for rebel sons

Once a child has joined the rebel group, such a child cannot listen to what you tell him. In fact, you then become enemies and they don't even come home. The community has been accusing and harassing the parents of the rebels claiming that they are benefiting from their sons in terms of money, yet in most cases such parents are innocent, as boys don't even step home; you wouldn't know whether they are alive or dead.

Fears for the future

There is not much hope for the future as there are just too many problems for this generation. The problem of AIDS is the most threatening. We seem to be wasting our time in the upbringing and education [of] our children. You have to nurse and bury your children one by one until you are left with nothing. You wish you never gave life. [AIDS] came with the war of 1986, because our women used to be faithful to their husbands. However, with the war, there were rampant cases of rape, and poverty caused many a marriage to break as women and girls turned into "camp followers" to avoid being raped. We even thought that the government sent only HIV-infected soldiers to spread this disease intentionally.

The upbringing [and education] of children is becoming extremely difficult because in the village we depend on our produce for almost all our income. During this war, our produce was looted by both the government soldiers and rebels; but these days the government soldiers don't take our food any more, instead they cheat us by buying very cheaply.

Women produce 70% of Uganda's staple crops; war disrupts this vital function
Ron Giling/Panos Pictures

I think children should be allowed to go back to school, even though some of them may be [over-]aged. There should be mass moral education for the youth because they indulged in activities like dancing and drinking due to lack of guidance, and yet they are too young for such things. All this started with the war when there was no money for school fees; when children don't study they become unruly and parents cannot manage them.

Development needs

The most useful assistance for the moment would be a better means of opening up the land, like a tractor hire service. We used to use ox-ploughs, but [since] our animals were taken by the fighting forces we use hand hoes and we cannot do much.

I know that the tractor hire service failed in the 1980s but at the moment the safety of the cattle is still debatable—unless all the rebels come out, as some of them are now doing. If this could

Most men never discuss money issues with women happen, then restocking would be a better option. [Otherwise] even the ex-rebels will find that they have nothing, with their homes destroyed. And if they are ready to rebuild their homes, then they won't repeat what they had done earlier to others—they would also be interested in acquiring animals. If all homes have cattle, there will be no inter-family jealousies—which were the main cause of the destruction of people's homes.

Almost every home in this village had livestock before, but they were all stolen by the fighting forces [or] our [own] neighbours. We had 37 heads of cattle, 45 goats and five pigs. The chickens were more than 50 [in number] and the ducks—about 20. Anyway, even the people who stole our animals are at the moment poor like us, because they either sold them for cash and drunk the money, or slaughtered and ate them. You see, such stolen property usually disappears just like that because of curses from the owners.

Men and money

[Later,] my husband returned to us. He went to town to find out about compensation from the government, but he never told me anything. You know most men never discuss money issues with women—probably because they think it will spoil their plans. If the compensation were to be given in the form of livestock then maybe we shall see [it], but if it is in cash then the money [will] be diverted for other things.

[My husband] still has no interest in cattle because he says some of these rebels still at large can steal them again. In fact, these days he is not keen on saving money. We use all the money we get, even though I keep telling him that we still have a number of young children and we should forget what has happened... but still his response to saving money and investing in something tangible is negative.

Sabina   UGA B1

36-year-old Sabina—separated, with four children—was abducted by rebels, members of the Holy Spirit movement (also known as Lakwena).

I was abducted around 2pm from my compound and taken to the rebel camp where I was left to stay in a hut [with] a man. At night he asked me for sex but I refused. We continued like this for a week then I had to give in—there was no way I could escape. So we started living as husband and wife. At one time I told him that I wanted to go back home but he threatened to kill me if I did such a thing. He was killed, just about the time when I left [the rebels].

When girls of about 14 were abducted, the [rebel] leaders would want to take such a girl for a partner even if he were aged. Should [she] refuse, she would be beaten in front of everybody till [she] agreed. Girls aged 13 downwards were not forced into sexual union; they were taken by the officers and used as house maids. It was the mature girls and women who suffered rape and forced sex.

Life with the rebels

I lived in the bush with the rebels from September 1988 till June 1989. The food we used to eat was raided from distant places and it was mainly cattle. During such operations, the girls would be taken to carry the looted property. For medicine, the raiders would go to government and missionary hospitals.

Money was robbed from buses. The **Holy Spirit** could say, "Go and ambush such and such a bus and you will get so much money." And this would come true. Or he would say, "Do not fight over your loot—if you do [you will lose it]." Sometimes they would come back with money packed in a big travelling bag.

[Sometimes] we would be on the run the whole day and only rest at night; there was not even time for cooking. [One] morning we heard bombs and gun shots and we ran till we reached a place called Amuru. Here we dug some cassava and as we were preparing to cook it, the bombs started—so we had to run leaving the food on the fire. We ran for a good distance and when we stopped to rest, the gun shots started and we had to run on. During these days we were living on boiled cassava because it was difficult for the rebel soldiers to carry out their food operations, except on some occasions when they would kill the wild animals from the game park. Everywhere we went, we were pursued by the NRA soldiers and we were worried that we were all going to be caught alive, because with only a meal of cassava per day our energies began to fail us and we [felt weak].

"A holy war"

Before going to fight, everyone would be anointed. This was done to cleanse us from all our bad deeds, like ill feelings towards each other. First we were sent to the stream to bathe; this was to cleanse all our sins. [Then] we assembled in the yard; oil and water would be sprinkled on us while we sang songs of praises.

Whenever we had been anointed, we would be barred from sex. If anyone disobeyed this command, then for men, during the battle, the bullet would precisely hit your penis. Or if you quarrelled with someone after being anointed, then the bullet

It was said that women were more courageous than men

would hit you right in the mouth. I saw these things happen with my own eyes. Even [if] a man caressed his partner, the bullet would hit his hand.

The Holy Spirit told us that we should fight with all our might for this is a holy war, and he came to preach the gospel of the Lord. **Kony** told us that with the power of the Holy Spirit rocks can explode, so we can use them as hand grenades against our enemy. Whenever there were preparations for battle, we would pray over a rock in the shape of a fist. But I did not see any explode. I don't believe in that.

Women as fighters

By the time I joined them, the Holy Spirit had stopped girls and women from fighting. It was said that they were more courageous than the men. They were also used for killing those condemned to death. This I learned through conversation with some of the girls who had lived a long time with the rebels. I said that I felt bad when innocent people were killed. One girl said, "What if it were in those days when girls would be selected to kill such people, what would you do?" I said I would pretend to have killed but let the person go! "How would you do that? You had to kill while everyone was looking. And if you refused, you would also be killed."

Views of the war

Some people in this district were double-dealers. They used to give support to the rebels to safeguard their [own] positions, in case [the rebels] won the war. Businessmen in Gulu town were giving us all forms of assistance and some of the more well-to-do villagers would give us food.

I don't take sides because I was with the rebels not out of my own [choice] but because I was abducted and now I'm glad that I came back alive! I don't even know why the two sides want to fight. [They are like] co-wives fighting for their husband's attention. I don't know where Kony is now. Since I came back home, I have been living mainly in town for fear that if I am caught again by them, I would get killed.

Blame from all sides

Some said that those who were abducted wanted it—which was not true for the majority of people, especially for women. Others were sympathetic and would say, "*Lakwena* has really made people suffer. I could also have been abducted." Why would a woman go in for all these kinds of suffering—like walking all day and night, forced sex and rape, or having to kill? Your feet could get pricked by thorns or stones, but you had to move on; if you said you were tired and could no longer move they would suggest that you could be "left to rest"... meaning you were to be killed.

How can anyone expect a grown-up rebel son to listen to his parents' advice?

The DA (District Administrator) said that the Gulu people were encouraging the rebellion; but I felt that such remarks were unfair because how can anyone expect a grown-up rebel son to listen to his parents' advice? [The DA] said that the villagers were the ones encouraging the killing, because they won't make alarms when the rebels are raping women or when they have killed. Even if one [sounded the] alarm, the NRA soldiers never responded!

The [worst thing about] the NRA soldiers was having forced sex with women one after the other. Men and women were collected during what they called a "screening exercise to flush out" the rebels from the community. The men and women were put in separate groups. Then in the evening the NRA soldiers started fucking the women in the compound. One woman could be fucked by up to six men; and this went on for three days. I saw these things with my own eyes, but I was lucky it never happened to me.

So I was hurt when the DA claimed that it was the women who were encouraging the killings, spreading the AIDS virus and encouraging the rebels to reach Gulu town because they knew them all. He felt that all who had taken refuge in the town should be forced to go back home [saying], "The rebels are your sons and why should you run away from your bad products?"

"Is rape a government weapon?"

He also said women should avoid getting contaminated with the AIDS virus. This annoyed me and I asked him, "How do we avoid getting infected with the AIDS virus? According to me it is the government which is intentionally spreading the AIDS virus by raping women when they go for firewood. Is raping one of the government weapons to fight the women? All these sufferings are being inflicted upon us because of our children's misbehaviour. We have a saying: if you have a dog which is a thief, it will one day land you into problems."

The DA asked me to prove if [the gang rape] was done by government soldiers. And I told him it was true because I saw a helicopter bring them food; the rebels never owned a helicopter!

Nighty   UGA F3

Nighty was abducted from her family compound by rebels, who then set fire to the house in which her mother was sleeping.

We walked for one day and night without stopping. All along, I thought I would be killed. We had been moving in the bush only, no path. The Commander told us that if they saw you trying to escape you would be killed. We moved for a long distance then three girls began to escape but they were caught. We saw the three girls bare-chested, brought before us.

The Commander said, "What did we say the other day?" "No one should try to escape," we answered. "So we shall kill these girls to show you that it is bad to escape," he concluded. We were ordered to watch. They collected big sticks and began to hit the girls with them. They were beaten to death.

We walked for a very long time. All along I thought of my dead mother and brothers who were burnt in the house because as we left our homes on that evil night, the house had already started to burn and the doors were closed.

After some time my legs were swollen and I could no longer move. So I was given a stick. I walked using the stick, until even my hands were bleeding. I began to think, now I cannot walk, neither can I handle the stick, what shall I do? If I shout I may be killed, if I run away I may be killed. Some of the kind ones saw that I could no longer walk. They decided to leave me with a certain woman as they continued their journey. This woman looked after me. She began to remove all the thorns [from] my feet, giving me warm water for bathing, feeding me... She was given a strong warning not to let me escape. They told her that, should I go, she would replace me. I remained with her for some time and when I was nearly recovered, [the rebels] came back for me.

Escape

We decided to rest and settled down after more than 24 hours walking. Where we wanted to cook there was no water, so six of us went to fetch some. Then one of us suggested we should bathe. No sooner had we finished than we heard gun shots. The NRA had attacked us. We began to run. As my legs were still very painful, and one of the other girls also had [difficulty], the other four girls left us behind.

We [kept going] until sunset and all that time we did not see any sign of human life. No food plots, no sound of goats or chickens. No path which we could follow. We were too thirsty to move anymore. But we pushed on. Then we began to hear something that sounded like a waterfall. We followed the direction and found a big river. We scrambled down to reach it, drank the water and poured it on our heads.

Next morning we decided to follow the direction in which the river was flowing, as we were unable to cross it. We followed it for a long distance. Then we reached a point where we could see the other side of the river and something which looked like a net. So we decided to try to cross from there. When we reached the middle we found that the water was too deep, so we went back.

We decided that whoever had put the net there, be it a soldier or a civilian, he would be the one to save or kill us. We sat for about three hours, then a woman came to fetch water. When we saw from our hiding place that it was a woman, we came out.

"Help us cross over to your side," we shouted. She jumped back terrified. She stood dumbfounded for some time then said, "Who are you?" We told her who we were and how we came to be there. She sympathised with us and she swam across the river to where we were and helped us.

We hid under a tree near her home. She began to look after us, bringing us food, water and any other assistance. She had no child. When her husband came, she called us to the house. We hesitated at first but picked up courage and came out of our hiding place.

It happened that the other girl's relatives were near to that place. She could be taken to them. I was the unfortunate one. My home was at least 50 miles away. All the same my hosts were so kind that they encouraged me to stay with them, saying that they would find means of making me reach home.

I began to live with them, going to work in the food plot with them and helping in housework, but I would sleep in the bush for fear of being caught again by *Lakwena*. One day the husband called me and told me that he was going to Awach, about 22 miles in the direction of my home. He would take me to a relative of his and from there, there were many people going to Gulu town [who] would help me.

He took me to this woman the following day. She had a son who was a cripple. She made up her mind that I would become the son's wife. Where we were, the detachment of the NRA was also near. Each time that someone came and told her that we could go she would say, "Let me first consult the gods to see if the way is clear." She would then say, "No, you should not go, the road is not clear. You might meet a misfortune."

After three days, her son returned from his hunting. That evening, she told me about her intention. I told her that I accepted but I wanted to see my people first, then I would come back. That same evening, a certain woman told me of her intention to go to Gulu and told me how I could dodge the NRA [and] pass the road block.

The following morning, my host told me to prepare food. She went to the food plot to weed some groundnuts. I took that chance and escaped through the bush until I crossed the path leading to the other woman's house. She was waiting for me. So we walked for about 17 miles. When we arrived in Gulu, she took us to her sister where we slept. I was very happy, thinking of how free I was again. I would go to look for my people again. I thought about my mother and brothers. My grandmother was still alive. I would stay with her until I found somewhere to live. I still had 10 miles to go in order to reach our home. The following morning I started my journey. When I had just gone 3 miles, I met my grandmother. She told me that they were living near there, together with my mother. So my mother was alive!

You can imagine what I felt. That was I think the happiest day of my life.

Easter   UGA C3

A widow, Easter has brought up two children of her own and four of her sister's.

The worst problems [for me] were at the time of the NRA. This was also the time I was left alone after my husband died. I felt very insecure and with no support. I used to think that if my husband was alive we could educate our children up to university level. Being alone, all the responsibility of feeding, dressing and educating the children was on me. I had also to accommodate some relatives who got displaced from Awoch. Each day I had to go to sell little things in the market and buy food for all of us.

I lost all my money [and] my husband's properties. My husband died in 1980 [in an] accident. He was the type of man who did not bother to keep money in the house and was not open to me as a wife. He had things and money which I could not easily trace. He died without disclosing his secrets. Luckily enough, I was already aware of his behaviour, and I had some small account of my own money which I kept myself. I gave it to my father so that he could use it for buying cows. After he died, I continued on my own to save money and buy more cows and goats, chicken and sheep. The money was from my [teaching] salary and from brewing local *waragi* (alcohol). I had already grown very strong, but the NRA came and destroyed all that I had accumulated for so many years.

Looting

A group of [rebels] came one time and tortured us for money. They came to the school and demanded school funds from the headmaster. [He] had just brought 300,000 shillings for teachers' salaries. They started by beating [him] so seriously that he told them that I was the one keeping the money. I told them it was not the duty of a woman teacher to collect salaries [but] I was terribly beaten [and] kicked. When they saw I could not produce any money, they decided to take [what they could find] and left. All the male teachers were taken up to the centre and tortured and later left to return home.

[Then some] NRA soldiers came and settled in the centre. As soon as they left, the *Cilil* returned to disturb people, accusing us of being friendly to the NRA. Most people found it difficult to tolerate and went to Gulu town.

Life as a displaced person in town

In Gulu, we had to face many problems. We [arrived] without any possessions. We had nothing to eat, let alone to wear. [We started getting] relief: one cup of beans and two cups of *posho* for each family. This was not enough because each family was very large. Later we had to sell our labour in order to get money. Some of this we had to invest by buying some beans from the soldiers then reselling among the displaced or in the market.

We returned [to the village] after the government started to resettle the displaced. The soldiers were sent first, then civil servants like teachers and nurses were asked to go. [Orphan] children have been sent to relatives or stayed on their own. They have a lot of mental torture and it is not very easy to handle them. Due to lack of proper care, some of them roam about and are very violent; some live by stealing in order to survive.

The fact that we have more women in our society than men today, [means] our lives are very difficult. That's why women have developed the idea of working in groups. In groups, there is opportunity to share common problems and discuss ways of helping [our] children. You find women in groups such as *Urib can* (Let's combine our poverty) and *Lacan kwo ki lwete* (A poor person survives with her own hands). So many different names have come up to indicate the ways women are looking [to help] themselves through their own efforts.

Children have a lot of mental torture; it is not easy to handle them

Alisantorina   UGA F1

41-year-old Alisantorina, separated from her husband, has four children.

We began to hide in the bush during daytime and return home only at night to prepare food and sleep, then go back to the bush at day break. We made small shelters near streams and valleys or deep in the bush where we thought it would be difficult for them to find us. [Soldiers] began to follow us by our footprints. If they found anyone they would burn the shelter together with you in it.

I found life was impossible so I decided to take my children to [my family] home. I went with them leaving my husband behind because, at that time, when it came to running away he would just take off on his own and I would have to run with the children.

When I reached our home, I found people [there] were also staying in the bush and cooking at night. In the bush you would also have to talk in whispers. If you heard any voice it meant there were soldiers nearby.

Forbidden from town by rebels

At one time the rebels ordered us not to go to the town any more. We obeyed for fear of our lives, and began to suffer badly. There was no soap, no **salt**, even no clothes for the children, because in the bush [they had got] torn. We decided to sneak to town once in a while to get the most essential goods. I collected remnants of cassava tubers [and made some of] our local drink to [sell] in town. When I was coming back from town, I reached a corner and saw some rebels—only 200 metres away.

Alisantorina ran but was caught by the rebels.

"Why are you running?" "I am running away from you," I answered. "Who are we?" "You are our people." I answered like [this] so I [would] not call the wrong people the wrong names, as both the rebels and the government soldiers dress alike.

[The rebels] removed the salt and soap and left the children's clothes [bought in town]. They warned me not to go to town again, kicked me, and showed me [their] *panga*, and I ran off shaking with fear. We continued with our saltless food and that was that.

Ordered to town by government

When the government learnt that the rebels had ordered us not to go to Gulu, they intensified the search for us and ordered us to leave the village, saying that should you be found in the village, you would be considered a rebel and killed.

I didn't know how I would feed my children if I was to go to

Gulu. In the village, even if we were living in shelters in the bush, *In the bush* we could go quietly to people's food plots, whether yours or not, *you have* and pick some remains of cassava and potatoes, or at least go to the *to talk in* forest and pick wild yams [to] cook and feed our children. There *whispers* were bananas too, or we gathered leaves to boil and eat. Where would I get all these things in the town? I made up my mind not to go, whatever happened. We decided to transfer to a new hiding place where there were no footprints because our old one had become easy to trace.

Later, Alisantorina realised that they could no longer survive in the bush.

I arrived at Alokolum Major Seminary where refugees like me had settled. I was like someone who was buried and exhumed, because the place was just too noisy for me—like a football field when one side has just scored. Anybody who spoke to me sounded as if they were shouting, because I had stayed for a long time without talking aloud. Even the children jumped if you spoke to them, as they were not used to loud voices any more. They thought whispers were the order of the day.

Jenneth   UGA G1

Jenneth is chairperson of the local Rural Development Committee and wife of an Resistance Council member.

When war broke out my husband was an **RC** secretary for information. He was viewed by the rebels as a government spy. One time when I was digging in my field with my husband, [and] my co-wife was sick at home, rebels came [to the home] demanding money, **salt**, and all sorts of things. The people at home were beaten, including my sick co-wife. One of them ran towards my field and signalled for us to run away. I tried but had a baby on my back who would not keep quiet, so I decided to just come out of hiding and go home. My husband hid himself near the field, though I had warned him to continue far into the forest.

I was met with a group of rebels demanding the whereabouts of my husband and threatening to shoot me if I could not show them. They demanded money which my husband got from the NRM. When I told them I did not know where my husband was and there was nothing I could give them, I was escorted at gunpoint back to the field. [The rebels] beat me and some suggested I should be shot for deliberately not telling them where my husband was. My husband could not bear it any longer and he jumped out and

We even gave the children soil to eat when things were very bad

said, "Kill me, leave that woman alone." They beat him, insulted him, tied him and forced him to move. [At] home he was forced to release salt and money.

Late the following day, we saw my husband appear, like a dream, for we had lost hope of his survival. So we prepared food, very quickly, and went away to the bush in hiding in case some other people might come back.

After some time they returned home, but her husband was taken again, and again released (because he was a relative of the local rebel commander).

We welcomed him and performed some traditional rites like slaughtering chicken and putting an egg for him to step on before entering the compound. In fact, to us he was like a person who had arisen from the dead.

The question now was where we were going to take refuge, since the problem was likely to occur again and we were expecting to die the next time. We tried running far away to relatives' homes, but people would not welcome us. Whenever we insisted on staying, the owners would pack up and leave us in their home, although we were running without our husband. As for him, he decided not to run to anybody's home but stayed in the bush.

Life in the bush

People had rejected me and my co-wife because we were an RC's wives and children. The only place where we could take refuge was in town, where government was operating full-time. In the villages, in most cases, people were confused and did not want to side with either government or rebels. When we saw that RCs and their families were being eliminated by rebels, we wanted to move to town where we would not be viewed as enemies. Because of the large number of children of my co-wife and me [12 in total], our husband said it would be impossible for all of us to move to town. He feared his children would die of hunger or disease in camps. So he constructed a small temporary shelter for us and he took off to town. He knew that the two of us would survive since we still had things like cassava in the field.

For almost a year, we lived in the bush. Our children even got used to the new home—where they never saw fire being made for fear that smoke would show people where we were. During all this time we rarely ate cooked food. [We even gave] the children soil to eat to quieten them when things were very bad.

Whenever the situation was a bit better, [we] would sneak home to cook. If I was the one to cook, [my co-wife] would stand in the middle of the compound and guard, looking in all directions. Occasionally, when things were not bad, my husband would also sneak home, mostly at night. He would bring us *posho* which was being distributed as relief in the town. He was very particular about the children, so he took a lot of risks [to supply] us with the most essential items from town—medicine and *posho*.

The children these days are lovers of guns and violence

Our children who were in school could not continue. None of them was abducted or forced to join either side, although the children of my co-wife were big enough. This was viewed as real luck.

In 1990, the situation improved and we all came home. By this time, our community started accepting the RC and their role. [But] the army believed that my husband knew about killing of people which took place near our area, [and] that he had never reported the presence of the rebels in his areas because he was collaborating with them. He was not alone; many RCs from different areas were thrown behind bars. He was taken in on 5th November 1991, and thrown out in July 1992.

Things are okay right now and I am optimistic that this peace will continue. However, the children we are bringing up these days are disobedient, and lovers of guns and violence. We parents have a big task to change this attitude of our children.

Rose and Olga   UGA C2

Olga is a widow; Rose is separated from her husband.

OLGA: We had a lot of problems from all the fighting forces here; both the rebels and NRA kept us moving up and down and running for dear life. [The *Lakwena* were worse than the earlier rebel groups,] they robbed people of their goats, cows [and] sheep. Government soldiers were doing the same. This left people without any livestock. Children now don't even know what a cow or a goat looks like.

Women really suffered because the responsibility of feeding the children and the aged was left to them. Most men were killed or ran away, which the women had never dreamt of.

ROSE: [After one serious fight between rebels and NRA in our village,] the NRA started questioning how these rebels could move through the villages to come and attack them. In retaliation, most civilians in the villages were victimised. The [NRA] started burning houses, robbing properties and killing indiscriminately. Even the

My father thought educated women become prostitutes

very old, the blind and disabled, who could not run, were killed. The government was convinced that the rebels were our sons, so all of us were assumed to be rebels. Yet these people came from different parts of Uganda and were using the forests to hide.

OLGA: The war that started during the reign of the NRM was the worst. I have not seen the man who is ruling now, and I really dread to see him after all that has happened to us. Even Amin only killed the people he wanted, not everybody. Women, the disabled and lepers never used to be killed by soldiers in the past. Women especially were feared, because it was believed that it was very difficult to perform the rituals when somebody killed a woman. Children were taken to be innocent, and the blind, crippled or lepers were respected. The NRA had no such fears. They killed without mercy. We still live in fear to this day. These soldiers were labelling all of us "rebels", including the women.

"Hopeless men, responsible women"

My father was a strong believer in traditions. Like most people at that time, he thought it was useless educating girls, because educated women become prostitutes.

ROSE: I was also convinced it was useless to waste money on a girl. Now I have realised the whole society was wrong in such thinking, because experience shows that most boys [and] men have become hopeless, while the women are very responsible and supportive to their families and even parents and other relatives. While I tried to work hard, my husband was very lazy and completely lacked development initiatives. When I tried to advise him about what we could do collectively in order to be able to afford school fees, he would tell me I was trying to dominate him. I then started struggling alone to support my children. [After the fighting ceased,] since the man continued with his irresponsible life, I found there was no point in keeping him, so we separated.

Development since peace

OLGA: Most women have become widows. The men who survived the wars are not being of any use to their wives either—most of them have become drunkards. The biggest problem for women in the past was dependency on their husbands. From the time we learned how to make things by ourselves through crop production and other income-generating activities, we have felt we can do a lot on our own. Some of us are doing petty trade, but this brings only very little profit.

Women have found strength working in groups. Now we are carrying [out] many collective activities—digging, different ways of generating income and constant discussions and meetings among ourselves. In my group, we are [taking] responsibility for looking after orphans. We feel that, poor as we are, we have to cater for the orphans by doing activities that can bring us income. We cannot wait for anyone to do it for us. Things don't come on a silver plate from nowhere.

We used to mock the refugees from Sudan, but now it was our turn

Bironika   UGA G2

Bironika, now in her late 50s, spent much of the war in hiding as a refugee in town.

[When] I registered as a refugee with my children, a whole bag of maize flour and a blanket were given to me. We used to mock the refugees from Sudan, but now it was our turn. [When in the bush] we lived like wild animals, sometimes depending just on [uncooked] roots and fruits. Even if one was courageous enough to live at home whenever a bit of peace [came], the moment [soldiers] found you, whether they were from the rebel side or government, they would either kill you or force you to take them to the *Aloop* (hiding places). If you led them to where they wanted, they would set you free but do a lot of damage to the people in hiding. [After] you would be haunted by the deeds of the armed forces you led. Where lives were lost, you would be hated by most of the people in the community. So people took a lot of care not to be found by [either side].

Being an RC

I became an **RC** secretary for women in the last RC election—in 1991. As I never went to school, there were better women who could have stood in my position, but nobody wanted to and I was pressed to accept. I did not want to [but] I told the community that I was already old enough, so let me hold the responsibility instead of a literate young one, since they were too young to die. The [memory] of what happened from 1986 to 1990 was still fresh— many people lost their lives for being RCs or relatives of an RC. Death of the RCs was by both rebels and government soldiers, [who] thought some of the RCs were collaborating with rebels. So the two parties fought the RCs almost equally, despite the fact that RC was a strong government organ for peace.

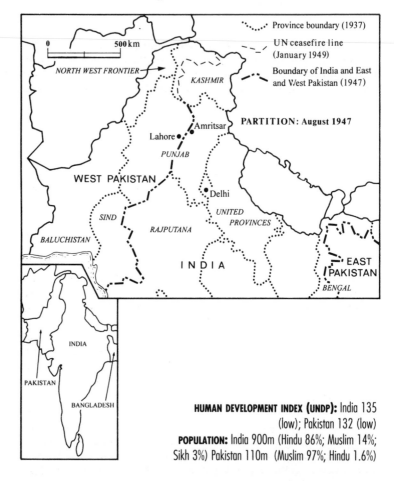

Province boundary (1937)

UN ceasefire line
(January 1949)

Boundary of India and East
and West Pakistan (1947)

PARTITION: August 1947

NORTH WEST FRONTIER

KASHMIR

Amritsar

Lahore

PUNJAB

WEST PAKISTAN

Delhi

SIND

UNITED
PROVINCES

RAJPUTANA

BALUCHISTAN

I N D I A

EAST
PAKISTAN

BENGAL

INDIA

PAKISTAN

BANGLADESH

0   500 km

HUMAN DEVELOPMENT INDEX (UNDP): India 135
(low); Pakistan 132 (low)
POPULATION: India 900m (Hindu 86%; Muslim 14%;
Sikh 3%) Pakistan 110m (Muslim 97%; Hindu 1.6%)

1858 British Crown assumes direct rule of India **1930-31** Mass Civil Disobedience campaign led by Mahatma Gandhi **1940** Muslim League declares formation of Pakistan to be its goal **1942** Quit India movement launched **1947** The Partition plan is announced, followed by riots in Bengal and in Punjab. Aug: Partition of India takes place; India and Pakistan (East and West) win independence from Britain **1971** After a bitter war, East Pakistan breaks away from West Pakistan and Bangladesh is founded **1966-77** Indira Gandhi prime minister of India; re-elected in **1980** Growth of Sikh separatism **1984** Government attacks Sikh militants in the Golden Temple in Amritsar; Indira Gandhi assassinated by Sikh bodyguards, leading to anti-Sikh riots; Rajiv Gandhi succeeds her as prime minister **1991** Rajiv Gandhi assassinated

~ INDIA ~

The Partition of India in 1947 marked the end of British rule. It also prompted one of the largest mass movements of people ever seen, as millions on the "wrong side" of the borders fled to the newly created nation states of Pakistan (East and West) for Muslims, and India for Hindus and Sikhs.

Thus modern-day India, as a discrete entity, is a relatively recent creation. The Indian sub-continent, however, has been the birthplace of some of the world's oldest civilisations. Many empires and kingdoms, predating anything comparable in Europe, had risen and fallen by the time the Europeans arrived, attracted by the wealth of resources. From the 1600s onwards, the British, Dutch, French and Portuguese competed for territory and power but by the 19th century, India was effectively under British control.

In the early 1900s, however, the situation was changing. Gandhi's policy of *Satyagraha* (passive resistance) to British rule was gathering pace and led to the Quit India movement. After World War Two, it had become clear that the European colonial era was finished. By this time, leaders of the large Muslim minority feared a Hindu-dominated India and demands grew for an independent Muslim state, Pakistan.

Prior to this, despite very real differences, Hindus, Sikhs and Muslims had lived together in comparative harmony. All communities needed the skills and services of the others for everyday life to function, although there was little intermarriage. But as Partition became a certainty, communal tensions increased, especially in Punjab and Bengal where the dividing lines were to be drawn. When independence came in August 1947 and Partition was put into practice, the riots and carnage were unprecedented.

Hindus, Sikhs and Muslims were forced to leave their homes, often overnight, and flee to the new "homeland". Over 10 million people crossed the border in both directions in the Punjab and another million changed sides in Bengal. According to some estimates, half a million people died and large numbers were forced to convert to the "other" religion. Thousands of women were abducted and raped, actions regarded by each community as a deliberate move by the other to dilute its purity. Many women committed suicide, some compelled to do so by their own communities to avoid rape or conversion. After Partition, both India and Pakistan launched a major operation to "recover" abducted women (regardless of their individual wishes and situations).

Partition had other consequences for women. Because of the disruption, education was often abandoned, and marriages could not take place. It was not until recently, however, that the work of recovering the histories of Partition began: for a long time families maintained a kind of silence, and historians were reluctant to tackle such an emotive subject and revive the trauma—rape, abduction, forcible recovery, inadequate rehabilitation—of women in particular.

Memories of Partition remain powerful, particularly for those who belong to north and east India, and tales of brutality as well as of deep and enduring friendships continue to be retold within families.

These memories were revived in 1984 during the anti-Sikh riots following the assassination of Indira Gandhi, then Prime Minister of India. Some years earlier, in an attempt to make electoral headway in the Punjab, Indira Gandhi had helped to build up the Sikh separatist leader Jarnail Singh Bhindranwale. This move rebounded and for many years the state became engaged in battle with the Sikh militant forces in Punjab, who demanded a separate Sikh nation, Khalistan.

Bhindranwale took over as his headquarters the Golden Temple in Amritsar, the Sikhs' holiest shrine. It was here that in 1984, the government carried out a major armed operation to flush out the militants, during which the temple was badly damaged and Bhindranwale killed.

In retaliation, Indira Gandhi was assassinated by her Sikh bodyguards in October 1984. Fanatical Hindus turned on the Sikh community (although Hindus and Sikhs are very close, with a great deal of intermarriage, and had been on the same side during Partition) and about 5,000 Sikh men were killed, mainly in and around Delhi.

Many widows, left to bring up families on their own, had to deal with the outside world and take on jobs, something they had never done before. The various relief organisations provided mainly practical support, but the women's needs went far beyond this. One of these testimonies (Mita) highlights how in many ways neither the agencies nor individuals involved had fully understood the consequences of the conflict for women, or how forms of compensation and support could create new kinds of conflict for them.

The Partition interviews were done by Poonan Joshi, and those on the 1984 communal riots were done by Mita Bose and Uma Chakravarti, both of Delhi University, with Urvashi Butalia, a feminist publisher, who also coordinated the work. Additional testimonies were collected by Teesta Setalvad and Farida Khan.

Nirmal   IND 2

Born in West Punjab (now Pakistan), Nirmal came from a progressive Hindu family who supported women's education and did not believe in the caste system. She was 16 years old at Partition.

Before Partition... we had a close relationship with two or three families, Hindu and Muslim. My mother's friends were largely, because they were teachers and colleagues, Muslim and Christian. And there wasn't even a question about the Sikhs, because the Hindus and Sikhs were as one, it wasn't considered that there was much difference... that they are of a different caste or group.

Before Partition we [identified ourselves as] Hindu and Indian. But if you ask me generally what I am, we are Punjabis. Our mother tongue was Punjabi, but people used to believe that Hindi, which derived from Sanskrit, was our national language. It wasn't merely a duty [to learn Hindi], it was part of our national culture. My sister studied **Urdu**, my father knew Urdu well. My mother knew and had a great liking of Urdu poetry. We used to sing *ghazals* (Urdu semi-classical songs).

In childhood, there was never any feeling [about the fact] that our neighbours were Sikh or Muslim, but it did make a difference. I was at the school where my mother taught. There was an Urdu teaching section and a Hindi one. I was in the Urdu section. There were two languages because after the Moghul empire, Urdu was the language that was used in the court, as English is today. But Hindus definitely wanted their children to speak Hindi and know about their religion.

I remember, I was only little, but at that time an incident took place... one Muslim had gone to a bookbinder, who was innocent, and the Muslim—I don't know why—knifed the bookbinder. And all the shops were closed—and a great panic spread. And the effect of this was that I was taken out of the Urdu section, and placed in

Initially it was all about nationalism ...then it became love for your own religion

the Hindi section of the same school.

But the matter wasn't allowed to spread, because the British still ruled. There was a curfew, and [it] was stamped down. But tension flared from time to time. Hindu fanatics and Muslim fanatics were always at odds. Those [Muslims] who were converted were from our people [Hindus], and they became really fanatical.

The rise of tension

Initially it was all about nationalism: how could we get rid of the British and get freedom? For this Hindus, Muslims and Sikhs made a great *sanyog* (sacrifice). People wanted the British to leave. This is our land... and then things began to change. I remember when I was in the seventh, eighth level... there was one Muslim girl, Ashraf. I still remember she would sit on the desk, punching her fist into the air. She would say, "We're going to get rid of all of you... Lahore will be in Pakistan."

Then the Jan Sangh (a right-wing Hindu movement—now the BJP) developed, and quite a lot of people supported them so that they could defend themselves. And in their hearts they were against the Muslims. At first it was "Desh Prem", love for your own country, and then [it became] love for your own religion.

And then some incidents started to take place. They began in the city. We lived two or three miles out of the city. It was a time of great trouble. You didn't know who was your friend and who was your enemy, what was in their heart and what was on the surface. But the ones who were real friends, whether they were Muslim or Hindu, their treatment with each other was very good. But when they realised that Partition was going to take place no matter what, then the people's confidence was shattered. Who knows what will happen tomorrow? In one way there was terror in their hearts, in another way there was no confidence about what would happen.

There was so much fear, in July 1947. There were about a hundred houses of Hindus and Sikhs together, but all the surrounding districts were Muslim. So those who had originally appeared to be friends, now there was a doubt in the heart about them. Those who were immediate neighbours, we weren't so scared of them. But those people in the surrounding communities —they were all Muslim, in them there was no trust.

People talk of Bosnia, but Partition was the first large-scale migration in the name of religion. Everyone blamed the British. The Muslims became their tool. It is the fault of our people [Hindus] too. The leaders didn't even slightly want there to be bloodshed... but when the British said we will only give you independence if **Jinnah** is given a homeland, well...

After Partition, we [were] most thankful to that Muslim neighbour to whom we tied a *rakhee*. He was our closest neighbour, who respected my mother and father as his own. He thought of us as younger sisters. That man told us, "We have had some secret meetings... I can't tell you any more, but no girl is safe, no matter how young she is, and it's better if you take the girls away for 10 or 12 days from here."

Women as commodities

It's the same from ancient history. All the invaders always understood women to be a commodity, not human beings. Muslims putting them in a harem—and the Hindu kings... Men just thought that women are a thing of beauty, or a thing to breed children. But [as to] why atrocities are committed against womankind, it is only because physically they are not as strong. Someone could abduct them and they can't protect themselves. What [can] girls do? And many girls committed suicide, [feeling] that it's better to die. My personal belief is that the poor woman who has been raped [should not commit suicide]... I'd call it a crime. Sikh or Hindu, the poor women were blameless during the time of Partition.

I saw myself the women whose breasts were cut off... "Pakistan Zindabad" (long live Pakistan) on their chests was written... but they were alive. I worked in the social services camp for refugees. [It was] terrible. Even when they were reunited with their own families, brothers and fathers weren't prepared to take them back... and so the refugee camps were built for them. One woman... Muslims had abducted her. When she was found, she was pregnant—but her in-laws said they'd only keep her if the child was destroyed. But look at nature. She didn't have another child. That child wasn't allowed to survive because it was the child of a Muslim... even [though] the woman had been [resisting]. And whatever her feelings had been, she was after all a mother. The same cases happened on both sides: that Hindus are made of gold and Muslims aren't, [this isn't true]. This happened everywhere.

At that age, 15 or 16, we didn't have that much experience of life. People had never seen this. Yes, coming home [from the camp] we would talk about it a lot... and then we would really give thanks to that Muslim man, that our honour had been saved. We lost our property and our money, and other things. But that which we saw... our hair would stand on end.

It took a great deal of time to feel again that we are human beings

The importance of honour

Honour [was the most important characteristic of being a woman]. This is the first instinct for any woman of whatever religion she may be... that nothing should be forced upon her... that she should be left alive, but her honour should not be lost... she should not be raped.

So when Pakistan was made we came to this side [India]. My sister and my mother, we came over on the advice of the Muslim neighbour for 10 or 12 days—but then we couldn't return, because they completely closed the border. My father was still on the other side. [We were separated] two months. We didn't know where he was.

Broken pride

My father told us about when he was in the refugee camp in Lahore. When [the food] was given... it seemed to [my father], "Have I become a beggar, that I should take food like this? We had our own house, our own servants."

He just didn't eat. He didn't do his hand like this [cups hands and holds them out as if begging], he drew his hand back. He remained hungry for two days. Two nights and three days he remained hungry. "I'm not going to say to anyone like this, that I'm hungry, give me food." When three days had passed he couldn't stand it any longer... and as he ate, he cried.

He used to wear a turban on his head, and now nothing. He didn't have any clothes... just a shaving box when he fled. He was gathering all his valuables, and the Muslims attacked. And he ran from there. I don't know how the sandals remained on his feet.

It seemed very strange to the Muslims, as it did to us when we came to East Punjab, that even Hindus could be this bad. It took [my father] a great deal of time to feel again that we are human beings.

Pity, but not respect

At that time, boys or girls or men, everyone was scared. Sikhs were most vulnerable, and girls were anyway. Being a woman or a girl, that was a curse then. I think even in the first world, when something happens it all ends up on the women.

When people saw the atrocities committed against women, did their ideas change about the treatment of women? No, they didn't change. They pitied those women, showed them kindness: but they thought of them as orphans, as deserted children who don't receive respect... as if something had gone wrong with them.

Physically they were hurt, but their hearts were so tortured. Some projects were started by the government to help them stand on their own feet. Some people did come in the community to help them. They looked after the small girls of five and six, and eventually had them married. Having found good boys, they even gave them possessions and dowry, but they did not say, " 'As with open arms' we will make you our daughter, and get you married."

Local people looked at the refugees with great contempt

Compensation

[Before Partition] my mother was a teacher. My father had his own independent business. But [after Partition] he couldn't carry on, because he had no capital. We had a very big bungalow. We had ancestral property in Vazeerabad, a hundred miles from there. All our family was educated. And so when we became refugees, and sometimes when we only had 17 *rupees* left, we'd cry that we have become very poor. And then my mother worked for just 40 *rupees* in a private school.

And we didn't have any home to stay, but the Muslim property that was allotted to us, randomly allotted. We are very fortunate to have that home. But it was very difficult to get it. People had to stand in a queue in the hot burning sun—and my father could not stand very long because he had a fever at that time—so we could claim compensation for the property which we left. He had to fill in so many forms, but he could only fill in one form, because he had a 104° F temperature.

[For the women alone] it was very difficult. They couldn't get anything. It was very difficult to stand in the queue with little children. And our own boys, they misused our own women. They insulted them greatly. The local people looked at the refugees with great contempt [saying] that they are a burden to us. They never wanted to help, except giving food at the railway station. But they didn't want [the refugees] to settle there.

Past and present

Some people couldn't regain at all: their lives were so shattered, they became [like] orphans. Those who were so rich became [so] poor that they couldn't cope. Naturally they couldn't rebuild that life again.

Now relations with Sikhs are not very good... now that Sikhs and Hindus are at odds, things have become difficult, because before, some families would have marriages between Sikhs and Hindus. But now people are adamant that Sikhs will marry amongst Sikhs, and Hindus with Hindus. And there aren't Muslims in the Punjab. But generally [relations] are good [except] when some case happens—for example, **Babri Masjid**. In their heart of hearts, in some of the localities, the people have got bitter feelings... they might be afraid.

It's not a
crime to
become a
refugee
People do tell the younger generations. It is a very natural thing that you should tell your children what your past is—parents should tell. It's not just part of history, it's part of their lives, and the influences remain for a very long time. Women and men suffered. Women and children really suffered, whatever religion they belonged to. The political parties couldn't or can't compensate for that time. Nehru came in a helicopter to the refugees to say, "You go back to your places..." and the people threw stones at him.

[Partition] can be summarised in one sentence; or it can be told in great detail. But I still feel great distress, that what happened shouldn't have happened. I think we should talk, we should talk about it very openly—we should know what happened at that time. And there is no disgrace in talking about that—it didn't happen to one or two people—it happened on such a large scale... it became a part of history. It's no cause for shame, what happened... and it's not a crime to become a refugee.

Harmej   IND 3

Harmej, a Sikh in her 60s, also crossed the border from West to East Punjab.

I was 10 years old when I got married. It wasn't the custom [to see your husband before]. No one asked the girls. I didn't really realise I was getting married; I wasn't even 11. I went to my in-laws five years later, at Partition. People were troubled about what to do with married girls. And so people sent the girl to the in-laws. And those who were engaged, they were married and sent off to the in-laws, because it would have been a problem to have the girls. [Parents] couldn't keep them, because the Muslims would abduct the girls and parents couldn't stand to lose their daughter. They wanted to make it the responsibility of the in-laws to look after her.

[When people started sending their daughters away] peoples' relations changed—with the changes in the nation we changed. Fear grew in the homes. Where the Sikhs felt "We are in danger" and the Muslims gathered together and spread fire in the villages, the Sikhs would form a group in order to save their girls.

Suicide as resistance

Then the Sikhs gathered together into *kafilas*. People were moving from village to village. It was a terrible situation. Muslims took away quite a number of girls—at that time some people threw their daughters in wells, rather than [let] the Muslims take away their

religion... their honour. They said that every man should try and save himself, but women shouldn't do anything by themselves. And so the girls would die [saying], "We don't want to go with the Muslims"... "We don't want to go from one religion to another."

On the run

It took one month to reach East Punjab (India). One person from the military and one on horseback travelled alongside each cart. Wherever the *kafila* stopped, we would sit down, put a few bricks here or there, and put a **thava** on and bake *chappatis,* and eat. And when it was time [to go], the military [escort] would rear up the horses and everyone would stand up, and us girls, sometimes they would seat us on their horses, or put the elderly women on a cart.

Every one or two days someone in the family would die

If there wasn't anyone to look after [girls of marriageable age], they would get them married. Many [marriages in the refugee camps] happened. Because if someone didn't have a mother or a father—a girl alone, a boy alone—they went to the refugee camp.

People died on the way because of the journey. Some people couldn't get anything to eat. Many people in our family died [of cholera]. Every one or two days someone in the family would die. As we were going we would just throw their bodies to the side as the *kafila* moved on. If you got left behind, how would you save yourself from the Muslims? There wasn't enough time [to cremate the dead].

The Muslims who came from the other side were also in a terrible state. One *kafila* of Muslims that arrived from the other side was half dead. [Near] Llayalpur—on one side a *kafila* of Muslims was coming and on the other side Sikhs. Although the military was with them, they were still killing each other.

Hameeda   IND 4

Hameeda was seven at Partition, a Muslim living in East Punjab, now India. Her family were close friends with a Hindu, who sheltered them for some time. Her family eventually fled to a camp in Nikodar, en route for Lahore in West Punjab (Pakistan).

The ground was baking, and on the road leading to Nikodar our feet were burning. My mother had a large pot of *panjeeri* (sweet made from semolina) wrapped in a cotton sheet, and my sister [carried] the passport and bank book and a small briefcase. So [to protect our feet] my mother took the sheet off the pot and would sometimes throw it under my sister's feet and sometimes under mine... sometimes under her own.

We stayed in the camp for two months, and we had no difficulties. When Vidhya [daughter of our Hindu friends] heard, she conducted a search to find us. Daily she would have her servant bring us fresh milk and then she said, "You used to come and [visit] us," and wept. So these poor things would come and give us everything.

The price of honour

[We heard about Partition through] the people who used to work in Jalandhar, my aunt's son. They would bring newspapers, and they would say how there is going to be an upheaval and there is great turbulence in the towns. Women kept stones and bricks on their rooftops. When the Hindu boys came [to Muslim homes], when they banged on the doors or made a noise, [the women] threw the stones down.

When the men came in a fury, they didn't see that this is someone's daughter or someone's sister. All they would see is a Muslim. They would come in a mob, and see that this is a Muslim village and these are the women of Muslims. The elders had said to [the women], if a Sikh comes near you, you should [kill yourselves]. There were some girls who were so honourable... when the Sikhs came—they died, they did not care for their lives.

The *patwari* (village head) had two daughters abducted by Sikhs. The younger was murdered. And the older daughter was married at the house of a Sikh. By the time I knew [the father] in 1960, he had already paid two visits to India, [saying] "My daughter should be returned to me."

Some [Muslim] girls in the neighbouring villages were brought back by the military. [But] many women were unable to escape. Their parents died suffering and weeping, [their] older brothers still longing to meet them. And some had children, and they were forced to stay in those Sikh homes for the sake of the children.

Mita   IND 1

In October 1984, after Indira Gandhi's assassination, Delhi saw rioting and looting on an unprecedented scale: about 5,000 Sikhs, mostly men, were killed in total. Several citizens' groups took up the work of relief and rehabilitation with the widows; Mita was part of one such initiative.

I started by helping some friends, but then after I went to the area I felt more strongly that I had to do something, that giving relief was not all... women needed so much more.

Lack of compassion

Remember it was dead winter: November—it was very cold that year. But the relief from the state was always very... grudging. I remember we felt that there was only one secretary [who] was very compassionate about these widows and he said right then that we should leave off all this [work] of getting these women who have never gone out of their homes to do a job—this is not fair, after all they have been through, to go out into the world and meet all sorts of harrassment. He said, why can't we just give them 50,000 [*rupees*], 60,000, some lump sum money. It's nothing for our budget. But I think he was very much in the minority. And the

First, the male relatives came and took over the women's lives

other people, I felt, were so "us and them" and grudging, saying they've got enough, and they would pull out all kinds of stray incidents and say, "Should those people get relief? And what about the ones the [Sikh] terrorists killed?" So generally, in the administration there was not a very positive feeling about the relief or compensation.

When we went to the riot victims, it was like another world... and this was only 10 to 15 miles from [where I worked and lived] and I felt a great guilt for that. That we have two worlds. So I wanted to learn, frankly. Slowly, over three or four years, I came to understand the problem, and the pressures.

I think [the prejudice] was not really so much anti-Sikh but anti-poor. To me, it was just this thing of "these poor people", and "what do they know? They don't know anything, they don't know how to live and they were living in *jhuggis* (shanties) anyway and what was the value of those *jhuggis*? Why should we give them so much?" And also this business of valuing a life at 10 [thousand *rupees*]: they gave compensation for injured at five [thousand] and death at 10, and then, about a year later, they gave an additional 10 because elections were close and... Some of the better-off women used to just sniff at it and say what is this 20,000 to us?

Family breakdown

Within the family... First it was the male relatives, whoever was remaining. They came and took over [the women's] lives. Then when I went three years ago, I found that a new phenomenon had started: our 12-year-olds had become 17-, 18-year-olds and my God, they were really harassing their widowed mothers. Popli's case was really sad. She had this son who must have been 18 and he was totally shiftless. He was just like a surrogate husband, he would wait around on the day she got her salary and beat her up and grab the money and go off. He got married [and] expected her to feed the family. This was happening in a lot of families, sons had grown up, and fathers-in-law, brothers-in-law [were pressuring them]... It's always a bad situation for them—and it was much worse because the standard structures had broken down and what came up in its place was even worse.

Worlds apart

I think the relief agencies were not able to handle this. Absolutely not. To all of us this was like Mars, this was a completely strange land, strange people. I remember I went with this one woman, very nice, genuinely wanting to help, she went with the best of intentions. But she said, "Look, they don't grieve, they don't

A Sikh woman and her children grieve for her husband, killed in the 1984 anti-Sikh riots in Delhi

Tom Haley/Rex Features

mourn." You know there was all this excitement in the refugee camps and the young girls and boys who had had five or six people in their families killed were unable to take it all in. And to them, all this attention that they were getting—or even the building they were staying in—was something quite strange and wonderfully different from the *jhuggi* they had been used to.

So this young woman, I remember her saying, "Look at these people, they don't feel anything at all." There were two young girls and they were trading numbers, saying 12 of mine were killed and only four of yours, which struck her as very strange. But I don't think it was strange. We were all stunned, in shock, and we don't understand too much, so we were all going through our own traumas.

We didn't understand, we didn't catch the signals of whether someone was suicidal, or sad, or going round the bend. We were just imposing our views... of what they needed, how to react and there were so many cases. I'd say that the **gurdwaras** were the worst. They just went around telling [the widows] don't do this, don't do that, as if they were children... It was as if they were just

We don't understand violence until it happens to us

something to be used because they had become of consequence, because they had value as symbols of the persecution of the Sikh community. In fact, I have my doubts about the role the *gurdwaras* played. They were extremely dogmatic... very authoritarian. They wanted to throw every other group out of the place, I remember. The *granthis* were total killjoys and always wanted to make [the widows and their families] feel they were victims, and keep them sobbing and weeping, making use of them.

So I don't think any of us, even the best intentioned, had any inkling of what this conflict was about, of what the victims were feeling, what they needed, who they needed. Their physical needs were met by the relief organisations and I think they were met very well: food, clothing, blankets. They needed more though.

I think we don't understand violence until it happens to us... We did get some counsellors, people who actually knew how to deal with depression, problems of excess of grief. I think even they were not able to understand, because this is such an alien situation they were not able to deal with it.

Had some justice been done, had at least half a dozen people been sent to jail or to life imprisonment or something, it would have been a kind of placating, a release.

Sense of injustice

They were all terribly shocked and were suffering from an acute sense of loss. One of the cases I remember is that of Gyani Kaur, who felt deeply upset at the fact that her husband was killed after the police had shown up. I can still remember her account of what happened during those two days of horror and as she told it she was totally oblivious of her surroundings. She went on and on for over two hours, slowly and meticulously recounting every detail, without making any distinction between the important and unimportant ones. Moreover, her meandering account of that night of horror was accompanied all along by a steady commentary comprising the feelings, hopes, fears, confusions she had undergone during that terrible time. It appeared that in her mind she often finds herself locked inside that phase and beset with bewildering questions for which she can find no answers...

Gyani, who is a simple rustic type, described the scene of the attack as one of a farmer harvesting—[the rioters] killed them as if they were harvesting the crop. She repeatedly expressed her sorrow and anger at the patrolling police who could have saved her husband. And this is what she tried telling the police commission... And the sad thing was that they didn't think that her account was relevant to what they were trying to find out. They were irritated with her long rambling account and they kept telling her, "Oh, we know this," or "We know that". But what she was trying to tell them was that her husband died in the *jhuggis* after the police came and were patrolling the streets. And this is what she cannot reconcile herself to.

She felt guilty: a feeling which was reinforced by all the other women

A mother's guilt: Shanti's story

Even though everyone in the area had lost someone or other, there were some special cases where those left behind [like Gyani] felt that what happened need not have happened. This is also true with Shanti whose husband and three sons had been killed. See, what was unique about her was that her two younger sons got killed, because of an unfortunate combination of circumstances.

The rioters were very organised and did not target children, but Shanti's husband kept his youngest sons with him. They ended up hiding with him and in the confusion they were burnt to death with their father and older relatives.

Her daughter, Babli, was the only one who knew that her brothers were inside that loft. But how does a little child like her get herself heard? She kept running about all the time while there was utter panic and bedlam. Later, Shanti came, and went all over the *jhuggis* looking for her sons. And then she found the bodies. She was... her daughter had told me... she was just sort of struck dumb since then. Later on, she was angry with Babli. She said, "Why did you not tell me, why did you not tell me?" and she used to take out all her bottled-up feeling on Babli.

I think she felt guilty for not having kept the sons with herself... But anyway she was just not able to recover. The fact that her younger sons were gone is something she just could not come to terms with. She just lost her will to live...

And it was a feeling which was reinforced by all the other women, by her community. What they would always tell her is, "What a fool you are—how stupid you are..." She would then blame her husband saying, "He is the one who kept them [with him]..." but that would not work. They would all say, "Ultimately you must be very bad to be so extraordinarily unlucky," or "You are a fool because you did not keep the sons with you. Nobody else's son got lost, all the other women managed to keep their sons. How come you did not know where your sons were?" And she took that guilt upon herself. I do not like even thinking about it any more... it seems to me that it was an unbearable sense of sorrow—unbearable grief. For her it was literally easier to die than

How can you put yourself in each and every woman's place? live and bear that any more... Because we had tried to tell her, "Who do you think will look after your daughters?" But she would say, "Well, I cannot help that."

You know I still remember the day I went after her death—we did not know that she had hung herself. It was ironical because we thought we were extremely successful. We had got therapists and psychiatrists to see her. And there we were with all kinds of things for her—clothes, an arrangement for rations—and we went and were told, "She's gone."

Shanti's sorrow was not just sorrow; it was this sense of inconsolable, irreparable loss. Literally, as if you have not put something away safely. It is like you had a purse and put something precious quite unnecessarily in that purse, and it got stolen—that kind of terrible gnawing loss.

Conditional relief

She could not get herself released from that feeling. She could not reconcile herself to it. This is all hindsight; because, when I think of it, I was also taking advantage of your average relief worker's stand. When you are dealing with so many people, how can you put yourself in each and every woman's place? All the time we were saying, "Yes, okay she suffered. But her suffering is kind of different from my sister's if she was suffering the same thing." I was expecting her to fit into a particular kind of stereotype... my idea of her.

We are a little patronising about our relief work—which is a very disturbing factor that I discovered through Shanti. [It assuages our guilt] and... also it gives us a sense of power, a sense of being in control, a sense of "Oh, how good we are" and that is what we enjoy. And they also know that and they play upon it... they say nice things about us which will feed our ego... things like: "You are the only one who does something, no one else does." And in some senses we can help—rather than sitting [at home]. My imperfect help to them is still something. If only one had not expected certain things from Shanti and given her a bit more unconditional sympathy. I think that even in the best of us, a lot of our sympathy, a lot of our relief is based on certain conditions.

This is one matter on which I have had some quarrels with others. On one level what [other groups] have done is very good and they have got tremendous experience—their methods of establishing rapport with the people are very good—but on the other hand they also expect people to conform with their notions of behaviour, with correct attitudes to men and women, and a host of other things. So as a result a tailoring school [did not even get started], simply because the organisers [said] the women are not in the correct frame of mind: "They are only interested in grabbing things."

Now for God's sake, this kind of remark does not take into account the fact of their already terrible situation being brutally aggravated by the tragedy they went through... so how do you expect them to be in a "proper" frame of mind? It is like saying, "If you are good, deserving poor—then we will help, otherwise we won't." That is the kind of thing which I have seen all along and which we have tried to avoid. But I wonder if this moral assumption is an essential part of social work—if [we] give, then you better toe the line. Otherwise...

If we give relief, then you better toe the line. Otherwise...

Hiding behind masks

This father-in-law of [Shanti's]—he seemed such a nice man. But later we were told that he used to taunt her, saying, "Why didn't you die, shame on you, no one else's little son died, why did yours?" So the picture we used to get—of all of them grieving together in a decorous manner—was obviously not the real picture. And it was only after I was in the community for three or four years that I started to see the face they put on for the middle class, for the *babus*. In fact they never let on any real emotion, any real grief, any real tension before the outsiders. "These are just people of authority, with so much money, let's grab from them how much we can." So in Shanti's case I think we were completely inadequate...

The need to counsel children

We felt that not one of the organisations paid any attention to the children. I just wanted to not leave them alone, because... I just felt like kicking myself after the Shanti episode, after Babli. We [did work with children] and included children of the attacking community [in our activities], because they were just as terrified, and just as traumatised. There was this one child, Suresh, he was very violent because he lived next to the *nullah* (drain) where all the men had been killed and thrown, so he was in need of help and relief, which none of these communities recognised. The actual witnessing of violence was too much.

Sexual violence

I think they put it aside (did not talk about it), because you know we were dealing with people whose relatives, very near relatives, had died. [But] the rape and molestation cases were more east

They did not let us see the real anguish Delhi, they weren't **Sultanpuri** side. But the reason why it didn't occur in Sultanpuri is quite clear. It was far too organised, the attack. [Had] the mastermind sat down and put rape on the agenda it would have happened. It's not anybody's goodness that it didn't. I think it simply didn't occur to the man who was masterminding things. It was so clear that only a particular profile got killed... here in the dark, in *jhuggis*, even if I were to go on a killing spree there would be at least five different kinds of [victim]. But if it's very well organised and orchestrated as this was, with police jeeps... actually patrolling and helping...

Suppressed anger

[The women] did not show anger in the ways that we would. They're just trained, I think, to never show anger. And when the anger would suddenly come out, it would be a good dramatic performance, or they did not let us see it—just as they did not let us see the real anguish. But the little boys felt tremendous anger, especially the ones who were 10 or 11.

I think the community had decided at that time that: we knew nothing, we were just going about our business, what do we have to do with the killers? They projected this kind of thing with the children... an apolitical image. [Yet] the women definitely did understand [who was involved] and they were quite angry about the fact that the police did not help them but killed them, and they were very full of anger with the shopkeeper who had a flourishing shop soon after [the riots] and the fact that [a politician, suspected of being involved in the riots] came and went in this great *gadi* (car), all of that. But... they have these very muted personalities, at least before us, where they don't let on what they feel.

Compensation brings pressures

I remember we used to keep going from house to house in the first year—there would be these strange, fat and middle-aged men, sitting in these two-roomed houses. A man always sitting there on the bed, with relief money coming in, mother getting it, all of the money going where it should... I really thought to myself, God knows who this man is, except that he was usually somebody they would say was a *jeth* (elder brother-in-law) or something, but whatever he was, he also had a wife and a family. I'm sure when I go back now I'll probably find some permanent arrangements with these [male relatives] having taken over. I'm keen to see which of the women have resisted and stuck it out on their own, and which have got absorbed within "happy" extended families.

Then they started having trouble with dowry... about three

years ago. Daughters had grown up and [prospective in-laws] were saying that four *lakhs* was not much, well... normal life had set in, with of course their own personal baggage of trauma continuing. Dowry demands, and shiftless sons, and male relatives...

But that in-law situation was quite odd, because you know, the [parents-in-law] were the ones who had suffered the losses [of sons], so there was a great deal of sympathy [for them]. There were a lot of such cases, where the wife was alive [and] so old people did not get compensation, but through social pressure the in-laws got a foothold into the house. So it was either the earlier hierarchies of power continuing, or it was a kind of opposite, a reverse, an injustice [the in-laws got nothing], it's very strange. But what is interesting is that at last it gave some of these daughters-in-law the money, and the chance, and the nerve to settle scores. With the compensation money in their hands, they had bargaining clout.

With the compensation money in their hands, they had bargaining clout

Gopi and Vidya   IND 5/6

Both widows of the 1984 riots, Gopi and Vidya belong to the Labana Sikh community, many of whom crossed into India during Partition. They speak of the changes in their lives in the 10 years since they lost their husbands.

GOPI: It is difficult to bring up a family on 1,200 or 1,300 *rupees* [a month]—how can you manage? For many years I had no job, so you do what you can, clean utensils, we'd get a bit from the stitching centre, a couple of hundred, and we never knew whether there would be food. We just had to make to with what we had. Then I got a job, and after a while, things got a bit better.

No one really helps. The *Nishkam* (local health and education centre) people get books and things for the children, but they charge them for it. We have problems with water, electricity, repair work, and then there is always the threat that they will ask us to pay instalments on the **house**, where will we pay this from?

The older daughter, Meera, I have married off. I spent my own money, but no one reduced it because of our status [as widows]—who will accept less? If we can't pay that much people will ask why they should marry anyone in our house. No one thinks these are the homes of martyrs; instead they think the women of these martyrs have money. They think we have a lot of money so we will be able to give a lot. And once our girls are married, they pester them for more money, more things.

Coping alone

[Before the riots] the men used to earn, the woman looked after the house, but now it is all on one person. You know there is that one thing, the support and companionship between two people, that is the key thing. We never felt any lack [of wealth], because there was that. In the early days when we were alone we used to feel very scared. We had no idea how to operate, what to do, how to travel alone. Gradually I learnt how to cope on my own.

For a few months [at work] it was quite difficult, I didn't know how to talk to people... but my office people were very kind from the start. They would help, they would advise me on how to deal with people. Now I like going to work... now even one day at home hangs heavy! It feels a bit odd, you feel suffocated. Going out, meeting people, talking, all this helps to take away some of what you feel inside. The unhappiness, the resentment, goes away.

Earlier [staying in the home] was a habit. I'd never once considered that I would get out and work outside. Now they are all my friends at work, and we socialise. They're all mixed: Sikhs, Muslims, Hindus. And no one cares about what you are. When you work these kinds of differences disappear.

VIDYA: You see, we have no choice. These children need to eat, and if we keep weeping they will starve. So, of necessity you have to stop the tears and get on with the work of feeding the family.

Today we have seen the world, Bombay, Delhi. Earlier we knew nothing, we didn't know this from that, we never stirred... When Gopi got a job she was ready to tear up her appointment letter [but] we managed to stop her.

GOPI: Well, we had never even seen the outside world. So I was scared. How will we go out, in buses, how will we get to work? Who knows who I'll encounter there? And I was so worried, I thought "better to die", so I decided to tear the letter up.

Mourning

VIDYA: The way our men were burnt, the way they died, the way their bodies were cut into pieces... you know we had never seen a body burning, women don't go to the cremation ground. But my man was half burnt, he was lying there and no one had even put a piece of cloth on him, and I then took my *dupatta* (scarf) off and gave it to my son and asked him to put it on his father, at least that way we would have put a cloth on him [because part of Hindu and Sikh ritual is to cover the body of the dead person with a cloth]. And the body kept lying there, a dog came and started licking up the blood, and then I thought: we can't let this happen. So we picked up our broken doors, and the wooden bed, and we put those on top of him and my son set fire to the body, with his own hands [because in order to release the soul, the body must be cremated.]

And then some days later we realised it was the **12th day** and we thought we should do something, and we got together and planned a bit. Then [our husbands' relatives, who would normally perform these rituals] came and said, "You didn't inform us and you have done this ceremony." We said, "You know, we have become this man's sister, father, mother." Whatever had to be done, we all decided to do, we thought we were the family now.

Later, [the relatives] kept saying we had not told them, but we thought, who knows whether they would have turned up or not? And if we had waited on them, our husbands' souls would have continued to suffer and would not have been released.

If we keep weeping, these children will starve

Remarriage

What help can another man give us? He will not give money, he will eat, he'll take money away instead, he may well be unkind to the children, but he will give that one thing.

Now at least our children are our own. Another man will fight, he will be violent, he may ruin your body, and everyone will get a bad name, your in-laws, others... And he'll start asking where did you go?—today you're late from work, who have you been with? After all, we meet people at work, someone may offer you a lift on their motorbike one day, you may go out, but there's no one to say anything to you. You are your own mistress. Yes, our sons [are sometimes critical of us]... but today we do what we want, we get what we need. Of course, there is a little restriction: you do want to do things, to eat certain kinds of things, but you stop yourself, thinking that that money can be better used. Who knows whether the son will give anything or not?

The sons' contribution

[A woman's earnings are a new thing so] some sons no longer feel the same sense of responsibility towards the family. This [complacency] happens in every home... in our homes. [Sons] do earn, it's not that they don't, but they will not take the responsibility.
GOPI: Yes, they contribute something, and when we want to make up a kitty (common purse) or something, they will contribute. But their contributions are often random. But there are others who are not [irresponsible]. They did not even ask us what we did with the lump sum money we got. They earn and give us something each day—if they can manage.

At the time when our men were alive, flour, ghee, oil, sugar,

We have all but held the criminals by the hand and pointed them out...

kerosene: all were cheaper. So even 500 *rupees* was adequate, now even 2,000, plus contributions from the children if they give, does not suffice. In fact, the money hardly lasts four or five days.

Relations with men

VIDYA: Several widows [have remarried], several are happy, others... Women were quite vulnerable, they'd go somewhere, someone would speak to them nicely, they'd get taken in. Several had children, others had to have abortions.

There were a couple of stray incidents in the office in the early days but not now. When we travelled in buses and were with crowds there were men who used to feel us up, make us feel dirty, and we used to sit together in the evenings, and say today this happened to us and so on... In earlier times, we had never gone out without our husbands. This was the first time we were actually out on our own. So when we came back from work we used to share what happened to us... and that way, by sharing and support, you'd conquer your own doubts and fear. And gain courage. Yes, we have shouted at people in buses, we've even hit them, complained about them... everything.

Justice

GOPI: It's 10 years [since the riots], but what have they done, we have all but held the criminals by the hand and pointed them out, but what has happened? The government certainly bothers us, if we don't go to court on the appointed day, we receive summonses. But what have they done?

VIDYA: We have given evidence so many times but nothing has happened. Instead of helping, they tried to trap us. People tried to persuade us to give false evidence, but we refused.

[**Rajiv Gandhi**] said, didn't he, that my mother has been killed and when a big tree falls, small ones also fall? But some sort of justice has been meted out, whether or not [the rioters] have got it. In Rajiv's death we see [justice]. You see the woman who killed [Rajiv], she was like us, she was tormented and sad like us, and we feel that fate has been on our side here.

So now we have also started believing that it was written in our fates that this would happen: that Indira Gandhi will die and there will be this kind of violence. And it was in the hands of the young woman [to avenge us]. She too had had her honour taken away, she had no family, she too was created by God to kill Rajiv Gandhi. She screwed up her courage, prepared the bomb and killed him and herself.

[Those five rioter we testified against—] yes, they are still there.

And that justice we did not get, that is true. But now we think they too are ruined in a way. Endless numbers of times they have been called to the court, they have had to pay up bribes... we feel they are not really alive.

We had forgotten to cry, we had no time to grieve

"A dog's death"

And we have still managed to live, to survive. God has at least given us this... and in a way our lives were put together again. But [Rajiv] died a dog's death. A leg here, a foot there, his stomach all over. Fifty people died with him and someone's limbs mixed with another's, a part of a body from this one, another from that one. What kind of death is that?

Our men died like that. We couldn't get to see their bodies, we couldn't perform the last rites. We didn't even get their ashes to scatter in a river.

"The riot widows"

The women refer to themselves as "widows" using the English word, rather than the Hindi. This is how the state referred to them, and the term has become a sort of marker of their identity. There is resentment among some extended families that the women are no longer defined as "wives of" the dead sons, but as women in their own right, albeit as widows.

I think nature made this word "widow" for us. When people see us they say, "Look, 'the riot widows' have come." Then it is used as a jibe—for example, my mother-in-law may taunt us with it. They say today these widows have become important, their men are dead, but they've got everything. Our sons don't belong to us any more, they don't count for anything.

My sister-in-law says this. Also, I find it difficult to cry and they find that odd about me. Recently someone was filming for television and I was told to cry a bit and I'd get to be on TV, but someone should have taught me how you bring on tears: I could not cry. So they didn't show it. I should have looked serious, unhappy. I told [my relatives]: "Look, I have work to do. I go here and there, I have children to bring up, so I won't cry. Don't say tomorrow that I don't have any regard for my husband." If I do cry it comes suddenly, something happens, and it sparks off my crying, but it does not come easily. If I sit in a corner and cry, who will feed these children, and look after them?

At that time this was the reality, we had forgotten to cry, we had no time to grieve because we had to get on with feeding the children. I had seven children. If someone was giving something, we had to get hold of it.

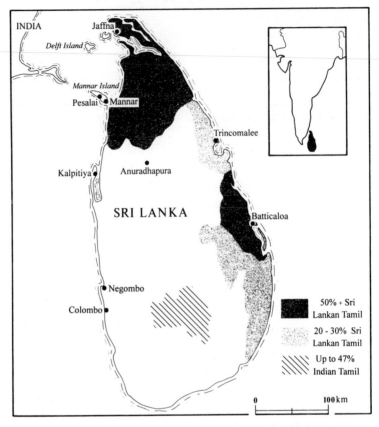

INDIA
Jaffna
Delft Island
Mannar Island
Pesalai ● Mannar
Kalpitiya ●
Anuradhapura
Trincomalee
SRI LANKA
Batticaloa
Negombo
Colombo ●

█ 50% + Sri Lankan Tamil
░ 20 - 30% Sri Lankan Tamil
╲╲ Up to 47% Indian Tamil

0   100 km

HUMAN DEVELOPMENT INDEX (UNDP): 90 (medium)
POPULATION: 17.7m
FEMALE LITERACY: 81%
FEMALE LIFE EXPECTANCY: 73.4 years

Early 16th century Arrival of Portuguese traders **1658** Dutch power replaces Portuguese **1815** Ceylon becomes a British colony **1840s onwards** Plantation economy (coffee, then tea, rubber and coconuts) worked largely by Indian labour **1931** Self-government; women get the vote **1944** Sinhala and Tamil recommended as joint official languages **1948** Independence **1956** Sinhala made the single official language **1958** Inter-communal violence **1970-1** JVP armed opposition **1975** Establishment of LTTE **1983** Inter-communal violence; increase of Tamil armed struggle **1987** Major government offensive against Jaffna; arrival of Indian Peace-Keeping Force **1990** Withdrawal of IPKF **1993** Assassination of President Premadasa **1994** President Kumaratunge elected; renewed peace talks **1995** Ceasefire

━ SRI LANKA ━

Sri Lanka used to be known as "The Pearl of the Indian Ocean", famed for its peace and beauty. After years of war, the name seems painfully ironic.

The multi-ethnic population is 74% Sinhalese, mainly Buddhist; 12% Sri Lankan Tamils, concentrated in the north and east of the country; and 5% Indian Tamils, originally brought over as labour for the tea plantations. Most Tamils are Hindu, but there are some Christians among both Tamils and Sinhalese. They amount to some 7% of the population, as do the Muslims.

Democratically self-governing from the 1930s, Ceylon negotiated independence from British colonial rule in 1948. It was renamed Sri Lanka in 1972. The official language was English, which gave disproportionate power to an English-speaking elite (containing both Sinhalese and Tamils); in 1944 the state council adopted a resolution recommending that Sinhala and Tamil be made official languages.

However, the resentment of the Sinhala-speaking intelligentsia at their exclusion from power found expression in a Sinhalese nationalist movement, demanding that Sinhala should be the only official language and Buddhism the state religion. The socialist Sri Lanka Freedom Party, which replaced the ruling United National Party (UNP) in 1956, immediately enacted a "Sinhala only" bill. Serious inter-communal violence erupted in 1958, but the bill proved to be only the first in a series of measures to entrench Sinhalese political, educational and economic advantage.

When the conservative UNP were re-elected in 1977, they pursued similar policies with equal vigour. By the general election of 1977, Tamil opposition had united on a moderate but secessionist platform as the Tamil United Liberation Front (TULF). Thereafter, Tamil militant groups, notably the Liberation Tigers of Tamil Eelam (LTTE or "Tamil Tigers"), founded in 1975, took up the demand for an independent state (Tamil Eelam) which would amount to one-third of the island. Increasingly ferocious inter-communal violence in 1977 and 1981, and the death of 2,000 Tamils in urban riots in 1983, provoked the Tamil militants to war.

In the early 1970s the situation was complicated by the appearance of an extremist Sinhala nationalist movement, the Janata Vimukhti Peramuna (JVP), formed mainly of deprived and disaffected Sinhalese rural youth. The JVP's brutal campaign, concentrated in the south of the island, was crushed with equal violence by the government. From 1983 onwards, there was a high level of violence on all sides—terrorisation of civilians, kidnappings, and on occasion as many as 1,000 political killings a month.

In 1987 the Sri Lankan army launched a major offensive against Jaffna, the Tamil stronghold. When this failed to quash the Tamil forces, the government reached an agreement with the Indian government (whose concern stemmed from the fact that southern India has a large Tamil population, increasing with the tide of Sri Lankan refugees), to accept an Indian Peace-Keeping Force (IPKF), supposedly to enforce a ceasefire. But the Tigers and allied groups resisted fiercely, and the IPKF, who had become deeply resented, withdrew in 1990. Full-scale war broke out again between the Tigers and the government; the Jaffna peninsula was blockaded, and regularly attacked. Some 800,000 people kept going under the autocratic rule of the Tigers with almost no water, power or daily supplies for four years.

The conflict was at an impasse and UNP President Premadasa stepped up the search for political solutions. His assassination in 1993 led to the election of a new president in 1994 who promised to bring peace. Talks resumed later that year, resulting in a cease-fire in early 1995. While retaining their objective of creating a separate state, the Tigers' have stated that they would consider a proposal for a federal state.

Conflict in Sri Lanka has left over 60,000 dead; as many as 500,000 people may have left the country, and 600,000 people have been displaced (75,000 are currently in camps). In 1989, one of the worst years of fighting, "disappeared" people from all sides numbered 6,000. Infrastructural, environmental and economic costs are enormous but despite the violence, democracy continued to function, and the economy in the areas under government control actually grew in the early 1990s.

These testimonies are from women from different communities in Sri Lanka. Most were not actively participating in the struggle. Many of their stories illustrate how the difficulties for women who become heads of household with little education or experience of work are compounded by social distrust of single women. The LTTE has brought some social gains for Tamils living under its control, overriding much of the traditional caste structure and traditions, while the Tigers have become internationally known for their 3,000 or so young women fighters.

Testimony collection was coordinated by Noeline Mendis in cooperation with the Social and Economic Development Centre, Colombo. Interviewers were Regina Ramalingam, Manel Perera, Francesca de Silva, Fara Haniffa and Manel Jayanthi. Additional interviews were collected in Jaffna by Subathira and Malini Shanmugam of the Centre for Women and Development, Jaffna, and coordinated by director Saroja Sivachandran.

Anthonicam   SRI 3

Anthonicam's husband died in 1986, shortly after being arrested on suspicion of being a member of the Tamil Tigers. She is a Catholic and lives in Pesalai, a fishing village in Mannar district, where much of the fighting took place.

In 1990 [when the LTTE and the Sri Lankan forces fought intensively in the North] we were forced to go to India. The bridge [to the mainland] was bombed by the LTTE. We were afraid of the future. We had nothing to eat. My mother, my children and myself all went to India. The [refugee camp] was alright, [but] what they provided was not enough for us so, though my son was small, he worked there. They gave poor wages, about 15 or 20 *rupees* a day, and with that we managed our needs.

About 40 families lived in a big hall. We partitioned sections with bedsheets, boards and sarees. At first we felt uncomfortable; later we got used to it. Most of [the other refugees] were from our village and so there were less hassles. We got transport and medical facilities, and help with our children's education too, so we were alright.

After the death of Rajiv Gandhi [1991] we were not allowed out of the camp for five months [because his assassination was blamed on the Tamil Tigers]. My children's education was affected—having them at home idling worried us more. Only little children could run around. Later we gave our consent in writing that we wanted to go to Sri Lanka and we came [back to Pesalai].

Managing back home

Here it's difficult for me to run a house. Nobody helps me. I am unable to search for work. I have to stay indoors, stitch or do some handiwork and manage my family. My husband had two trawlers, but we lost everything. I wrote for compensation but I never got it.

I have the talent, but not the means

For the past four years I am trying to obtain some pension from the fish canning factory where my husband had worked, but nothing has materialised so far. I go to each government department and they say, "We will give you," but I've got nothing so far. The Fishermen's Society too promised me a loan, but I have yet to receive it.

But if I get some compensation for my boats, I can cope. I am trying to negotiate a loan and purchase a boat and employ a person to manage. I have the talent, but not the means. In 1989, the IPKF burned my shop. We went to put out the fire, but they shot at us. No compensation for that either.

The most affected [by the situation] are the women. If the men are not permitted to go fishing, then how can the women run the family? Ours is deep sea fishing and they have invested a lot of money on motors, nets and boats. But the Navy now [prohibits] fishing. It is permitted only on one day of the week [and not] at nights. Earlier our women never went to the seashore to help, but now, since times are very hard, they go and work with the men. The cost of living is very high now—and the women are afraid to send the men alone since they may be taken into custody. The men go to the sea but the women attend to tasks like making dried fish. If they have grown-up children, they are worried about sporadic arrests. They are affected mentally too.

All the time we hear gunfire. We can't get out after dark. No freedom. Always frightened. We can't sleep at nights and can't live peacefully during the day. When the children go to school we panic till they come back. When there is an emergency, one child in the hospital and one in school and one at home, we wonder what we should do. When we all stay together we are at ease. Daily there is some sort of tension. We don't know when we will be allowed to live peacefully.

Farida   SRI 2

Farida is a Muslim from Mannar district.

We left home because the army was shelling. One of the shells fell in front of the house. From that time we abandoned our house and our belongings. We were in Erukkalampiddy for five months then were chased away [again].

When the LTTE ordered us to vacate, immediately, we came with what we were wearing, not taking any valuables. Meanwhile the LTTE wanted us to write in a document what we are taking and what we are leaving behind, and they wanted us to hand over the keys of the house. If we were taking gold, only one and a half sovereigns per person was permitted. Hence we had to leave everything and flee. We had problems with the LTTE before that. Often they'd come and ask for two or three parcels of food. They'd bring a newspaper and ask [a high price] for it. We were afraid, hence we had to oblige.

Muslims and Tamils were so united for generations

[When we were leaving], my school principal hugged me, cried and said, "What help can I give you?" All the teachers came to meet me. They said, "This same plight will come to us too. We are helpless. Please don't worry." Everybody tried to console us. My children's friends stayed with us till the end to bid goodbye. [These were] Tamil children, Tamil teachers, the principal a Tamil [nun]; they consoled us.

[Muslims and Tamils] were so united for generations. If somebody dies in their house we feel that someone has died in our house and we visit their house. Likewise for a wedding, they invite us to take part in the meals. We moved with the Tamils just as we would with our own Muslim sisters and brothers.

The Catholic priests approached [the LTTE, asking them not to act in such a way] but the LTTE didn't give in. What they did was to prolong the deadline to vacate. They gave us time, but nothing else. Everybody toiled. The priests tried to help us. Even the boatmen said, "Don't send them away. We will not take them in our boats." But [the LTTE] wanted us to go.

[The bridge connecting Mannar island to the mainland had been bombed so] we hired a boat—500 *rupees* per passenger. We spent a lot and it was raining heavily. [The LTTE] examined everything we were taking. We brought our belongings in a polythene bag, even that was checked. We carried two or three sarees to change, and everything got soaked in the rain. For 23 hours [until] we reached our destination, we had no food or drink.

When we came to Kalpiddy people were put up by those who knew them. Me too—I can't take my children to unknown families. A family known to us sheltered us in the principal's house. They gave us a place to sleep and forced us to eat... but we were not in the mood to eat, we drank watery tea, and ate some biscuits. They gave the children bananas, mangoes from the fridge and the lady said, "They look like my children."

Displaced in Colombo

We came here on the 1st of October 1990. I am staying with my sister [in the house of a man who knows] my brother-in-law. We are six and there are three more families living upstairs with us. Downstairs is occupied by the landlord and there are 18 of them. We do not know when they'll ask us to vacate and if they do we will be on the road—there is no other way. We are not paying any rent. They are good-hearted people and since they know us well, they've helped us.

I'm here in Colombo only for the sake of my children's education. Otherwise I would go and settle in a village. Colombo is really difficult. Every morning our children need 40 *rupees* as bus fare. [And my sickness is] expensive! I spend 100 *rupees* a week for my tablets. How can I bring up my children? I have lost all my belongings. I do not know when I will have a normal life. I think constantly of all these uncertainties.

No support or compensation

Among the people who came from Mannar many are living in refugee camps. It's they who get help from the government. Others are being helped with pots and pans and food items too. But up to this day we have not received help [because] we are accommodated in this house. It's not that nobody knows that we live here. We've told so many. We haven't [registered our names]. We don't know where to register. Since we lost everything, we need everything. We had to buy our own [reed] mats to sleep, and charitable people gave us bed sheets. For the damage caused to our house [in Mannar] we applied to the Ministry of Relief and Rehabilitation but so far we haven't received any help from them.

Where can we go for a job? Even for [my husband] to get employed in a shop, whom can we approach? This is a new place for us, and we are unknown. [Teaching] at home is a possibility, but we have no furniture. If he goes [out] for work it would be difficult for me. I am unable to do anything for myself [because of my illness]. So he is staying, helping us, and that's how we are spending our time.

Elise   SRI 11

Elise, 34, lives near Negombo. Her husband was one of 23 migrant fishermen killed by the LTTE in 1990.

We received 50,000 **rupees** [compensation from the government for my husband's death]. But my step-sister took it, promising to return it [but she did not]. [Before that] I sold the boat and we also found some money Anthony had hidden in the hut. I have assistance from my younger sister [who is a housemaid in Oman].

Each of us received 600 *rupees* [from the Church] at the start [and I had] 5,000 *rupees* as funeral expenses. [The village] all got together for the burial—not with money, but they attended to the chores of burials and alms giving. It was a collective funeral.

We avoid houses where there are males, due to gossip

Grief shared

Because it was a group [who suffered] I was able to bear the sorrow. But if it was similar to the tragedy my sister faced [who also lost her husband in crossfire], I could not have gone through it. [She suffered alone but] because it was collective mourning, we did not feel it so much. But today, when I have to face my children's problems, my grief surfaces.

In the night I feel that I am alone with my three children, and when the children get ill I miss my family, though neighbours assist me. That is when I feel the pain of the tragedy. My husband, his father, my father, his sister and brother all died that day.

Suspicion of a woman alone

The women who suffered the same fate have a tendency to visit each other. We avoid going to houses where there are males, due to suspicion. The woman next door is suspicious about my dealings with her husband who is old. If I speak to him his wife argues with him, accusing him of spending for my needs. Due to this irritation I am nervous to talk to men. Even for an emergency I would think twice about calling a male to assist. It is only with those who have suffered the same fate that I could share my grief and talk freely.

All types of false allegations are levelled at me. I think people feel that I am doing well and that I am prospering by false means. I have the [gold jewellery] that he bought me. I preserve it and never pawned it. This appears to be an irritant factor in the village. If a [male] neighbour or anyone comes over to my house they believe it is due to a relationship. Hence I am unable to seek their assistance. I have to live in isolation. When we are at the bus stop, people working in the neighbouring factory offer lifts to Negombo. Even such a trivial act is frowned upon. Therefore I feel I am in no position to stretch my hand out to anyone, even for an emergency. If mishaps come my way I have to face them alone.

My step-sister has written to my sister abroad also accusing me of friendships. Even if I seek a man's assistance to mend a broken fence, people gossip. My sister has replied showing anxiety about news she received. Because of this situation I feel it is best to attend to my chores alone and prevent gossip.

People have a misconception that I have everything I need.

They think I have money since I built a wall around my house. They are also prejudiced by the fact my sister is abroad. But they do not understand that she too has to live. Even my step-sister has communicated to others that I have money. That is why she got her husband to borrow my money and did not return it. But only I know the hardships I have to endure.

Economic initiatives

[I reared poultry at one stage but] it is difficult to obtain a profit through that venture. We received 3,000 *rupees* as assistance for the project. But due to the high cost of poultry feed it was not successful. No one instructed us. We applied the basic knowledge we had and we never profited.

My step-sister took my money and tried to persuade me to go abroad. But no one assisted me in a way I could live in the village, care for my children and earn. I planted banana trees but the monsoon destroyed all my plants. Rearing animals is also a difficult task as my compound is small. Fencing them in does not seem a good way to rear them.

Accepting his death

They buried [him so] soon, it remains a dream and I wonder whether it really took place. I do feel his absence going through financial difficulties, but that he is really dead appears to be a lie.

The last rites were performed in haste. They brought the corpses and buried them within one hour. Wednesday evening they had been killed. Thursday they had been taken to Kalpitiya [the hospital and town nearest to the incident]. Friday morning they brought the corpses to the village. Within an hour they were buried. We were not permitted to bring them to our homes.

Rathie   SRI 5

Rathie, 42, left Jaffna for Colombo, where she earns her living by sewing. Her husband left her 14 years ago.

By God's grace at home I had my three acres of land and a big house. I have 27 coconut trees and four mango trees. I never bought coconut for cooking. The paddy was more than enough for me. If somebody came and asked for half a measure of rice, I could give them. I had no problem regarding food.

[I left my village] because of the problems [there]; and one of my sons has gone away from me—to serve the country. So I brought my other son to Colombo. I can't stitch all the time, my

eyesight is poor, I can't earn. I have been badly beaten and I am *I fed the*
physically not fit. That's why I came to Colombo.   *LTTE. I don't*

I've undergone sufferings that a woman is afraid to speak of *deny it*
publicly. I told [my attackers], "Brothers, what is the difference
between me and your sisters?" But they said, "Shut your mouth,"
and scolded me with filth.

The [IPKF] always came and treated us cruelly. So the LTTE
boys thought I was badly treated and to stop it they planted a land
mine about 10 yards from my house. Suddenly the army came by
and the LTTE boys triggered the mine. Only one of the soldiers
died. The army set fire to my fence [and home], but since my
house is of brick it escaped... they burnt all the photographs in the
house, the roof and my sewing machine. I was teaching 11
children sewing. Everything was smashed.

Boy soldier

My son hadn't joined [the LTTE then]. Nobody was favouring the
LTTE at that time. They had nothing to eat, nobody would feed
them. I felt that my children and the LTTE were the same. I fed
them. I don't deny it. I was ill-treated because somebody reported
this to the army. The neighbours got together and said, "She is the
person who protects the LTTE and gives asylum to them."

When I cooked, the IPKF would come. They would ask, "Why
are there four plates for three people?" Our boys came and spoke
to me saying, "*Akka* (sister), we won't allow anything to happen
to you. Don't worry. Since you have helped so much we won't
abandon you." When the IPKF visited, somehow the Tigers
came—disguising themselves as old men—to find out what
happened.

My children were small. I was alone. The IPKF commander
would come to my house any time he wanted, even at midnight.
When he beat me my youngest son felt hurt. "Where are the Tigers
who came just now?" they would question. Because of this, my
[10-year-old] son got frightened. "If we are living, we should serve
the country. There is no point in living like this," he said. He
became so frustrated that it made this small child join the LTTE. I
didn't send my son to make him a hero. My son wanted to join,
and I was not in a position to bring him back.

My son is still a baby. So far he has not sustained any injuries.
He is being praised as a clever boy. I think since he is so young they
won't send him to battle fronts—with that hope I live. [I couldn't
try to bring him out because] I was in the political committee of
our village. I have given my house for their office.

We have lost   *"Others should not starve"*
the peaceful   Even when [the IPKF] beat me, nobody came. One day at about 9
life   o' clock, seven trucks and seven armoured cars came. After the
IPKF left, people came one by one. They said, "If you had listened
to us at that time... by not feeding the Tigers, they would not enter
your house. If they plant a bomb in your house, it is not only your
house that gets demolished, the neighbouring houses too. You
have no husband, and since you have no daughters [either], you
have the courage to accept the Tigers. Why else should they come
to your house only?" They were not bothered about my feelings,
but their questions started irritating me. So I told them, "They'll
come again. So you please all go away."

I have helped so many. I have given money to people to send
their sons abroad. I have taken money on interest for others and
even if they don't pay the interest I have paid it myself. But nobody
seems to help me when I am in need. Since coming to Colombo I
have helped five or six people to go abroad. I have no necklace, no
bangles. My brothers and sisters hate me because I help everybody.
What I feel is when we are eating rice and good curries, others
should not starve.

[The Tigers] will bring us to a good position. How many other
mothers, who have only one child, have lost them? We [cannot]
say, "Our children should not go, but others should get us our
[independent] state." Such thinking is entirely wrong.

Kokila   SRI 17

Kokila, 43, is Tamil and the principal of a displaced school in Jaffna.

We have lost the peaceful life. That is a big loss. Tension, stress and
grief, all these are here. I lost my own house. Lands have been lost.
Banana, onion, chillies, beetroot and palmyrah land have all been
lost, except for their memory. When we were displaced we
couldn't bring anything with us, only human relationships. Books
of value we'd collected are also lost. When we think of it we feel
sad. [But] comparing our lives with those who are in the refugee
camps, we are satisfied.

Contribution to the struggle

I think all those who chose to live in Tamil Eelam, instead of
fleeing to foreign countries or Colombo seeking a good life, are
participating in the struggle. To head an establishment providing

Life goes on in the ruins of Jaffna
Martin Adler/Panos Pictures

education to poor children is a participation in the struggle. When I undertook the responsibilities as a principal there were three displaced schools functioning under one roof. But I managed to get

It is a relief my school into a separate building.
to face the   I have published four short story collections and two novels.
army with Two more books are yet to be published. But there is a shortage of
your own paper due to the blockade. I am writing articles on psychology too.
weapon What I am trying to convey is that human beings have to respect
fellow human beings. I wrote a short story called "Burning", about
the psychological impact of war on women.

The changed status of women

Before the struggle started our society was very conservative and
rigid. Women had no place among men. They would not talk with
their head up. Who thought that they would take up arms? But in
the last 10 years there has been a tremendous change. We see
young women in the battlefield fighting equally with the men. [It
is] the need of time. Now women all over the world participate in
armed struggles. Why not our women? Instead of dying screaming,
being raped by an aggressor army, it is a relief to face the army with
[your own] weapon.

Our women have proved that they can do anything. [Now]
women can go anywhere during the night. They can drive vehicles
without any fear. Men are scared to abandon women after loving
them. It is a big change. Our women are going to police work. This
was not there before. Many women have lost their work like men,
but others are working as saleswomen, journalists and in small
industries. I appreciate their heroic acts, self-confidence and the
sacrifices they have made for the land of their own. They protect
not only the land, but also the entire women of this land.

Women expect a revolutionary change in the society—I hope it
will come. Freedom struggles never fail. We will have a bright
future. But the question is when.

Vinothini   SRI 18

Vinothini is a Tamil activist in Jaffna.

[I was] working as an **ayurvedic** doctor. Why did I get involved in
this struggle? Because of my love for the country where I was born.
There is a need for it, people are suffering and economically
deprived. So it is a must that every Tamil should participate in this
struggle. [I am working for] freedom of our land and people.

I look after the injured combatants, political campaigning,
propaganda, pre-school education, and conduct public meetings.
[Through my involvement with the movement my] self-

confidence developed, to meet people and do social work. [My family] don't like me working all the time with the movement—my son feels he is being neglected. But I can't help it, I love it.

It is unavoidable [that widows and unmarried women are on the increase due to this war]. Women should learn to stand on their own feet. [People suffer a lot from this war] but we cannot avoid this. We have to protect our land and people from our enemies. We have to sacrifice our life for this purpose. We too have our rights to live in this land—no one can deny that.

Anu   SRI 19

Anu, a Tamil, was an undergraduate at Jaffna University.

[My] ambition was to become a doctor, [but I couldn't]. Every year the marks for entrance to the university differ, especially for Tamils. We have to wait nearly three years after the A-Level exam to get into the university. I did not want to waste my time idling.

Of course [Tamil students are being deprived by this education system]. I completely reject it. Every student must have the right to continue his or her education. I am worried about the younger generation. [Discrimination in education] is a reason for [them] to take arms against the government. I know many students who got frustrated and joined the liberation struggle.

We have given enough time for the politicians to solve the minorities' problems. But they failed. The war has to find a solution. I grew up with the struggle. I know how the Tamil community has been hated by the Sinhala politicians. Vandals and hooligans raped, looted and killed innocent Tamil civilians during the 1958 and 1983 riots in Sri Lanka.

"Women are the most affected"

My mother's income is enough [to pay for my education]. But she cannot save even a cent for dowry or anything. [The dowry system is] not yet abolished. People's attitude must be changed, we can't abolish a social system by making a law.

I don't have time to think about [marriage]. Anyway it's going to be difficult for us. Many boys have migrated and are living in Western countries. Here, most of the boys are involved in the liberation struggle. You see many unmarried women in this region at present. Women are the most affected by this war. Most have become breadwinners of families. They have to do everything.

Memories of war

We have seen only destruction and human deaths in our life. We are not afraid

We lived in Delft. But when the Sri Lankan army occupied the place, in 1991, we ran away, leaving all our belongings—now we live in Jaffna. We, young girls, ran out first for safety reasons. You know how the armed forces behave with women.

We ran out to save our lives. While we were running there were planes bombing all along our route. We cried and ran. On our way, there were a few children who got injured, lying there and looking for help. But, in fear of the bombing planes, we didn't even look at them and ran away. It still hurts me.

I sometimes think of joining with the freedom struggle. We have seen only destruction and human deaths in our life. We are used to it. The experiences we had have given us confidence. Now we are not afraid. This is the reason our young girls are also willing to join the struggle.

Manorani   SRI 12

Manorani's son, a journalist, was abducted and killed during the JVP's campaign. She founded an NGO, the Centre for Family Services, to provide psychological and economic rehabilitation to families affected by political conflict.

When this terrible thing happened to me, I was taken away from my home, I lost all my possessions. [I went abroad for one year, but] I don't like living in another country. And nobody, but nobody, has a right to make me leave my country for any reason.

[When I returned] I was unable to pursue my normal and professional life [as a doctor], due to death threats. And I realised that if I could be so disadvantaged, how much worse it could be for women in less advantageous positions. In villages, most [women] have their home and a few paddy fields—[we both] have some means of supporting ourselves. The thing was—to use a new word— to empower them. They had to overcome their grief, and suddenly they had to learn to accept [the] new position of sole decisionmaker in issues such as children's schooling and children's problems.

Learning to be heads of the household

I remember the very first meeting with the first group. The women did not talk at all. We had to ask questions and extract answers from them. When I visited them after two or three months the difference was phenomenal. They discussed amongst themselves, came to collective and individual decisions about their own income-generating activities, and several ideas were thrown up.

[There are] two things: the women are socio-economically and psychologically disadvantaged. Children are quite adaptable to new situations. The mothers bring them along for meetings and we have playgroups for them. When the children first come in, they have their eyes fixed on the mother when she is disturbed, but when the mother comes out of this depressed [state] the children automatically come out of it themselves.

[A stable economic situation] is the main priority to start with. They are unable to maintain the family—feed the children and till the fields and do all the chores—[so] they get into a worse psychological state. Despair adds to the grief. But the moment they are involved in income-generating they move on, and it is group therapy as well when they find that there are other people who... it's a support system. From whichever side [they have suffered] political violence, all are concerned about similar issues.

[Even] soldiers' wives [who get a pension] need help to use it profitably. Giving them money is insufficient. It is like a woman deciding to grow yams: if she does not have the labour to cultivate, it's futile. If they say they can make garments, you have to make sure they can make garments that can be sold.

[These] women's development societies have to be registered to obtain funds through a bank account, and don't forget they have to deal with cheque books and accounts—all things they are not accustomed to. So it is a whole educational process.

"Women shed the same tears"

It is so good for them to meet in a group. They do not feel isolated. They gain stature in the village, where [before] the villagers may have shunned them. At the beginning [that] did happen. All the assassinations and abductions were political, done by the JVP or government forces. And it has helped the families of the JVP come back into the mainstream, and take their place in society again. The women realise that this is all one problem that they are facing, and is not their fault.

My battle cry is "Women are the ultimate victims of political violence" and through them children become the innocent victims. Take Iraq or any war... the women have to bear the brunt of it and carry on. Take the refugees... in a tiny little space they hang a saree and make a space for the family, cope with the children, cope with the unemployed man who gets frustrated.

This is one of the reasons I feel that women should be the

Women are the ultimate victims of political violence

The need for counselling is not seen from the outside pushers in the peace process. They understand what conflict means to the family. Look at the soldier's wives and mothers—they too suffer, like the women affected by the JVP problems. All women shed the same tears.

[In our women's groups there is] a whole group process which includes every individual. Nobody is teaching, only guiding each other to make their own decisions. The women in the villages have an immense amount of potential. If you take the refugee women— that they keep sane and survive is amazing. A strong motivation is the socio-economic build up. They come expecting hand-outs and they learn to earn and participate in a growing process.

They never get back to their old selves but become new people, because they take a new place in the family structure. The village structure is more difficult, but the fact that they can earn their living and involve themselves in other activities without being dependent on the village gives them their own place and status. They are recognised in their own society.

Coping with grief

[Losing someone this way] is a devastating sorrow because it is arbitrary—it is not like a person dying of an illness. And this terrible thing of the house being invaded, and your child pulled out of your arms at gunpoint... a denial of one's own right as a citizen. And from that arises a... you feel disadvantaged to start with but it is the beginning of asking for justice.

I was so much better off than the women isolated in the villages, being able to talk about the tragedy and express my point of view. The ability to go public, that kept my sanity. It is impossible [to stay quiet in such a situation]. I read books too, especially a beautiful book, *Mothers of Argentina*. All they did was to walk round the square wearing white scarves and from that they started their Mother's Front.

I am slowly starting to earn my living again, [although death threats are not comfortable things to live with] if you take them seriously. Being able to practise my profession gives me back my strength and makes me feel whole. Being a doctor was my life for 40 years.

Grief... those who work with [the women's groups] seem to think they do not have any grief. I don't appear to have any grief. I function, but it is there. If something goes wrong or a child gets ill, then it will resurface double, so it has to be addressed. Counsellors go and chat and... let it come out as a catharsis. The need for counselling is not seen from the outside. There could be many who weep tears into their pillows. Normally the village

women scream and cry, but those who have lost dear ones through abductions, disappearances and arrests have been denied that—mostly there has been no funeral or body to weep over. They have been deprived of showing sorrow, and it has been suppressed. This is soul-destroying.

The disappeared: "there has been no funeral, no body to weep over"
Martin Adler/Panos Pictures

[You have to] try not to get destroyed, which is not very easy. Always one has to give expression to grief. You must be able to work through it. You can convert that emotion into something positive, make a life for yourself, building the old fabric into the present. Taking the love and memories and building a fabric again for yourself is very necessary.

For each person their grief is unique. The ability to form and progress in a group is rewarding and that is what our whole group is about. That is why we call it the Centre for Family Services. A family may be without one member, but it still continues to be a family and it is as a family they have to progress and not as

*I can still see
him turning
and looking
at me* individuals. And the groups are made up of families; so the structure gives them emotional and psychological support. Asian [women] have managed to keep their special perspective of being the gentle sex, the one who provides love, the one who builds the family. All the more today, it is necessary for women in this country—of all races, religions and social strata—to stop and think where we are going.

Rita   SRI 13

Rita, 42, is a member of a women's group organised by the Centre for Family Services. Her son has disappeared.

There was a court case. It was in 1989. While we were coming back from the courthouse, a white van stopped, and they held a gun to the chest [of my son] and took him. I was with him when it happened. One of them held the pistol to my chest.

We went to the police, then we went to Boossa [detention camp]. We went to Anuradhapura. We went three or four times to Boossa. Wherever we went, they told us that he had not been brought in. [When] he was taken, I went to the Seeduwa police station. But they said that he had not been brought in. They said that we had to come back in three days if we wanted to make [a complaint]. We went back in three days. Up to this day there hasn't been any information as to his whereabouts.

Endless enquiry and expense

Well, we always did this mattress and pillow manufacturing. I have two sons—the two brothers used to do it. They were doing well. But after my son went missing we had a lot of expenses... to look for him, to make enquiries. Then for about two or three months we couldn't work. Wherever we heard there might be people [detained]... we went. We are still looking.

I can't even remember some of the [places of worship] I have visited. How many times did I go to soothsayers? I can't even remember. Every soothsayer always said that my son was alive.

After he was taken away, the people in the neighbourhood started looking at us strangely and treating us differently. We had lots of financial problems and we went down in life and so people... well, no one tries to help. They all want to see us in the gutter. Now it is one of those boys who was very friendly with my sons— who was always with them—that is our biggest competitor. Sometimes we think that it was he who would have been behind my son's disappearance.

In Seeduwa, there are still plenty of people who were heavily involved in all this JVP activity. They are still roaming around. If there was really law and order would these things happen? [We have always been supporters of the UNP but] we will never give our vote to them again. When we heard that Premadasa died... we were rejoicing.

He was 22 when they took him away. I can still see it. When they stopped the van, one of them jumped out and held a gun to my chest. My son, even after they took off, looked behind to see if they had shot me. I can still see him turning and looking at me.

If not for the children I would have ended my life

Jayanthi   SRI 14

Jayanthi has two children and lives in Negombo. She lost her husband during the troubles between the government and the JVP.

On 4th April 1989, my husband left for work at the government hospital. That evening we heard that he had been shot and killed. But they did not show us the body. It had been put in the mortuary... I have no idea how I came back home.

They didn't say why it was done or who did it or anything. Those days my husband was the head of the UNP Committee. A lot of people said he was killed because of a personal grudge. Then they said the government did it. I have really no idea who did it or not. All I got was the dead body.

Survival

When I am at home... it's not so bad during the day, but after 6 pm I feel like I am waiting for someone to come home. The person who did this thing—he will pay for it. If not in this world, then in the next. If my husband had been killed because he had done something wrong I could have borne it. But he never did anything of disrepute. There was no one who did not think highly of him, either at the hospital or at the village.

Those first nine months we suffered a lot. We didn't even have enough to eat most of the time. If not for the children I would have ended my life. I talk to a lot of people who have lost their husbands like this. They all say the same thing. And at least I have a steady income and some sort of stability [with a pension and compensation]. But often there is an emptiness.

It's not so bad when I am with people in a crowded place. But when I am at home in the nights I always remember. Even the

In the past I was shy and scared; now there is not a bit of that left in me

children remember. I keep losing weight and I feel like I am wasting away. Sometimes I wonder why I am still going on like this... There are children who don't care for their parents. I don't think my children will be like that but sometimes I wonder. How do I know they will not leave me?

For a while I stayed at home and cried a lot. The pain only increased. Now I am in a state where I can laugh and talk and act normally. And since I started going for all these committee meetings I have realised that I am not alone. There are so many people like me. And people who had worse experiences.

Fears and frailties

My son looks exactly like [his father]. He is very tall for his age. Now I am a little frightened for him, whether the same thing will happen to him. But how can you keep a boy indoors all the time? He always tells me where he is going. So I don't want to tell him not to go, because if he goes without telling me I wouldn't be able to bear it.

You know the other strange thing? I lose my temper so quickly now! The smallest thing makes me so angry! I know it is a bad thing but I can't help it. Before, even if [my husband] got [home] late from work I would never get angry. I would just ask him jokingly what happened. Now if my children get late I am harsh. Then later I would go to the room and cry because I yelled at them. I don't know what has come over me.

I got some training and I work about twice a month as a sort of a family health worker [at the hospital]. It's good, I like what I do, giving injections for various things. I have hardly any time to stay at home now. Even when I am home I have much work. Sometimes I am so pressed for time [and] I don't feel like eating. So I drink tea. I exist on tea.

As long as I know that this or that committee is doing good work I join it. Even if I am not going to get anything out of it, I join if I can contribute something. Actually, in the past I never used to talk—I was so shy and scared—but now there is not a bit of that left in me.

Shanti   SRI 15

Shanti is the administrator of the Family Rehabilitation Centre (FRC), a centre for trauma counselling.

Our target groups are detainees, widows, orphans, refugees, displaced people, youth in rehabilitation—and anybody who has been in any way affected by the war.

Really there are many widows; some do not even know that they are widows because their husbands have disappeared. We came up with the Empowerment Programme. The objectives were to help widows and make them independent and strong [enough] to lead their own lives. You know that widows in Sri Lanka are *persona non grata*. We have had a lot of success in this programme and [some widows] have become leaders in their villages. In each area we selected the motivated ones for training in Colombo. Those trained—about 600 to date—are sent back to their villages as change agents.

[Change agents are key figures] because if I went to a very poor widow's house and said, "Look, we can help you," she will think that there are strings attached. A woman who is already a widow, if she reached out to another and invited her, saying, "Come, I have already been helped," there is a greater response.

So one objective is empowering, the other is ethnic harmony, as these women are from Sinhala, Tamil, Muslim and **Burgher** communities. We do not have a programme unless we have three ethnic groups present. The third aspect is that we try to involve the medical, educational... government networks. This makes it easier for [the women] to receive their compensation and [learn to deal with the [government] officers.

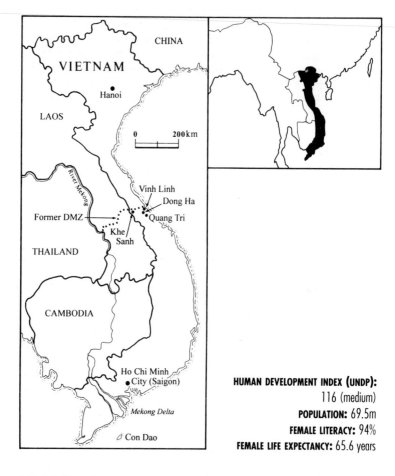

HUMAN DEVELOPMENT INDEX (UNDP):
116 (medium)
POPULATION: 69.5m
FEMALE LITERACY: 94%
FEMALE LIFE EXPECTANCY: 65.6 years

111 BC Chinese first conquer Vietnam **981 AD** Chinese expelled **939-1945** Vietnamese dynasties **1847** French first invade Vietnam **1867** Cochinchina becomes French colony **1930** Indochinese Communist Party and Vietnam Women's Union founded **1941** Ho Chi Minh forms League for the Independence of Vietnam (Viet Minh) **1946-54** Franco-Viet Minh war **1954** French defeated; Vietnam divided into North and South **1955-56** First US military advisers arrive in South Vietnam **1959** Vietnam war begins **1964-65** US begins bombing and sending large numbers of troops **1967** 485,600 American troops in Vietnam **1968** Tet Offensive; tide turns in Vietcong's favour **1975** Fall of South Vietnam **1976** Vietnam officially reunified

~ VIETNAM ~

Vietnam lies along the eastern coast of Indochina, a country of rice paddies, rivers, lakes and ponds. Water is so important to Vietnam that the Vietnamese word for country—*nuoc*—also means water. Although the Kinh majority dominates the fertile coastal plains and deltas, more than 54 ethnic minorities inhabit the mountainous regions that cover almost two-thirds of the country. An agricultural country with 80% of its 72 million people living in rural areas, Vietnam has recently become one of the world's leading rice exporters.

Vietnam's strategic location and its enviable fertility have resulted in a succession of power struggles reaching back 2,000 years. Much of the country's history is concerned with the Vietnamese peoples' struggle to define and rule their own nation and defend it against invaders.

The Cham Empire, influenced by Indian culture, occupied most of southern Vietnam from about 2 AD to the late 15th century, whereas China ruled the northern part of the country for nearly 1,000 years from 3 BC to 939 AD. Vietnamese history is full of stories of heroic uprisings against the Chinese; one was led by two noblewomen, the Trung sisters, who tried valiantly to repel the Chinese forces but failed. The rebellions finally met with success, however, and the Vietnamese ruled their own land for about 400 years. This golden age ended when the French occupied the country to establish a strategic and religious sphere of influence in Indochina. The French were temporarily replaced by a Japanese occupation force during World War Two. The war for national independence, led by Ho Chi Minh, began at this time and finally succeeded in ending the French colonial domination. Independence was achieved on 20 July, 1954—but with a divided country: North Vietnam above and South Vietnam below the 17th parallel.

Political and economic differences characterised the two halves of the divided country: North Vietnam a socialist country with ties to Russia and other eastern bloc nations, and South Vietnam a capitalist country with ties to the United States and the West. Initially the US provided only financial support to the Southern forces fighting against the Communist guerrilla Vietcong, but the US finally became directly involved in the fierce and protracted conflict, known in Vietnam as "the war of American aggression". With the fall of Saigon in 1975, the country was finally united under the leadership of the Communist party based in Hanoi. The war had cost the lives of two million Vietnamese.

Vietnam is one of the poorest countries in the world, largely due to the events of its recent history. Rapid socialisation (for example, the forced collectivisation of agriculture in the south after reunification) led to economic upheaval. This was exacerbated by the US' refusal to re-establish relations or help with post-war rebuilding, and by a trade and aid embargo imposed by the US and supported by other Western countries and ASEAN (the Association of Southeast Asian Nations). A new cycle of war, marked by Vietnam's invasion of Cambodia and China's retaliatory attack along the northern border, side-tracked Vietnam's post-war energies away from economic development.

In 1987, Vietnam established the policy of *doi moi* (renewal), a doctrine of economic restructuring similar to the Soviet Union's *perestroika*. With the eventual dissolution of the Soviet Union, Vietnam's reliance on it for economic assistance came to an end. Vietnam turned to China to resolve the Cambodian conflict and establish relations. These changes opened the way to negotiations with the US and helped to bring about the lifting of the embargo in 1994.

Vietnamese women stepped from a strong wartime role into a position of relative prominence in unified Vietnam. However, in the years since reunification, the representation of women at national, provincial and district levels of government has declined. Recently, literacy rates have fallen for women, especially for minority women in remote areas.

Since 1987, socio-economic reforms, progress toward a market-led economy and increasing foreign involvement have changed the face of urban Vietnam. However, restructuring also has negative aspects, many of which are felt more severely by women. The withdrawal of government financial support for most aspects of life has brought hardship to many women. A widely shared belief is that men's work is more important than women's work; this attitude persists despite the fact that in many households women's incomes from household sector activities are higher than the earnings of male family members. The Confucian view of women as dependent and submissive is still present, in spite of the attempts of the Socialist state to eradicate it.

The following interviews were conducted throughout the country by a team from the Women's Union (WU). The WU, whose headquarters are in Hanoi, is a mass organisation representing the women of Vietnam at the commune, district, provincial and national level.

The testimony collection was coordinated by Truong My Hoa, president of the Vietnam Women's Union (WU). The interviewers were Luu Thi Kim Oanh, Le Thi Ngot, Pham Ngoc Anh and Doan Thi Binh Minh of the WU research department, and Le Thi Ro, Nguyen Thi Buong and Do Thi Hien from WU provincial branches in the South.

Lanh   VTN 8

Lanh is 83, and lives in Ho Chi Minh City.

I was [first] asked for help [against the French] by a revolutionary. He asked me to help, so I did, but with no idea of what I was doing until, say, 1932, '33, '34. Then, they proposed to admit me into the Party. "Admit me into the Party?" I said. "What for?"

They appreciated my work. After [I joined] they made me responsible for 30 families. If there were any policies or resolutions, I had to tell them about them. We'd gather in one place, but pretend we were doing something else, and as we did I'd tell them about the Party.

When I was in prison [I met] Khai. Later on I learnt she was a member of the Party committee. She told me a lot of things so I began to have a revolutionary awareness. Khai was sentenced to death. I fainted when they shot her. It was terribly painful to watch. Love between revolutionaries was very profound. I still remember it as if it happened yesterday.

In 1940, 1941, many of our revolutionary activities were defeated. My husband and I were both arrested. I was released but my husband was sentenced to 10 years in Con Dao prison. When we parted I was holding my child. We just stared at each other as we couldn't say a word. It was 1941 then. He died in 1942. The day we parted is still so clear in my memory, as if it were just yesterday. I'll never forget the moment we looked at each other for the last time. He looked at the child. His eyes were filled with tears. I'm unable to describe it. We knew we were looking at each other for the last time in our lives.

Torn loyalties

I brought my children to Phuoc Ving An to stay and took part in revolutionary activities. When I had an assignment I always had to think a lot about who'd take care of my children... There were two

I had two thoughts: one was love for my children, the other was the revolution different thoughts in my mind. One was love for my children. They were the dearest things I had and it was very hard to leave them to live with other people. Eventually, I decided to send them to my brother and sister's house [because] the other thought was the desire to participate in the revolution. I decided to put aside my [family] feelings to complete the work I had been assigned.

Nowadays, when I think about that period I feel sorry for [my children]. They lacked so many things. They didn't have the love of their father and mother. How miserable and how poor they were then. Now my three eldest sons are dead. It's really painful to think of them.

They were so lonely. The love of their uncle and aunt could never make up for the losses they had to suffer. Oh God! That difficult period is over now. It's impossible to explain... Sometimes I had to go on for months and couldn't visit my children.

Activities against the US

During [the war against the Americans], I carried out agitation and propaganda among enemy troops around **Cu Chi**. I didn't meet the enemy soldiers myself. I just helped our cadres to meet and talk with them. There were no men doing this work because it was very dangerous for men. It was much easier for women. I helped them make contact. When they sat down to talk in the shadow of the trees, I went home.

I remember **Uncle Ho** saying: "The revolutionaries must try their best so that people miss them when they leave and love them when they stay." People in the area loved me very much, even though they didn't really know me. I never told my relatives about my work. I just kept it secret. So only the people in my organisation really knew about me; my relatives never knew. We had to be very sensitive otherwise the enemy might arrest us.

In my whole life, I was most pleased with myself when I was arrested in 1959. In my house there was an underground shelter of the district Party committee. I was [arrested and] beaten so hard I couldn't move, but I still felt happy because I didn't give away any information [about it].

Strategic hamlets

Their plan to set up **strategic hamlets**... that was our biggest concern. They forced the people to build the hamlets themselves then sent in their so-called cadres to live among them and control the people. They didn't allow people to go out. Revolutionaries told people to protest: "What will we live on if we stay here? We must go out to cultivate the fields." Eventually, they had to let people go out. But we had to inform them when we'd come back.

Having set up the hamlets they sent in the so-called "black clothes cadres". Every day they sat around and tried to court the wives of our cadres. Their aim was to ruin the lives of those women. Those who thoughtlessly agreed to be their wives were very unhappy.

Sometimes we were successful because our demands were accepted but sometimes we were struck and beaten. They painted on our shirts and hats: we usually wore two or three shirts so we could just take one off when they painted it. They painted to mark [us]—usually words against communists. Just like prisoners who bear the word PRISONER.

The happiest occasion of my life was Liberation Day: 29 April, 1975. I went along to welcome the revolutionary troops. I was so happy. It was as though I was walking on air. I was too happy to eat or drink... About a month after that I became ill. I was so happy I became ill.

Losses and pain

Through my own life I have experienced all the difficulties that Vietnamese women had to face during wartime. We were jailed. We were captured and tortured. We were terribly miserable in

Interrogation
Topham

Not only did
they torture
us, they used
to lure us
with sweet
words

prison, especially when we menstruated. There were many other women in the same situation as me. The enemy used every means to treat us badly. Not only did they torture us but they also used to lure us with sweet words.

One could easily compromise if one was light-minded. They often said: "They persuaded you to work for them. Now you're captured where are they?" They tried to make me deeply resent our cadres and revolutionaries. I answered, "I don't work for anyone. No one told me what to do. We cannot stand to see the nation under America's oppression. We're indignant at the injustice so we fight. No one asks us to do it."

It's impossible to tell you all the difficulties, losses and pain we had to endure during the wartime. So the government's attention to us can only comfort us a little. But I know we have no other choice. It's our obligation to sacrifice our personal interest for the nation. Nothing can make up for our sacrifice. My husband was arrested and killed. My children died. [But] if no one dared to sacrifice, we'd never have independence. I don't regret anything about that.

Ban   VTN 20

63-year-old Ban became involved in revolutionary activities at the age of 18. She was three times imprisoned and tortured under the French and American regimes.

Uncle Ho said that women were the powerhouse of the war. I found that women who were instructed under Uncle Ho had a very deep hatred of the enemy. They considered death as light as a feather, so they were ready to rush into danger. In many face-to-face struggles and even demonstrations we were terrorised by helicopters and US tanks.

Women and liberation

When our country was liberated, women's activities and organisations were transferred to the younger generations. They were in a bad way. Nowadays, women are not aware of their responsibilities because they are not so well-educated or trained. I think they have forgotten the golden words of Uncle Ho: "Heroic, Firm, Faithful and Clever". Today's girls know about karaoke, videos and cassettes, but forget about their studies. They do not understand the importance of women's role. But since the '90s, women's activities in my commune have become more forceful.

There have been meetings and awareness campaigns. I do believe *Life,* from now on our women will hold onto their revolutionary *movement,* tradition and work closely with each other in the women's *all activities* organisations. *happened underground*

An   VTN 1

An was active in the struggle against the French from the age of 16, and then against the Americans.

After 1953, peace was restored in the North. The country had been divided into two zones. Then the war happened in the South. Along the demarcation line the enemy directed its guns toward the North. Women's activities were to mobilise for production, and to prepare women for fighting if the enemy tried to attack. In 1964, when the enemy attacked the North, the women were ready. Vinh Linh [where I was living] was on the demarcation line. The American aggressors used chemicals to destroy the life of the people and the trees. They tried to turn Vinh Linh into a bare hill.

Evacuation

We and our organisations dug tunnels, and life, movement, all activities happened underground. A lot of families were afraid of living in tunnels; they divided up to live in two or three tunnels, so they would not [all] be killed at once. Vinh Linh had a policy that schoolchildren had to evacuate to other provinces to continue their education. Women could only fight and serve the war if their children were safe. Women didn't want to leave the fighting, but we made the job of evacuating the children a duty, so they accepted it and left with the children. Nursing mothers were evacuated to the North too. In some cases, it was compulsory to take the baby from his working mother. So the women had an agreement that a nursing mother with two babies of her own would withdraw [from the war effort], and those who had only one baby would send the baby away. Our women evacuated as far as Tan Ky district. The whole [procession] went on foot, because we feared that vehicles would be easily detected and bombed. Children were put in two baskets and the women balanced them on a pole on their shoulders. One- or two-year-old children sat obediently in the baskets, but the smaller babies were not disciplined enough to sit still. They wriggled and cried, so the mothers had to use an extra basket as a lid and keep them between the two. In the sky, the bombers were cruising and the babies were

We loved crying. The mothers had to suffer all this, just running, running
each other through the ditches.
in secret   So families were separated; the husband stayed in one place, the
wife and children in another. I had three children: one stayed in
Tan Ky, one was with relatives in Hanoi, I stayed here, and my
husband worked in the South.

Revolution and romance

Though I look after [my disabled husband] to the best of my
abilities, I have a secret memory of my own. During the war with
the French I loved a man in the next village, called Phuong.

My uncle was faithful to the revolution, but he did not want me
to join in, instead he wanted me to stay at home to work, and he
wanted a nephew-in-law who could work for him [—my father
was dead]. He insisted on matching me to another man. I was
angry, and I borrowed money from my aunt to buy *betel* and *areca*
nut to refund the engagement gifts. My uncle had to give in. He
said: "I made a match for you and you did not listen to me. I
declare that you are not my niece." He spoke thus, but I still went
with the revolution, and so did Phuong.

We loved each other in secret. When Phuong's mother died I
dared not attend the funeral, but I went to the tomb to light
incense sticks several days later. Whenever my uncle saw us
together he rebuked me. Phuong joined the army in 1947. He sent
me letters from the front. In 1949, his sister-in-law came to my
house, proposing the marriage, and my uncle had to accept.

I didn't have enough money even to buy an aluminium dish for
him. We only had our love to exchange with each other, nothing
else. He was faithful to me. Girls in the enemy areas were rich; they
gave him clothes and soap but he refused everything. Friends tried
to match him with other girls, but he said he had a wife at home.

Whenever I heard about the stationing of [his] regiment I found
my way there immediately. Sometimes, when I got there, the
regiment had left. Letters we had, but meetings we did not. In 1951,
he was killed in action. Correspondence was still difficult at that
time, but when I didn't get a letter for several months, I did not
know what had happened. Then I got a letter with strange
handwriting. My body shook. I opened it. It read, "Comrade An,
Phuong went to the battle at Phu Thiet, Quang Binh province on
October 10 [and was] badly wounded. He handed over his bag and
said: 'Common things should be sent to the unit. And what is
personal will be sent to Tran Thi An'." The mementoes he left were
not much: a watch, an army hat, a notebook and a volume of poems.

For several months afterwards I couldn't sleep. My sleep was full of dreams. I would hear somebody sounding like Phuong shouting, "Hey, An!" I jumped out of bed and ran out, but saw nothing. Later I realised that it was only my imagination.

Women were the powerhouse of the war

My love for him was so deep that I thought I would never love anyone else. But in 1961 I married Dung, who used to be Phuong's friend. His former wife was my friend too.

The first night beside Dung I saw Phuong in my dream. I ran after him saying: "Phuong, darling, Phuong!" He raised his hand and said, "You are married, what are you running after me for?" I kept chasing him and he cried, I did too. Dung woke me up and asked why I had been crying. I thought if I told him the truth it would not be nice for our first night together. So I said that I dreamt I saw a buffalo attacking me with its horns and I was afraid. Occasionally I see Phuong in my dreams now. Once I saw him in the garrison, surrounded by trees. Suddenly I heard a loud noise and woke up, then I regretted losing the image.

Blood and bone

The war needed the men at the front. Young women had to join the fighting. Behind the scenes were the middle-aged women. Women stayed at home, fed the babies, looked after the house and also joined the battle. Supplies were limited because the production was destroyed by the enemy. We paid for the fight with blood and bone, and we paid for the production with blood and bone too. When we worked in the fields, we'd carry a stretcher with us. If someone was killed, one person had to carry the dead one home and the others would continue [their work]. The hard work was done by women. In the hard, bitter war, women had no opportunities of being trained or informed by newspapers or radio.

Life in the underground shelter brought a lot of diseases. We lacked the facilities for medical treatment; we had to give priority to wounded combatants. Women's diseases were left to cure themselves. We did have rice, but we lacked cooking facilities and nourishing food. People's health was eroded.

Life was harder for women from the South whose husbands were posted in the North or fighting at the front: they were arrested and imprisoned. Anyone connected with the revolution would be beaten, imprisoned [or] raped so they'd be forced to get divorced, [or separate] from their husbands.

After 20 years of separation, the country was reunited. When women met their former husbands, they found out that the men were not faithful, they had married new wives. Some faithful

Without the strength of women, how could the men fight well? husbands came back to see their former wives old, diseased [and] exhausted, due to bombing and imprisonment. Some women [had been] raped. It was a big problem: if a husband knew his wife had been raped he would be ready to divorce her, and raped women were afraid of being laughed at, so it was necessary to help them, [and] encourage the husbands to treat them well.

I saw advantages too. The role of women was highlighted and admired [in the war]. Without the strength of women, how could the men fight well? The resistance war created favourable conditions for women to build and defend the country.

Help for war victims

After the war, when my husband and I met again, all our possessions were in one kitbag. Then the local organisations and the state and our friends helped us. One person gave us a table, another a bed, another gave us chair, so we had enough furniture. I tried to raise poultry, plant vegetables, and encouraged the children to share the work.

We had a little savings and support from the organisation to get a discount on buying construction materials, and workers came from the state enterprise, free of charge. Now I have a three-room house and a television set for my husband to watch, because he is an invalid.

Talking about help, it was great, coming from friends and comrades who had been with us during the two wars against the French and the Americans. The presents are of little value, but it's the comradeship that counts. Bombing and shelling are no more, but the comradeship is still deep.

My husband gets the most support. The Office of Labour, Invalids and Social Affairs gave him a wheel chair so he can get around. The social organisations are acting on the slogans: "Eating fruit, we think of the planter of the tree," and "Drinking water we are aware of the source."

[After the liberation] in 1977, my health was not good so I was allowed to retire from work. I came back to Dong Ha town. Here in a new place, I thought I should go to the other women, not just wait for them to come to me.

I went and asked for the head of the women's association, and I told [her] that when there was a women's meeting I would like to attend. So, on Vietnamese Women's Day (20 October) she invited me to give a talk about tradition. Then in 1978 I was elected to the executive committee of the women's congress. When talking about retirement [before] I felt downhearted. I thought I was out of action. However, now that I participate in the women's association, retirement doesn't bother me.

Voc   VTN 2

31-year-old Voc is married. She talks of the effect of bereavement on her family.

I was still small during the war, but I remember [what] my mother told me. My father joined the army in about 1958. I was born in 1963 and my father sacrificed his life in 1967—but we did not receive his death notice until 1971. During that period there were death notices of many, many people. Father's came with those of three of [mother's] brothers. We thought that mother would never recover from such bereavements, nor would my grandmother.

Losing father meant we lost a big part of feeling like a family, which could not be replaced. Mother told me that my younger sister was only 25 days old when father came to say goodbye [for the last time]. I felt sorry for little sister who never saw his face; at least I could think of him. Now, I can't even remember his face. The biggest loss for us was losing father, especially when we heard our school mates calling father, dad—we could never use the word.

My family was very poor because we did not have a father, so poor that when I started secondary school, we could not afford a bicycle and I had to walk the 10 kilometres to school, which was really hard, especially on rainy days. I had to compress rice mixed with paddy bran into pieces to bring to school for lunch. I felt embarrassed eating with friends so I ate my lunch alone. Those whose fathers were still alive had clothes and other things that I did not have and that I dared not ask for from mother. In my friends' families, they had fathers when they returned home, they had fathers to look after the house, to repair this and that, to repair their bikes when they were broken.

When it is rainy and windy, those who have men in the family would feel differently; for us, mother is the only shelter so she had to go out even in heavy storms. I remember the worst typhoon around 1985, 1986. We were terrified. Mother told us all to come to her room. As soon as we did, the house collapsed. Three of us were left with almost nothing. If father was there, he would have fought the wind and used ropes to support the house. People in our neighbourhood saw our misery, they helped put things in order and then returned home for lunch. They [saw] that we could

In those days, people's attitude to daughters was hard not afford to feed them, so they took lunch in their homes.

In those days, people's [attitude to] daughters was hard, and mother became even more disappointed that she didn't have any sons. Because of this thinking and her illness, our economic situation at home could not be improved. Although we tried to convince [mother] that sons or daughters were both children, we still saw [how] that preyed on her mind. Her mother-in-law had such feudal ideology. [She] has been living with us for more than 20 years, but now she says she's moving to my cousin's—our uncle's son—because he has sons... grandmother is like that and mother the same. Mother kept torturing herself about not having sons; the more she thought of it, the more upset and distressed she became.

In my small village, there were 10 families living near each other. Nine had revolutionary martyrs. There [is] one widow who had no children. She had no choice but to ask for foster children. Some women received their husbands' death notices when they were too old to remarry, so they have to live on alone.

Xot   VTN 4

Xot, a widow in her 50s, took an active part in the fighting in and around Saigon.

Nhuan Duc commune was a **heroic village**, in the commune of **Cu Chi** where the fighting was very intense. We built a network of underground tunnels. If we hadn't dug them we wouldn't have survived. Later, old ladies and children could not stand staying in the tunnels, they had to go into the **strategic hamlets**. The young people who joined the revolution had to live [in the tunnels]. You couldn't make any smoke. If the enemy discovered a trace of smoke they would shoot and bomb. We cooked at night. Sometimes we had to stay in the tunnels for a whole week without a bath. It was a terrible hardship for women especially when they were menstruating. I bore my two sons underground.

Hatred

1963 was a miserable year for me. I was far from my children and my husband had been killed. I was 23 and I joined the revolution solely to take revenge for my husband's [death]. I wanted to kill all the enemy. I couldn't express in words my overwhelming hatred against them.

As far as I am concerned, although I am a woman I was brave. *I put a timed*
In 1973 we were still fighting tanks. There was a women guerrillas' *explosive on*
anti-tanks team. We put timed explosives in bunches of vegetables *one of their*
to kill the brutal aggressors, because of their barbarity. We put the *motorbikes*
mine into a basket to make it explode on the route which the
enemy always patrolled.

Tricks and talk

There was one thing about being a woman which favoured her
participation in the struggle: it was easier to get close to the enemy.
Sometimes we disguised [ourselves] as regular citizens, coming from
the town to the countryside. I'd carry a basket of tomatoes on my
shoulder, or custard apples or several kilos of fish. The enemy looked
down on us, but we infiltrated [their ranks] more easily than the
men. We sometimes brought old ladies to speak to them. As for the
junior soldiers, we talked with them [ourselves and had] success.

The first success in fighting against the US forces was in
propaganda; the second was the combination of combat and
propaganda—with guerrillas behaving in the day like mothers and
sisters, and when night came we went to destroy their posts. If this
[form of attack] was not possible, we had to use other means. It
might be face to face combat. I personally put a timed explosive on
one of their motorbikes. When they started the bike, the bomb
went off—just an example of hundreds of tricks and schemes. We
fought in unexpected ways. The beautiful make-up box was stuffed
with explosives, pushed into the handbag which we left where
they were eating. Twenty minutes later it was sure to explode.
Fighting that way unnerved the enemy, [more than] battles full of
explosions.

Once we had a battle in Trung Hoa. They'd found out that we
were infiltrating, delivering rice and ammunition in the night. The
next afternoon they laid an ambush. I didn't know how to warn
our men about it. We crawled from house to house and got the
mines they had laid. We threw grenades. The [enemy] were killed,
five of them. Our men heard the explosion. They stopped trying to
get in—they would have been killed if they had.

Effects on children

I sent my children to my parents, one to mine, one to my parents-
in-law. I joined the battle and tried to find time to see them. I sent
rice and money. When my children were a bit grown up I didn't
have much to say to them. They were children standing at a
crossroads. They lived in the enemy's land. I loved them but I had
to leave them for the liberation of the country.

We threshed rice, carried rice, and had no help from any man

[The biggest problem now for the families of martyrs is] unemployment. Companies are having to lay people off. There are very few jobs. The children of these families are not properly educated or qualified.

Bao   VTN 21

Bao's husband died during the war, leaving her in a "strategic hamlet" with a baby daughter.

It was very difficult in the **strategic hamlet**. Their soldiers guarded all the roads. My comrades asked me to come to Tan Phu and help the people there. The comrades were hungry. My aunt also told me: "Only you can do this work. They'll die if you can't bring them food. They haven't eaten for three days." So I cooked a big pot of rice and one of sweet potatoes. I bought a kilo of dried fish and fried them and then put [it all] into jars. I was known by the soldiers. If they asked me I would tell them I was just going to the fields.

It was twilight when we reached the subhamlet. I rowed the boat to the canal edge and hid the jars where I knew the comrades were hiding. They could creep up and take the food when night fell. If the soldiers had seen us, they would have beaten us to death.

Whenever we worked in the fields, the atmosphere was tense. The soldiers wouldn't let us bring too much food with us, just enough for one. If you brought a bit more, [they] would make you eat it all and only then let you go. They were hard times. We were all wives of fallen soldiers. We threshed rice, carried rice, and had no help from any man. The comrades hiding in the bushes had nothing, so every morning we would bring rice to the fields and go without food ourselves. They found fruit for us. The comrades asked: "You bring rice and go without food, so how can you go on working?" We said: "Don't worry, we only do without at midday. If you go without food all day you won't survive. Please, eat this. We'll eat in the evening when we return home."

Deceiving the enemy soldiers

We had a very narrow social circle, we didn't dare make too many friends. I simply said my husband was a soldier and had died. I didn't dare say he was Vietcong. Sometimes the [enemy] soldiers came. My sister's husband was a [Vietcong fighter] too and he is still alive. The soldiers watched us very carefully, and our children, so we were in a miserable situation. They came and asked where our husbands were, why we had children and no husbands. I said mine died during the war and my sister's husband left her. They didn't believe us so they asked the children. I didn't let my daughter call me "mother", so she called my sister "mother" and me "aunt". [The soldiers] came and asked her, "Where's your father?" And she said, "He left us and went with another woman."

Some women went to see their [Vietcong] husbands and became pregnant, so they had to pretend they were someone's concubine. At that time men were invalids or disabled, there were no able-bodied men because they [were all fighting] for one side or the other.

There was a man called Nam Nhanh, unmarried. Tu Nhung went to see her husband and became pregnant. She begged Nam Nhanh to accept her as a wife but he felt ashamed and refused, so she had to find another man, a married man, and became his concubine. Enemy soldiers knew we were Vietcong wives but they had no evidence. We suffered a lot of humiliation having to say we slept around and got pregnant; we didn't dare say we had proper husbands, so it was a hard time for us.

Mobilising the wives of South Vietnamese soldiers

In general, wives [of soldiers of the South Vietnamese army] were not bad; it was the circumstances that made the soldiers fight, but they were kind to their families. Step by step, we organised these soldiers' families. We were more skilful and more cautious [with them than with revolutionary families]. I said we knew their husbands had to fight, that their families had contributed to the revolution before. Sometimes we got them to visit their husbands and call them back. Then we would [take] them to the revolutionary base.

One time we took over a whole post without a shot being fired. We took cakes and meat to [the enemy troops] at *Tet* (New Year). ·First we let them eat, then we'd begin to talk. We moaned over the situation. We said, "Now that you're in the army, your parents must be worried about you. If something unfortunate happened to you, your families would bear all the pain, so stop now and go back home to your families." They saw that we were kind to them, they took our advice, gave up their posts and we led them to the revolutionary base.

Silent grief

When [I learnt] my husband died, I was struck dumb and I couldn't say anything. I couldn't even cry. People around me said: "How can she be so calm? She doesn't cry or say anything." The pain hadn't hit me yet. After some time I thought about his death

We suffered a lot of humiliation having to say we slept around

I wept in secret. I didn't dare cry in public and was pierced by grief. I wept in secret. I didn't dare cry in public, people would watch me so I wept in secret at nights.

Now our country's liberated, women can cry in public when their husbands die, but back then we couldn't do it. We wept in secret in the shelters; if somebody came we wiped our tears dry. If they asked we wouldn't dare tell them why. They were such hard times. When a husband or son died one felt such a wrench in the heart, but one couldn't cry out.

Women's "weakness": persistence

Till I die I'm going to try and do everything. If they assign me three or four tasks, I'll try my best to do them. If we accept work, we [women] try our best to do it: we don't accept and then give up. This is women's weak point. We're not like men: they'll accept a task, but as soon as they see alcohol they'll forget about work. We women, when we commit ourselves to something, we try our best despite all the hardships. We're so persistent, we can't say "Let it be".

During the war women participated much more [than they do now]. Because they belonged to revolutionary or soldiers' families, they were very active. Now, I see women participating in activities but not with the same enthusiasm.

[After the war] the Party and the state weren't so thoughtful about the way they settled some things. [They] didn't forget the families [who had suffered], but some things were not settled properly. Women's needs were not adequately met, so some women became discontented and gave up. During the war they would not have flinched at anything. I think if women hadn't helped, our soldiers and guerrillas would have had many more problems.

Qualifications, not courage, needed now

Women's abilities are limited, because they're not well-educated. Now, one can't do anything without qualifications. In our time, we didn't know our letters, we were just brave. We didn't fear death or prison so the Party didn't disparage us. But now they want ability; we don't have it, so we have to give up our positions to the younger generation.

Since the liberation, some women often complain when something isn't right. I say to them: "Have you forgotten what you said then? You said you could bear anything. Now you complain at every shortage... Since the liberation we're in dire straits [but] we'll improve our living standards step by step. There's no reason to complain." I remind them of those hard days of the war when they used to say, "I just want to sleep in a bed, I could eat rice with nothing but salt, I could walk for a whole month..."

Nam   VTN 12

Nam lives in a "thankful house". She describes the affect of Agent Orange on her husband, her three daughters who died and her two sons, aged five and three.

My husband returned in 1976, a year after peace. He proposed to me and I agreed because I thought he was a man of good qualities. We got married when he was on leave, [then] he returned to his unit. I had a baby the next year. The first child was very weak so I had to stop taking part in **social activities** [and] stayed at home to look after her. I only worked to earn our living.

He took another leave of absence in 1979. I gave birth to my second daughter in 1980. My friends assured me [she] would be stronger. [She] was born normal, but compared with other children she was still weak. I thought she was weak because her father had just come back from the front and hadn't recovered yet. I didn't ever suspect he was infected with orange poison (**Agent Orange**).

Husband's and children's illness

In 1982, my husband finished his military service and returned home. Our third daughter was born in 1983. The two elder children were getting weaker and weaker. I wanted assistance when he came home [but] on the contrary, by 1983 he too was sick. All his hair fell out. His skin was full of blood and pus. We'd no idea about this kind of disease. We thought he just suffered from some kind of dermatitis because he hadn't got used to the strange water in the South that he'd used in the army. I tried to buy him different kinds of treatment but he didn't get better.

In 1984, my husband even peed blood. He was so weak he had to use a walking stick [and] I had to support him when he went out. That year was so harsh for me. But I still tried to find the right medicine for them. Each of them was given a different remedy. There were always three or four pots of medicine in the kitchen. But medicine didn't work. My husband could only use traditional remedies because he couldn't adapt to Western medicines.

My eldest daughter was becoming weaker and weaker. Her muscles shrank every day. She was all bones, her eyes protruded. Visitors were moved when they saw [her] . They gave us money or rice. I [was ashamed] as I was still young and strong but had to receive assistance from my neighbours.

My situation was desperate. I got some support from the government and local union, but it was just a small token in

I blamed myself...Now I know they died because of the orange poison comparison with the medical costs. I produced almost a tonne of rice that year but I couldn't pay any tax to the cooperative. I told the cooperative chairman, "If you sympathise with me, please give me tax exemption this year. I'll pay the debt next year." The cooperative didn't ask for my production tax that year.

I'd nothing left to sell. I didn't have any rice left. I went out to the garden and picked some fig leaves for my children. I'd no money to buy medicines. I'd borrowed hundreds of kilos of rice and hadn't paid yet, so I daren't borrow any more.

Sometimes I cried through the night. I blamed myself for not knowing how to bring up my children. At that time we didn't know about the orange poison. I thought my children died because I didn't keep my house clean or didn't give them hygienic food. My house was close to a cemetery so I thought I had to move it to another place. Now I know they died because of the orange poison transmitted from their father.

"Like a herd of pigs"

I remember 1985 the most. We were destitute then. All three children and my husband were sick and had to stay in bed all the time. [My] three daughters were blind. They couldn't feed themselves. [They] peed and defecated in bed all the time which made the house smell horrible. No visitor could stand it. The mats and beds were rotten. I had to have my children and my husband nested in the corner of the room with dry leaves. They looked like a herd of pigs.

I was extremely desperate. I couldn't ask for any more help because everyone had helped me. During those years I didn't dare go to any meetings or festivals because my appearance was terrible. All my clothes were worn out and smelt of excrement and urine. I thought all my children and my husband would die in 1985. If they'd died they would've been happier. The longer they survived, the more unhappy I was.

My eldest daughter died in 1986, the third in 1987. The second child went blind and her muscles shrunk, and then she died. My husband's health was getting worse and worse. It was so painful. I thought no one in the world should have to undergo as much pain as I did. I'd been trying my best. I worked day and night but I couldn't improve my living conditions [and] meet the cost of the medicine.

When my children had all died, my friends advised me to have another child. In 1989, I had my fourth child, a son. He was born stronger than his sisters. He could see his way when he was walking. I was so happy then. I believed in science so I decided to have one more child. I gave him every kind of immunisation. He was born stronger than his brother, but in comparison with other children he was still weaker. His eyes were not very good. He was not as bright as other children.

I've stopped hoping he will recover and help me

Moved by my situation, the Women's Union advised me to ask for help from the communal, the provincial and the central Office of Labour, Invalids and Social Affairs. The communal Women's Union and the communal Invalids Council also supported me. In 1990, I received aid from the government. I've found this assistance most helpful. They gave my children clothes. I've also been given money to care for my husband and children every month. I was given a **thankful house** too.

I still haven't paid all the debts, but my situation's much better. My burden was shared with other people and I felt relieved. But I'm still very sad when thinking of my future. I'm still strong, but when I get older and weaker I won't be able to rely on anyone. My husband can walk now, but sometimes he suddenly collapses, he has aches all over his body. At such times he needs to be assisted. So when I have to go to work I have to ask my mother to come and help him. My two sons are getting worse: if they go out of the house, they are in danger as they cannot see and hear properly.

[Because of the war] I lost everything in terms of spiritual life and material life. Yes, I had a husband, but in name only. When he returned from the front, he said he'd fought in the Khe Sanh front. But when I asked him about the details, he got angry. I thought he'd got angry because he'd just come back from the front. I wasn't aware he'd been infected by orange poison.

Our emotional life was badly affected. I never had a chance to enjoy happiness and sympathy from my husband. I'm living with [him] now but we're like strangers. I just live with him because of my conscience. I could care for him, but he could never care for me. I never complained. He suffered a lot himself from the war. I've stopped hoping [he] will recover and help me.

The war took everything away from my family. I lost my husband, my wealth, my happiness, my future and my love. All the money I'd earned has been spent on medical expenses. The aftermath of the war was so severe. The chemical war was so terrifying and devastating. I hate the enemy. I wish I could have killed all of them.

Thom   VTN 11

Thom, 40, was disabled during the war.

Our hope as young women was to join the army and serve at the
front. Only those who were 45 kilos could join the army, but I was
only 41 [kilos]. Most of the women were not heavy enough. At the
time, there was a movement in my hamlet for young people to
serve the struggle by maintaining roads. We sent in our volunteer
applications, but they did not accept us because we were so small.
Eventually, we went to the President's house together to ask him
to call us up. Some days later we were allowed to go. We were
taken to Vinh. When we arrived it was getting dark. That night we
slept outside, we just lay in a field. I thought it was a grass field.
Only in the morning did we realise it was a cemetery.

We walked for a night and a day until we reached the military
region. The camp was empty. No beds, so we had to sleep on our
raincoats. That night it was drizzling, and it made the ground wet. We
were so tired we weren't aware of anything. Jungle leeches stuck on
my back. I felt cold but didn't know what they were. I touched them
and tried to pull them off but they seemed stuck to my skin.

Some days later we went to the jungle to cut down some trees
to make beds. A girlfriend from the same village and I used an old
bed that the soldiers left. Every night we felt itchy but we didn't
know it was because of bed-bugs. Then we saw them on the
blanket—it was terrible, first we took them out and killed them,
then we had to burn them. After a few months, both of us got
malaria. Our hair fell out. The roof in the camp leaked badly. My
friend slept deeply, paying no attention to the rain, but I could not.
I was awake all night, trying to patch the leaks.

The road that we'd been sent to repair was an earth road and there
were many bumps and holes because it was the main supply line. Our
duty was to keep the surface good, and a brigade took on the main
job of repairing the embankments after each wave of bombs, so the
lorries could get through. It was really hard work, loading [heavy]
stones onto lorries. We did it continuously for a month. We worked
every day, with no day off—but it was wartime.

Once they dropped so many bombs that we couldn't stay by the
road. We had to move to a cave in the mountain. A team of four
people was sent to live near the road; I was one. We had to make
a shelter beside the road and stay there. Whenever the road was
hit, we went out to repair it, even during the night.

After a month the road was totally destroyed and we were

needed to help rebuild [two roads elsewhere]. I was ill with a fever. [I was weak] so I only carried my clothes; other women carried rice for me. We walked through heavy rain, fire, bombs, and helicopters. After three days we got to the [work] station. We laid stones and repaired drainage systems and holes. On that day they dropped fragmentation bombs. I was hit in the stomach.

A mother and her family flee their burning village
Kyoichi Sawada/Topham

After an emergency operation in a field hospital, Thom was moved several times from one hospital station to another to escape bombardment.

All the doctors and nurses looked after me very carefully. I couldn't have a bath or wash my hair. I had lice—there were so many that they crawled down onto my face. My friends combed, washed my hair, and took out a bowl of bloody hairs and lice.

No hope for a family

The war deprived us of hope—the hope of having a family. You know the state gave us compensation, but it was a small thing compared to our losses. I think that women should have a family.

Men who are wounded like me are still able to marry It's the best. I had to suffer so many losses... Men who are wounded like me are still able to marry, and when they get ill their wives and children can help. I am still single and I live with my old mother. I have had several operations, but my wound is not curable—the doctors can't remove all the pieces of bomb. When I had to go back to hospital, I stayed alone [there, because my mother is too old and my brothers have their own families]. Sometimes I had to ask for the help of other patients in the same room... I only want to die, but how can I?

Thuy   VTN 15

Thuy used to work under the Saigon administration. Her husband was a lieutenant in the South Vietnamese airforce.

For two years now, my family's life has been stable. But in the past, we had a lot of problems because my husband had just been released from **re-education camp** so he often felt inferior. But later, when I got a job, thanks to the great support of the state in general and from women in particular, things improved. Now my husband no longer feels inferior and with the family's help, he now has a stable job as a driver.

[When my husband first began paying attention to me] we were studying at school and I did not yet love him. But my mother liked him very much. [She] wouldn't allow me to marry any man except him. But I couldn't marry Chau because I didn't love him. In my book, marriage is for love, not for a parent's satisfaction.

After that, he joined the army. When he came back, he was like a hero in my eyes. He looked very vigorous with an American kitbag in one hand and an airforce hat on his head. His image really touched my heart. I fell in love.

I went to work at a US Agency as a trading cooperative accountant at Dong Du Regiment. I felt permanently sad. As you know, people working for Americans were often looked down upon. [But] I still had to go to work, regardless of other people's opinions. Some of my cousins followed the revolutionary course; while I was doing such a well-paid job, I wondered how people could survive under such hardship. I was still young, and my understanding was limited.

When I got married, my husband asked me to stop working. You know, any newly married couple will be unhappy if they have to live apart, and my husband was quartered at Phan Rang airport.

Fear of reprisals

I had been told that when the communists arrived, they would kill all the men who'd served the old regime and remove their wives' finger nails. I thought it was just exaggerated rumours, [but my husband] was frightened of being killed. He asked whether [we should take up the offer of going] to the US. I said, "No." Staying at home we could work on the field to support our family. Even though life was hard, at least we were living near our parents, sisters and brothers who would share our hardship.

I used to feel inferior because I had served under the old regime

When he had to attend the [re-education] course, he said he would come back after a week. But he didn't, [and] I didn't receive any news. I felt worried and regretful, fearing he might be killed. Finally he came home after 30 months. The government displayed great tolerance towards what my family had done against the revolutionary cause. I myself should not have been employed because at that time officers' wives were not trusted.

Opportunities under the new regime

I often used to feel inferior because I had served under the old regime. At that time I'd hear a lot of propaganda about socialism, but I had no clear views on it. I also heard of the campaign to develop the new economic zone. But I thought, instead of settling down in such a remote area, I would [prefer to] live back in my home village, **Cu Chi**, where I had land.

[People] told me that kindergartens were recruiting teachers. Working in private schools was poorly paid at the time. But I thought I had to do something so I could report it to the local authorities. By doing so, my husband could perhaps be released earlier. This was one of my primary motivations [as well as] the chance to participate in **social activities**. It was particularly important for me because of my complex about being deserted by society. It is incredible for me now to have such glorious days. Nobody would have thought that the officer's wife would be recognised as such a good teacher. I find that my case is rare. The revolutionary government has proved that people who make an active contribution can get recognition, even though they have a chequered CV.

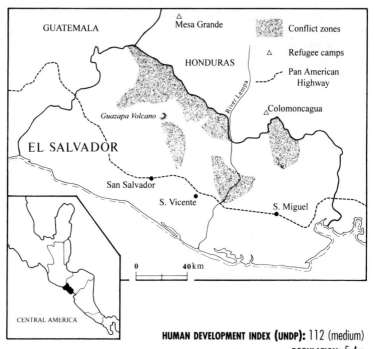

HUMAN DEVELOPMENT INDEX (UNDP): 112 (medium)
POPULATION: 5.4m
FEMALE LITERACY: 71%
FEMALE LIFE EXPECTANCY: 68.2 years

1838 Independence **1932** Peasant revolt under Augustín Farabundo Martí **1961** Formation of Christian Democratic Party (PDC) **1964** José Napoleón Duarte (PDC) elected mayor of San Salvador **1974** Fraudulent elections **1980** Jan: second junta formed with Christian Democrats. March: assassination of Archbishop Romero; third junta formed with Duarte a member. May: formation of FMLN **1981** FMLN launches "final offensive"; Robert d'Aubuisson (implicated with death squads) organises National Republican Alliance (ARENA) **1984** Duarte becomes president **1987** Esquipulas II Regional Peace Accords; mass repatriation of refugees from Mesa Grande camp in Honduras **1989** Increase in tensions; Alfredo Cristiani (ARENA) elected president; FMLN launches major offensive **1990** Series of UN-mediated peace talks begin **1992** Jan: signing of Chapultepec Peace Accords **1994** March: elections—ARENA victory over FMLN coalition

~ EL SALVADOR ~

In January 1992, with the signing of the Chapultepec Peace Accords between the Faribundi Martí National Liberation Front (FMLN) and the government of the Nationalist Republican Alliance (ARENA), the most brutal 12 years in El Salvador's history officially came to an end. The civil war, which caused the deaths of more than 70,000 people, was rooted in the country's economic and social polarisation.

For generations *Las Catorce*, the mythic "Fourteen Families", had owned and controlled most of the land and national wealth. When urban and rural workers first rose up to challenge the feudal structures, their claims were silenced by the infamous *matanza* (massacre) of 1932: an estimated 30,000 people died.

The post-World War Two wave of industrialisation and democratisation in Latin America did not completely pass El Salvador by. The 1950 Constitution, for example, established women's right to vote and there were some legislative reforms which favoured the working class. But the mood of the military regime swung from concession to repression.

The 1960s brought new political and religious ideas. The "theology of liberation" took root in the impoverished rural communities, where its progressive teachings struck a powerful chord. To women in particular, a philosophy which equated morality with social justice had considerable appeal. Many were encouraged through their readings of the Bible and the outspoken homilies of Archbishop Romero to engage in the struggle and, in some cases, to take up arms.

Throughout the 1970s, despite the intimidatory tactics of the military regime, a growing popular movement developed from the ranks of disaffected rural and urban workers. Fraudulent elections throughout the decade, however, kept any real political opposition at bay. Peaceful demonstrations by workers, teachers, peasants and students were violently put down and popular leaders were killed or "disappeared".

At this time, several leftist groups appeared who promoted and practised armed struggle as the key to social and political change. The campaign for social justice embraced by the mass movement found an echo in the political and economic demands of these guerrilla armies. When they came together—the Armed Force of Liberation (FAL), the People's Revolutionary Army (ERP), the Popular Liberation Forces (FPL), the National Resistance (RN) and the Central American Revolutionary Workers Party (PRTC)— in 1980 as the FMLN, the students, workers and peasants from the beleaguered popular movement were willing recruits.

Social and political tensions reached a climax in 1979. This same year saw the United States step up its military and economic aid to the Salvadoran government—support which was to become a major influence on the scale and nature of the war.

The early 1980s were marked by unprecedented levels of brutality, as the US-backed regime attempted to undermine the guerrillas' social base by employing "scorched earth" policies and death squads. Over a million people—one-fifth of the population—fled the country, and thousands more were internally displaced. Camps were established in Honduras for the thousands of women and children refugees.

These camps would become famous for their high levels of organisation and, later on in the conflict, for the voluntary mass repatriation of refugees. For many Salvadoran women, camp-life had its positive aspects. Through the programmes of international solidarity groups and NGOs, they had the opportunity to extend their education, developing new skills, for example in healthcare, animal husbandry and popular education, and to take on non-traditional leadership and economic roles.

The FMLN became a legal political party in 1992 and in the general elections of March 1994 gained 21 seats (against ARENA's 40). But the war has plunged the country into economic crisis. The neo-liberal policies of the ARENA government, despite producing an encouraging annual growth rate and stabilising the balance of payments, have resulted in high levels of inflation and unemployment, which are shouldered disproportionately by the rural poor. The virtual paralysis of the government's land transfer programme, and delays and distortions of other compensation and rehabilitation schemes, have led to an increase in crime and unrest.

Women are playing a major part in the country's reconstruction. Empowered by their struggles in exile, many expect and are prepared to demand a better future, as the interviewees bear witness. For the 1994 elections, over 40 women's groups came together as *Mujeres 94*, presenting a common platform to all political parties and campaigning around such issues as human rights, land rights, legal discrimination, domestic violence and reproductive health. However, the extent to which *machismo* and the dire economic climate overshadow these developments is yet to be determined.

The interview collection was coordinated by María Candelaria Navas, a sociologist and consultant on gender. The interviewers were Liza Dominguez Magaña and Edy Areli Ortiz Cañas, sociologists at the Instituto de Investigación, Capacitación y Desarrollo de la Mujer; Ana Patricia Quezada Tejada, social anthropologist; Ana Kely Rivera, journalist; and Paty Otero, of the NGO Mujeres por la Dignidad y la Vida.

Nubia   SAL 12

Nubia's experiences are perhaps typical of many Salvadoran women her age (30s). Her role in the early part of the conflict was to "organise" the masses and prepare people militarily for war. She also trained as a first-aider, was a refugee and was repatriated in the mass returns of 1989.

I was the eldest in my family and when I joined up I didn't even want to tell my father or mother. I did it behind their backs. If they knew, they wouldn't have let me participate because if you were involved in politics, if you said things against the authorities, it was a crime. They used to think I was going out with my girlfriends. They didn't know where I went. My mother punished me, but she couldn't get the truth out of me; my father made me tell the truth because he hit me hard.

When I told [my parents] I was going to be posted far away, my father terrified me when he said, "Look! They'll kill you and I won't hear anything about it [because] I don't know where you're heading or where you're going to stay." And he began to tell me about what had happened when **Martínez** was in power. "The memories live on," he said. "Those holes in the ground are the ones where people used to hide... They say they killed pregnant women, young women were raped..."

I decided to remain working in the **zone**, preparing people for what might happen: how to defend themselves from a mortar attack, how to arm and disarm, how to attack, what to do in a mine field, and things like that. I learnt the tactics and then I passed them on. The young people joined straight away as combatants, and the civilian population joined in because their sons and daughters were there and they had no alternative. They helped by providing food

Strategy, everything was part of a strategy and being on the look-out for the army. Our job at the time was to protect the masses. We told people not to wear red because they'd be noticed from far away. They had to wear green. They weren't to put clothes out to dry anywhere where they might be noticed. No fires could be lit. Strategy, everything was part of a strategy.

Standing up to the enemy

Do you remember the time when there was an amnesty law? It was in '83. They captured 75 people and I was among them. My mother was there too. We were at the lake, about 400 of us, and the soldiers were up on the cliffs. They started dropping mortars on us, and shooting at us. Then they started flying overhead in a light airplane and calling out for people who'd become guerrillas to surrender... [saying] they wouldn't be killed or harmed in any way, you know the kind of thing. But nobody came forward. There was so much propaganda about the enemy and everyone was terrified of them. Then the attack began, goodness, how many were killed! I got everyone to throw themselves on the ground but the swines continued shooting, dropping bigger and bigger bombs, and the children were crying. The more they cried, the more they shot. And then they began to shout, "Guerrillas!" and they swore at us, "You sons of bitches!" Then they started calling out the names of their battalions—"Atlacatl", "Pipil"—so we realised there were lots of them. "Give up," they shouted and went on swearing at us.

Eventually I forgot my fear. "There are no guerrillas here!" I shouted back at them. "We're just women and children and old people." "Why are you running away then?" they taunted. "Because you're killing innocent people," we said. "If we were guerrillas we'd be armed and we'd shoot back. Look for the armed guerrillas, not the ones who are unarmed!" I was no longer afraid. We tried to escape, forcing our way through big bramble patches; we were covered in scratches. I was still wearing combat boots, and at that time, if you were found wearing boots, you'd be killed. What did I do? I took them off and threw them into the water so they wouldn't find me wearing them. I continued barefoot.

Capture

They took us to the military headquarters in San Vicente. They told me I had to take them to the shelters where the weapons were hidden and to show them who the leaders were and loads of things like that. I said I couldn't because I didn't know who they were and as I was telling them, another soldier arrived. "Who's this bitch?" he asked. I think they had their eye on me because they had probably recognised my voice from when I was shouting at them. "Listen, we don't like the way you're talking to us. Watch out. You're a woman." "Yes!" I said. I was still talking loud. "Yes. It's true. I'm not a man like you, but I'm made of flesh and bone like you. Things hurt me the way they hurt you. I have a right to speak. You're telling us there's an amnesty, that you're going to forgive us, that you're not going to harm the people, and so on and so on... Where's the amnesty law you're talking about? What rights do you respect?" I carried on talking and my mother trembled. She told me through her eyes not to talk to them that way, but I had no fear at that moment. I wasn't afraid of anything.

I'm not a man like you, but I have a right to speak

Parenthood

I left [all my children] when they were babies. I had three when I was in Honduras [as a refugee]. I felt awful [leaving them] because we knew that in war anything could happen. At that time I regretted giving birth. But at the same time I said, "I know if I leave them there they'll stay alive." There was plenty of food there, medicine, everything. They provided milk for the mothers who took care of these children. They were well looked after.

All of [my children] had the same father. Unfortunately, we always seemed to be apart. We'd see each other every two or three months. There was a time when eight months passed without us seeing each other. That's what it was like because he was never in one place.

*Nubia is resettled in El Salvador (in the **Nuevo Gualcho** community) in 1989, where she works as a health promoter.*

I began to notice things [in the community] were breaking down. There were some people who were politically organised but later, when outsiders began to arrive—people who'd never worked as part of an organisation or anything—negative things began to be seen. There were men who'd take advantage of the young girls; other men would see what these guys were doing and want their piece of the action. These bad examples ruined the whole community. Before, everyone there was well organised.

The community board used to meet on their own and there were some things they kept to themselves. They'd receive all the delegations [from abroad]. They didn't tell us if aid was coming but we'd see it arrive. Until today we haven't seen anything of that aid; they didn't give anyone a cent. If you said something they didn't agree with, they'd say you were against them and that you were on the enemy's side.

It's our right
that the
government
admit to the
destruction

Demobilisation and fragile peace

The children got annoyed when they saw [their father come] home: they didn't recognise him. Even my youngest girl was angry. She told me, "Just wait for my daddy to get back. I'm going to tell him another man's been here." To his face they'd say, "Go to hell!" And then he'd say to them, "No, children, I'm your father. It's me—Daddy." "No! [Go away], you old bearded man!" He always had a beard but it had grown even longer. [It was] not until the old man, their grandfather, told them that he was their father [that they accepted him]. If he hadn't done, they would have gone on being angry, jealous.

When the Peace Accords were signed, the first thing I thought was that the enemy would try to take advantage, that they would see us disarm and then attack us the same way they did when the death squads started up. After all, these are enemy tactics: let them disarm and then we can easily jump on them. I never stop thinking that the death squads could start up any time.

It's the men who do most in the community. Many women don't want to be on the same level as men. I don't know why they don't participate. It's probably because their *compañeros* don't allow them to. On a positive note, [we have] the elections. All this time during the whole of the war, none of the women who participated in the struggle were able to vote for president. For me, at my age, this will be the first time I'm going to vote.

I have faith that things are going to change, but they won't change overnight as the saying goes. After 12 years of war, the country is in a state of ruin. I hope the incoming government takes direct care of the needs of the poor, people like us who've been displaced. We've suffered so much... our houses have been destroyed. It's our right that the government builds houses for all the families whose houses they destroyed, that they admit to the destruction. There is support coming from other countries but the government does what it wants to do. They don't know how to distribute aid to the majority of the poor. They carry out the odd project... but it's mostly a PR exercise and nothing more. They only do things so that other countries think the Salvadoran government is doing something, rebuilding El Salvador. They've put up big signs, saying they're doing things for the people, building latrines, respecting people's rights, but it's a political manoeuvre, pure propaganda. My idea is that this [testimony] is read in other countries so that people understand the reality. It's all lies. What does the government say? That they're rebuilding, that they're working in the zones. But we haven't even seen them here.

For me, peace and reconciliation mean that if you say peace, there won't be any more deaths, abuses against the people. Reconciliation means that we have to trust one another. As far as my dreams are concerned, I'd like all of us to have a job, or at least that us women earn the same as men; that our work is recognised as men's is. At least [my *compañero's*] sacrifice has paid off. I'm giving my work for free. No one says, "Here, we're going to recognise what you do. Take this [money]." I do what I do because of my awareness and understanding that people get something out of being involved. But I see a lot of people who are disillusioned, they don't want to get involved in the community's work because it's not something that will benefit them as individuals.

Suyapa   SAL 13

Despite her commitment to the cause, Suyapa, 22, spent most of the conflict in exile, to be with her mother.

As a family, we were politically organised from the beginning. When the death squad came and painted *el mano blanco* (the white hand) on our door [we knew] it was time to flee. The white hand was a signal to leave your house within 24 hours and it was painted on all the houses of the families who were politically organised or where there was someone in the house who had some political attachment or other. At the time, my elder brother was secretary of the student movement in Arcatao, so we were marked from the beginning. The soldiers would go by and fire into the air near the house before painting *el mano blanco*. It was a way of frightening us all—psychological warfare—so that we'd reject our political beliefs or leave the house... On that same morning, there were lots of families whose houses had been marked. Crowds of people began to leave.

Forced to move

During the first **operativo**, we were left without a father. My brothers stayed in the **Frente**, and me, my mother and another brother who was young like me—I was eight when my father died—had to take refuge close to the Honduran border. The repression had reached critical proportions by that time. They'd attack by dropping mortars from helicopters and planes which would go round and round all day. All the inhabitants living there would have to look for ditches or **tatues** which the people dug. Sometimes we'd spend up to three days at a time buried in the ditch.

Many didn't want to become refugees; they preferred to risk death

Things [got even worse] and we fled to Honduras, although some people stayed in the community despite the bombings. People stayed because of their love for their land. Many didn't want to become refugees, because [they] had been refugees before during the so-called 100 Hours War (El Salvador-Honduras, 1969). They had already experienced the torment of living in a foreign place. They preferred to risk death while defending their land.

Camp life

[The NGOs in Mesa Grande refugee camp] tried to get everyone to invest some time in studying. I went to school for two more years and then I felt the need to do something [for] the people in the camp. So I asked if I could start working as a pre-school teacher. I was 13. I was given two months training and then I took on two classes and went to classes myself in the afternoons. That's how I kept myself busy all through the week. Most people joined the different workshops to learn one trade or another.

Life in the refugee camp, if you didn't try to adapt, was incredibly hard. I was distressed about being in a strange country, even though I understood why I was there. It was awful, that feeling of imprisonment—there were 10,000 of us in seven camps, and we were not allowed to leave the compound. I wanted to go back to the **zone**. The only thing that stopped me was [my mother]. She didn't have another child to look after her, to comfort her, because my brothers were already in the *Frente*. Even though I so wanted to go and play my part, I didn't do it then because of [my mother]. I remained as a refugee until they decided to repopulate some areas. "Listen, mother," I said. "I'm leaving in that **return**. Either we go, or you stay, but I'm not being a refugee one day longer." There were lots of us who had decided that way. Then my mother said: "You're right to think the way you do. We're not doing anything in this country, let's go back. We have our own country and we have a right to live in it." So that's how we came back, around 3,000 of us.

The return

Our return was not without difficulties. The government didn't want to give us a permit. When we signed a petition to inform them that [we] were returning home, [President Duarte] publicly announced that he didn't know there were 11,000 refugees in Mesa Grande. But we told him loud and clear that we were coming back whether he liked it or not.

That's when we began to ask for international support and the repopulation board was established, which was the one which

began organising the returns. UNHCR (United Nations High Commission for Refugees) were between the devil and the deep blue sea: either they obeyed what Duarte was saying about us remaining as refugees, or they responded to [our] anguish and petitions. And so a whole process of international negotiations began with the different humanitarian organisations.

[When we] arrived in Guarjila, we found the military there. We were terrified that the army had the nerve to be there—it was because of them, because of their repression, that we had been driven away from our native lands. A mass was said, of welcome and victory—it was a victory to have returned home. That's how our life as returnees began.

Mary   SAL 1

Mary, 58, was displaced many times during the fighting, but always within the conflict zone.

Before the war started, we were a very close family. We worked in the fields and lived on what we grew there with our children. But then the lands became so expensive to work and [the landlords]

Every living made us work from sunrise to sunset. Some of the boys saw the
creature need to expose these injustices—because they were young they
they saw dreamed that life could be different. So when war was declared,
they killed they had no other option but to get involved—they felt they were
being so unfairly persecuted. As their parents, we too were obliged
to get mixed up in the war. After that, all the happiness we had
known disappeared.

Why should [the army] have been after my children? No
reason. Except that at that time, some people would point the
finger so to speak, and all for a few cents, that's all they'd give
them; they'd sneak on someone they were enemies with, or on
someone they didn't get on with. That's how so many families
were destroyed... by lies. Even if a family wasn't mixed up in
anything, they were labelled as subversives and guerrillas, and
therefore the whole family would have to flee.

Scorched earth

In '83, the "scorched earth" attacks began. Those who didn't have
a *tatu* to hide in went to the shores of the lake. Those of us with
tatues, took shelter. Then the army came and totally scorched the
earth, as they said they would. There were dead chickens, pigs,
horses, cows—every living creature they saw they killed and then
set fire to the hillsides... everything was cooked in the flames.

They denied our existence. As far as the president was
concerned, there were no civilians, no old folk, no children in the
conflict zones. The troops were doing what they had to do because
[they said] it was only guerrillas who were there and not children,
mothers, old people, or innocent people. And that's how they got
away with their indiscriminate attacks.

I talked to [my children] when I realised things were becoming
serious. They used to say they were going out. So, I asked the
oldest one, Heriberto, what he did when he went out at night. He
replied, "Mama, I cannot tell you." But as a mother, you always
know when your children are up to something. One day I realised
what they were involved in. I called them together, the three
eldest, and said, "Listen, children. I've never seen a war, but my
father used to say that war was a terrible thing, a sad thing, its
consequences are manifold. It'd be better for you if you went
somewhere else, to a place where the war cannot reach you...
You're young and single, you can read and write." "Mama, if we
don't stay to defend those of you who can't defend yourselves,
[who will]? Because it's not just you who is suffering, it's a whole
people. There are children watching the consequences of

indiscriminate killing; mothers, children and frail old people unable to defend themselves."

We are all some mother's children

I begged and pleaded with them so many times to flee from the war. I told them I didn't want them mixed up in the trouble but their answer was always the same. So I said, "Well, children, I have said what I wanted to say to you. From now on, what you do is your own business. I shall suffer the consequences. But if this is what you want, then so be it, go ahead." They clapped their hands and said: "Thank you, mama. We wanted you to give us this freedom, because we cannot stay here with our arms folded." This is why I feel the way I do— because they died how they wanted to die—defending a people unable to defend itself.

A mother's grief

[My daughter] wrote to me saying, "You are the mother of guerrilla soldiers, and your first child has fallen, my little brother. But you must be prepared for all of us to die." She told me that I had to be strong: "Remember, guerrillas never cry. Be strong, because he is not the first one to fall. Thank God he died as a fighter rather than a thief."

She died in Las Guaras. It felt the same, but worse. The girl and I had been so close. When she joined up, she said to me: "Listen mama, as soon as the war is over, I'm going to get married, I've already chosen the guy. Yes, he's a good looking fellow—he'll get along well with you. We're going to have a little house with a garden round it and you'll be there with the two children we are going to have." That's what she used to say. I felt awful... But she'd told me that guerrilla soldiers never cry and so, little by little, I got over the worst. She had died how she wanted to die. She died on a good day, 14th September, Independence Day.

One day some troops appeared [in the village]. They had a chicken with them and they asked me to cook it. I felt sorry for them. I'd never distinguished between the way I treated people. We are all some mother's children. The soldiers were also somebody's sons, and that they were undoubtedly suffering like everyone else.

I've never known that feeling of resentment, because I followed God's word—and in our generation, it was His word which mattered. The war and everything else that has happened was written. Neither one side nor the other can be blamed for it. The guilty ones are the ones at the top. They'll no doubt be enjoying their meals while they decide on their plans. The poor little

I'd prefer them to kill me rather than fall into the army's hands

soldiers, sons of poor parents, meanwhile are dying on the battlefield. And so I told them I'd cook for them.

No better than before

I am [afraid the war will break out again] and it's not just me... I hear other people saying the same thing. The injustices are worse than before. There might have been some economic development, but development in terms of equality, nothing has improved... I, for one, thought that when the conflict was over the first thing the government would do would be sort out the housing problem; that the workers would be paid fair wages; and that they'd use their laws to sort out the municipalities. But it seems otherwise. I tell you, there are only a few who gained anything from the war and they wouldn't mind if it broke out again. War ends up sorting out those who are already sorted and disrupting those of us who are already disrupted.

Carolina   SAL 21

Carolina, 37, talks of her desire to take up arms and her military exploits, and openly about sex and sexual politics within the guerrilla movement.

There were 11 brothers and sisters [in my family]—only three of us are left. All of them died fighting. [My brother] Mateo, well, that was his *nom de guerre*, he was one of the first men to become politically organised in the village. I remember being at home and [him] rushing in and saying, "Mother, do you have any food? Please get some food ready for me and my two friends who are here with me." He never said who they were. [But] we had noticed that he didn't dress like he did before—he used to wear shoes then and he'd pack a change of clothes if he was going out. He'd changed, he looked different, he looked like a real worker.

Inspired by her brother's example, she joins the FMLN when she is 22.

First a fighter

I was primarily a combatant. After that I went on to learn other kinds of skills. Since the **Frente** recognised that war prevented many of us from getting our diplomas, they've always taken this into account and given us the chance to work in all kinds of fields. While I was here, in the mountains of Morazán, and in Colomoncagua as well, I went on training programmes in radio-presenting and editing—so I can now work in radio or as an editor for a paper or something. I should like to thank the *Frente* because

they didn't just teach us how to use a gun, to shoot, they taught us so many other things which are useful to us now.

Guerrilla family
Martin Alder/Panos Pictures

As I was young I didn't have any fear. I never stopped to think I was going to die or anything like that. But I was always afraid about being captured. I used to say I'd prefer them to kill me rather than fall into the army's hands. There came a time when [it wasn't safe for me] to live at home any more. That's when I went into the bush. I'd come to see my parents clandestinely. When I saw my mother I cried for her and she cried for me. She said if she was ever killed by the army, that I should not be distressed. She trusted me because she saw in me a strong spirit. Those were almost the last things my mother and I said to each other. I was about to become fully involved, and ready to take up arms.

"Blue jeans, beige shirt"

In the beginning, my responsibility was for organising the people—we were assigned the task of having 50 new recruits in 15 days, another number in 12 days and so on. And it seems like I did a good job with the people—I got a lot politically involved. After this, I moved on to the armed faction, the ERP. I used to really love doing the kind of individual activities, like when Ana Guadalupe Martínez (FMLN leader) was in San Salvador. It was one of the first times I'd seen the armed units [in operation]. I liked her self-confidence, her uniform and everything. That's when I decided that I wanted to be like that. I used to like the uniform of blue jeans and beige shirt and the early weapons. When I joined the guerrilla I already knew how to handle a G-3 and all kinds of small arms because my father used to own some. When they gave me a '45 it wasn't anything new to me. What I did want was to carry an Uzi [machine gun]... and they let me. I had it for about seven months. We started from scratch and as the people started supporting us, things began coming together. The ranks grew until we finally became an army. I say all this because it is what I experienced personally and I loved it. I really wanted to become a guerrilla soldier because everything was done in the name of the people.

My first experience of death was when I was with the *LP-28*—the massacre of 29th October, 1979. My first two brothers were killed there. I'd been taking part in the huge demonstration and we were ambushed. When I saw my brothers had been killed, and all those *compañeros*, huge piles of dead bodies, I tried to take my own life. I went running zig-zag into the crowds, among the dead. But the bullets just whistled past, singed my hair... I have the shirt as a memento, because the bullets went through my shirt. I did it on purpose when I saw my brothers dead. I wanted a bullet to kill me so I could lie beside them. But nothing happened to me. I felt that I had grown as a result of this experience and felt stronger for having seen my brothers dead... and my *compañeros*. "I can't leave now," I said. "I must go on. I must do something more."

Children

I have three children and six adopted children who were left orphaned. Only eight are with me because the one I had before the war was only two when I joined up. He's a young man now, he's 17. The *Frente* allowed mothers to breastfeed their children for six months. After I'd looked after [my second] child for six months, they gave me another two months as encouragement. It was hard with children in the guerrilla, dragging them through the mountains and all that, so we took them off to Colomoncagua [refugee camp]. They had a mother's committee there whose job it was to take care of these children. But when the mother of [my adopted] children was captured, the *Frente* said I could look after them for three months while they found a new way of rehabilitating the children—organise where they were going to stay, who was going to bring them up and so on. The children started getting used to me and it [would have been] hard if the *Frente* had decided, "No", [but they didn't]. "If the children don't want to be separated from you, keep them, we'll support you." But the *Frente* had so much to do at that time that there was no way they could help me with all those children. So I made it my own responsibility... those five boys and a little girl and the one child of my own...

"Love slows you down"

I'm single, but I'm with someone so to speak. I say I'm single because my *compañero* is in the US. He's been living there for 14 years. He was my first *compañero*, the father of my son, but the organisation wouldn't let me be with him because he wasn't politically involved. We loved each other a lot and when I left for the mountains I spent three months crying over him. After that, during my time in the popular movement, I met a *compañero* who was a high-school graduate. When you are young you have a lot of sweethearts, but my first love was the one I really belonged to. When I became politically involved, I was going to marry this *compañero*—the one who belonged to the same organisation. But on the day we were going to get married... by five that afternoon he was dead.

I'm really not ashamed of having had different fathers for my children, because it wasn't me, it was imposed on me by the war. Every kind of relationship between men and women changed during the war. For example, I was used to making love at home with my *compañeros* on a bed. Making love in the bush was quite different, but nice when the *compañeros* knew how to make you enjoy it. With the tension of war and knowing that the enemy could jump on us at any time, you couldn't hang around naked for too long, nor was there much foreplay! Things were done much more quickly. There was also an order which said that nobody could be naked, everybody had to be ready with their clothes on. So we did it quickly. In the really difficult times, there was no love-making. But if we knew we weren't going to attack or be attacked, there were more opportunities for caressing. I never liked making love without caresses. If there are no caresses, it's not worth doing anything. I've always felt good if you can talk a lot and be caressed and not simply wait for the man to take his underwear off and do it. So I didn't really enjoy love while I was a combatant. When it comes to it, there was very little I did enjoy.

Another thing was that you didn't spend much time with your **compa** at the camp. However you look at it, being in love slows you down and stops you doing what you ought to be doing. That's probably why the *Frente* decided it was better if we were separated. It's not like nowadays, when there's time for it.

I'm not really ashamed of having had different fathers for my children; it was war

Things have changed. I feel I have to behave like a lady

Civilian life: a different style

We demobilised on July 30th '92. But I'd stopped being a combatant in the latter part of the war. I was in other, more important structures than being a combatant. I'm ideologically prepared, and militarily, but not politically, so I'm learning new things from people who have the experience. Most of us, the ex-combatants, don't know anything about politics.

One of the most serious problems is economic. We demobilised after 12 years of war, no one had money. When we arrived back in the **zones**, everything was destroyed, we had practically nothing. Personally I realise that there won't be any support for us. I don't sit around hoping they'll say, "Listen, you have to do this and we're going to help you with that... We're going to cover your fees so you can study." There's nothing like that. I don't think it's because the *Frente* wants to leave us on our own. It's just that they really don't have the means. Sometimes people say, "The ex-combatants don't have shit and the officers drive about in cars." But these men need a car, borrowed, rented, I don't know how they get it—they need to move around. They're different from me. I'm never going to discredit the *Frente* or anyone who's been a leader. I don't think it's right.

Things have changed. I feel in civilian life that I have to behave like a lady. I can't joke as much as I did before—we used to joke a lot with the *compas* to pass the time more happily. In the military, I learned to give orders and to be ordered and I got used to it. Nowadays I must be careful when I talk to people who weren't in the war, and even with those who were—the political world is very different from the military one where we'd go around talking abruptly to each other, giving harsh orders. I've had to change and it has been difficult for me because sometimes I like calling people *vos* ("you", informally) and I like them calling me the same. But there are many people who you can't address as *vos* and so I go around excusing myself.

"If you drop it, it breaks"

I have come across this word "reconciliation" in the *Frente*. It's a positive word. Do you know why? Because it's lovely to make up with someone who's been offended. Before the war, people always argued over everyday things, over children, animals, a piece of land, and now, over all these things, I sense reconciliation. For me it's the most beautiful thing in the world, reconciliation, caring for each other like brothers... And then there's peace... there's something about the word peace that stops me seeing it as simply a nice word. Building it, making it and not allowing it to collapse is very difficult

to do. Peace is like something made of glass: if you drop it, it breaks.   *Peace is like*
I would like to say the names of my relatives who have died. My   *something*
mother was called Feliciana Díaz, she was born in Delicias de   *made of glass*
Concepción, Morazán. My eldest brother was called Juan Bautista
Díaz and he fell in combat in Usulután and the second one was
called José Santos Díaz and he was killed in the October 29th
massacre in San Salvador...

Carmen   SAL 11

*Carmen, 42, spent much of the war in San Salvador, working
underground for the urban guerrillas.*

We used to celebrate God's word... and we began to see how things
ought to have been and how things really were... how the
government abused us. Through our study of the Bible we began
to discover how they wanted us to remain ignorant. When we
realised all the injustices the rich were guilty of, we woke up.
That's when they began saying that we were subversives, and the
repression began.

When there was time, some people would work on the land.
But if we were forced to leave on **guinda** we had to leave
everything. If we managed to harvest something, we'd eat it, and
if we didn't, sometimes [the soldiers] would arrive and set
everything alight. They'd set fire to the *milpas* (corn fields) or if
they didn't, they'd take the corn and leave us without a thing.
That's why we often went hungry. But we always tried to keep
working to support ourselves...

On *guinda*, if a **compañera** was pregnant, there was nowhere to
take care of her, no medicine or anything. There were times when
we had to sterilise the umbilical cord with hot ashes. We just
sharpened a knife, boiled it in hot water and cut the cord.
[Someone] would grab the child and someone else would pick the
compañera up and carry her.

To the city

I came to San Salvador in '83. We had no house, no money,
nothing. Three days after [our other son] was born, [my husband]
was captured and put in prison. Who knows who betrayed him?
There are so many people and so many people know you.

I didn't even have a cent to go and see him, not for the bus, nor
to eat, nothing. "Oh, my God! What am I going to do?" I
wondered. [Someone lent me a few cents.] I saw people going by

with pastries and I decided I'd look for the place where they got [them] and go and sell.

I woke up early in the morning and asked a woman to take care of the children. "Don't you have a basket?" the pastry woman asked. "No," I said. She took out a really dirty and stained one, and put the pastry in it. Then I went off to market. I sat down to sell and a woman came up to me and said, "You won't sell anything in that! Look, I'm going to sell you a small basket. When you're doing OK, you can pay me back." And that's how I began to earn at least enough to pay for sugar and to feed the other girl, but I still couldn't afford to go and visit [my husband].

Urban guerrillas

I collaborated with the urban guerrillas of San Salvador. My work involved moving equipment to [different] places. Even my husband [now released from prison] didn't notice what I did—you had to keep your involvement very hidden. I'd go out with my basket as if I was going out to sell. But I'd also perform the tasks they'd asked me to do. He wasn't aware that I worked. He's only just realised now because I've told him.

At the beginning I had problems with him. When he noticed I was going out, he used to ask me what I was doing. Sometimes I tried to explain, but since men aren't the most understanding... But then when he realised, I told him to leave me to do what I felt good doing. I said I couldn't do what he wanted me to if I didn't feel right about it. That's when we started having disagreements. Eventually, after I'd tried so hard to convince him and he kept saying "No", I stopped taking any notice of what he said. Finally he gave in. At first he'd say: "What are you doing? Aren't you taking care of the children?" "I struggle", I said, "because I don't want them to suffer as much as I have. If my parents had struggled before, I probably wouldn't be doing what I'm doing now. But since they didn't, I'm doing it for my children." It was my job to convince him and other people to do the same. Because if people never participate, they never understand.

Better to forget

Later, we decided to come to this zone because I was working with the FAL and they decided to repopulate this place. Another reason was because I didn't want to go back to where I came from—it would make me remember the members of my family who had died, and think about them a lot. It's better to forget.

I've been given land. At first they didn't include me [on the lists], it was only [my husband] who was included. On the day the man who was dealing with the land arrived, I asked: "Who's on the list? You must include me, because he might be here today but not tomorrow, and I'll always be here with the children—and I'd be left with nothing. I've fought hard for this land." Eventually they put my name down.

If people never participate, they never understand

Discrimination

Women have always been marginalised, even though they have always worked as hard as men. Since we love our people, we worked together and we thought that everyone would gain from it. We've all been through the same process and we've all paid dearly for it. When it comes to it, some have been acknowledged more than others. OK, so some of us didn't take up arms, but we exposed our lives and it's God's miracle that we're alive. And sometimes they don't consider that.

Men don't want to work in health, because they're not interested in helping others. "Health?" they'll say. "No thanks." Because it means giving of yourself, doing what others don't want to do. That's why the whole area of health is undervalued. That's why us women do it. I've been working in health for two years. We've commented on that too, how our work is never acknowledged! When aid arrives, they never say, "Let's give this to the women because they've worked so hard." Aid always seems to get to the NGOs, but for us...? That's why they've set up the inter-communal board so that aid will get to those who need it, not to the people who drive about in cars and all that.

It's been difficult to get people organised, particularly as far as the women are concerned. Most of the men don't want a women's organisation and that's probably why we haven't been acknowledged for so many things. Our little shacks are almost falling down, there are no programmes specifically for women. That's what we've been arguing about. There were people here saying that feminism was this and that... And we've always defended it. It doesn't mean you have to be anti-men: it means you have to convince them. I tell people about my own experience, how I tried to make my *compañero* understand and how now I go wherever I please, do whatever I please. If he doesn't have anything to do, he takes care of the children and things like that. He now knows that this is what I want and this is how I feel good.

Peace does not mean we must forgive the wicked things [people did]. But we must try to understand those who want to see change. [We must] continue our struggle but not through arms but through our voices, our thoughts.

Rosario   SAL 15

Rosario, 37, was a refugee in Honduras.

As refugees it was terrible because we didn't know anything about our [family] from one moment to the next. We didn't know if they were living or dead, thinking that even if they tried to visit us they might be killed.

When we arrived at Mesa Grande [refugee camp], I felt close to the end. I thought we'd never get out of that hole. Particularly when we saw there was wire all the way around. If someone tried to get out you'd hear the loud shots as they were killed. And the [Honduran] soldiers would come into the camp to intimidate us. But although we were afraid, we never stopped fighting. We continued to prepare food for our boys, because they were always coming and going to the [conflict] zone. We embroidered protest sheets to denounce what was happening and we'd send them with the *internacionales* (foreign workers) who'd come to the shelter. And there were times when the soldiers would come to search, and so that they wouldn't find the sheets—because if they found them they would have killed us—we'd wrap the sheets around us, and we'd put our skirts over the top to cover them. We were in a continual state of fear.

First I did embroidery, then I joined the tailor's workshop where we'd sew clothes secretly for [the *compañeros*], and the rest of the time we'd make clothes for ourselves. You wouldn't earn a cent for it, it was simply for the work. We didn't have to worry about food but sometimes things were tough because they hadn't brought enough supplies. By the time Friday came along, many of us were left without a grain of corn, but we'd get by. But we were always working, because there were training workshops, some where people would learn and others where things were produced. Men worked in garden produce, and what they produced was shared out among everybody. No one worked to produce things to sell; no one earned a cent. People worked only for everyone's general consumption.

Homecoming

We've had losses and gains in equal measure. It used to be rare to find someone who knew a craft or could even sew. It was even rarer to find someone who knew how to operate machines. Today, the majority of women could work in a tailor's shop [and] there are opportunities now to develop a whole number of jobs. In the resettled communities, it's *campesina* (peasant) women who are giving the classes. Although they don't earn a salary like the professionals, we still feel it's a big achievement for us. Some men see what's going on and think that it's a positive step. Others think women now feel superior to men. There are others who don't mind either way. Like everything, it takes all sorts—not everyone thinks the same.

We must continue our struggle but through our voices, our thoughts

Dolores   SAL 3

Dolores, 23, was a combatant from the age of 11.

Now I'm old I say I'm going back to my childhood. I sometimes act as a girl because I spent my childhood in the war. For example, I sometimes see toys and I feel like playing. I have a little teddy bear and I like playing with it. My brother is that way too, we both have the same story—he says he feels like playing with toy cars and he sometimes chats as if he was a boy. We didn't enjoy our childhood, we spent it as if we were old people and that's why it all comes out later on.

Arms to protect

Since I became involved with the military, my aspiration has been to join the PNC [*Policía Nacional Civil*]. So my ambition is to get though the ninth grade and then join the police. I want to make my career within the PNC, which will still involve carrying arms. I still want to work with weapons and to relate with *compañeros* because I got used to being just around men during the war and only wearing trousers as if I were a man. I still like being around *compañeras*, but I prefer being with *compañeros* as if we belonged to the same sex, that kind of thing. That's why I hope to join the PNC. The PNC is responsible for everybody's rights, including women's. I mean, if a criminal rapes a woman, I've got the right to tie him up and do what I want to him because I'm a police officer. That's what concerns me, abuse towards women, because men often don't take it seriously enough.

Esmeralda   SAL 22

Esmeralda, 24, joined the FMLN as a teenager.

I felt terrible because I had never been apart from my mother. All I did was think about her. [My brothers] tried to comfort me by saying, "This is the way things are. War is like that." [The FMLN]

I never wanted to carry guns told me to take a first-aid course. I worked as a *sanitaria* (first-aider). Then they decided I should take a course in anaesthetics. I was really nervous but I learnt step by step... They said that you'd learn more by practice. You were really afraid you would overdose on the anaesthesia and that the patient would die. But I was fully trained after six months and I worked as an anaesthetist until '88.

Women and men

In the FPL army, there'd sometimes be discrimination. For example, every time there were **guindas**, [the men] would take off... and the poor women who were cooking would be left behind. Some **compañeros** took advantage of the girls. They'd say, "We're here, all alone. Why don't you come to bed with me?" And there were girls there who hadn't had any experience, so... If you were lying down, stretched out, another man would come and lie down with you. But this didn't happen for long. We spoke with the people in charge. We said to them: "Look, this *compañero*, on such and such a date, came to where I was sleeping and tried to take advantage of me." So they began discussing it in the assemblies, which everyone had to attend. We women spoke out against it. We told the people in charge that it couldn't go on. "We're putting in as much as you are," we said. "We can't allow these *compañeros*, just because we're here without our mothers and fathers, to take advantage of us." And so they put an end to it all.

It also happened that some girls realised they were free (away from the parents), and they'd have a relationship with one and then the other, and there were probably things going on which weren't right. For example, if there was a girl who was like that... nobody went up to her to say: "Look, *compañera*, what you're doing is not good." What they did was laugh at her. When she'd had three or four blokes, they'd say, "Look at so and so. She's had so many men..." [This went on] among men but also among women themselves.

Bearing arms

I never wanted to handle a gun. I used to say, "What use is it to me? If the time comes, I won't know how to shoot. What if I miss someone and shoot another?" Once they almost forced me to carry a gun. One week later I said to them, "Take it back or I'll throw it away. I'd prefer to give it back to you now rather than hear you complaining later on that I've left it somewhere." In the whole time I was there, I never wanted to carry guns. I just carried my medicine, and the first-aid kit.

After-effects

Three months ago I started to get this problem. I went to bed with a terrible headache. After the pain, I felt like throwing up and then I started shivering, as if I had a high temperature, but I felt cold, and sick and dizzy—really awful. They called the woman working in health and she gave me pain-killers and some tranquillisers. Since then, the pain hasn't gone away. I don't feel like doing anything... really unmotivated to work. I keep forgetting everything. The doctor said that it was probably traumatic epilepsy. He explained that it was caused by the war. He told me I had to rest... that I had experienced many things... that I should try to regain control of my life, but that it would be very difficult.

My *compañero* came home after he'd been demobilised. He is war-crippled. He can't work much because he is injured in one arm and the other arm is completely dead. So, economically, we have problems. You sometimes worry because the children are growing up and need more things, and what you earn is practically nothing.

Lessons from war

On the one hand, I feel we have learnt something about what living in this country is about... how some people have more opportunities than others and how people from poor classes live. The other thing I learnt I guess was about health. I also learnt how to work, how not to be self-conscious. In the time I've worked with the organisation, I've stopped being scared. [I've learnt] to speak out in front of people, to know more things, about others as well as myself. Because there are a lot of things one doesn't know, that one's ignorant about, superstitious.

Personally, before I had this [health] problem, I felt fine, happy even. *Púchica!* We had finally achieved what we'd been fighting for. I decided to learn and find a way of giving something to the other *compañeras* who haven't had a chance to know about their rights. For the coming generations it's important they understand what we've been through, so that they don't repeat what has taken place. So may the new generation be more aware and may the gains of our generation be continued by them. If we forget history, we forget everything.

I've stopped being scared. I've learnt to speak out

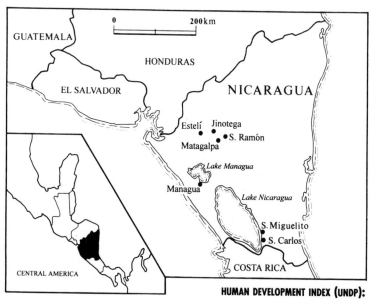

HUMAN DEVELOPMENT INDEX (UNDP):
106 (medium)
POPULATION: 4.0m
FEMALE LIFE EXPECTANCY: 67.8 years

1821 Independence **1912** US Marines begin 20 years of occupation **1932** Peasant revolt led by Augusto Sandino **1933** Creation of National Guard; Sandino assassinated **1956** Somoza assassinated; succeeded by son Luis **1961** Formation of FSLN **1972** Earthquake devastates Managua; martial law declared **1974** Somoza re-elected; FSLN raid in Managua **1977** Opposition mounts to Somoza regime; major FSLN offensive **1979** FSLN enters Managua and installs revolutionary government **1980** Ex-National Guardsmen established as counter-revolutionary army (Contras) **1984** Daniel Ortega elected president **1985** US economic embargo declared **1987** Esquipulas Peace Accords; first discussions between FSLN and Contras **1990** Feb: Sandinistas defeated by Violeta Chamorro's UNO party in national elections. March: US trade embargo formally lifted; Contra demobilisation officially ends; army initiates plan to cut its ranks in half

— NICARAGUA —

As the largest country in Central America, situated in "the backyard" of the United States, Nicaragua's history since independence from Spain in 1821 is dominated by its resistance to US intervention.

Widespread exploitation by US enterprises, feudal conditions and the example of the Mexican revolution, led the poor and landless to rise up throughout Central America. In Nicaragua, in 1932, a peasant army under Augusto Sandino threw out the US Marines who had occupied the country for nearly 25 years. Before they left, however, the Marines installed the National Guard, with Anastasio Somoza as its head. Sandino was assassinated the following year and Somoza appointed himself president. Although he was later assassinated, he was succeeded by his sons; with US support the Somoza family controlled Nicaragua for 45 years.

Somoza ran the country like a personal fiefdom. But the post-World War Two economic boom in Latin America brought pressure from the Nicaraguan people for democratic reform. Somoza responded with increasing repression and throughout the 1970s thousands were tortured or killed. Social protest was led by the Sandinista National Liberation Front (FSLN) which took its name and inspiration from Sandino. Peasants, students and poor urban workers took up arms; many were driven underground. Women played an important part in the struggle. Some 30% of FSLN combatants and leaders were women; many more were messengers, took charge of supplies and kept safe houses.

Unlike neighbouring El Salvador, however, opposition to the ruling regime was not confined to the working classes. When the FSLN marched to victory on 19 July 1979—the War of Liberation —they had the support of the traditional political parties, business interests and the progressive elements of the Catholic Church, who had also suffered at the hands of Somoza.

The FSLN government embarked on a programme of social, legislative and political reform. This included a national literacy campaign, redistribution of land, setting up national health and education services, and establishing a new constitution. Women in particular secured important new rights, including the right to own land, equal pay, and improved maternity services.

There were also many problems, including rising corruption. The new government's lack of experience and inability to carry out much-needed reforms, as well as the dire economic situation reinforced by the US blockade, soon threw the country back into war. The ex-National Guard re-formed with US backing as the "Contra" (later known as the National Resistance Army) and fought against the Sandinista army. Most of Nicaragua's adult men and many young people were drawn into combat on one side or the other.

The upheaval of war opened up opportunities for women in the new social organisations, agricultural production and government administration, while they continued to shoulder family and community responsibilities. Women's increased awareness of their rights and abilities also led to the creation of numerous feminist organisations outside the official party structure, laying the foundation for a powerful women's movement which continues to influence the national political and social agenda.

Throughout the 1980s, neighbouring El Salvador and Guatemala were immersed in civil war. Honduras was flooded with refugees and had become a military base for the Nicaraguan Contras. Costa Rica was also home to significant numbers of Nicaraguan refugees and migrant workers. Peace became a priority for all countries in the region. The five Central American presidents signed the Esquipulas Peace Accords in August 1987, providing a basis for ending the conflicts and for initiating national dialogues.

Although this began immediately in Nicaragua, it was only in February 1989 that the Central American presidents finally moved on disbanding the Contras. The US maintained the economic blockade and financial support to the Contras until the national elections in February 1990. It had become evident to most Nicaraguans that the only possible route to ending the war was a change of government. Despite a flamboyant electoral campaign by Daniel Ortega of the ruling Sandinistas, the US-backed Violeta Chamorro of the National Organised Union (UNO) party was voted president, promising peace and national reconciliation.

Five years on, structural adjustment policies have virtually dismantled social services. Three-quarters of the population live in poverty, with unemployment running at over 60%. In some parts of the country, both Sandinista and Contra ex-combatants, frustrated with the government's broken promises, have taken up arms again. Delinquency, violence, corruption and fear are widespread.

Women, whether Sandinista or Contra, have led the reconciliation process in the community and at home. The testimonies recorded here are with women on both sides. They talk mainly of the conflict during the "revolutionary decade" of the FSLN government.

The interviewers were Mercedes Ríos, Magda Torres, Teresa Chamorro, María Esther Quintana and Flor de María Zúniga of Mujer y Cambio, a feminist research centre in Managua.

María Alicia   NIC 12

María Alicia, 30, joined the Sandinistas before the overthrow of the Somoza regime. She continues to be a supporter of the FSLN party.

I am going to tell you my story from the time we became involved in the war, from 1977 that was, because from then on it was always a question of war.

My parents were accused of collaborating with the Sandinista Front. The [National] Guard came and took all of us—children, women, old people. We were held [prisoners] for three months. My father was in jail for a year, and they tortured him. He was [eventually] set free, mainly due to my mother's efforts. [She] was the only one not arrested, because she wasn't there at the time they took us. First they freed the children. At the time, I was barely 12 years old. Many girls my age were raped.

Collaborators

Once we got out of jail, we could no longer live [in the village]. We had to move here to San Ramón. It's true that at the time my parents were collaborating by giving food to [the Sandinistas]. As my parents would say, "We are all human, and everyone needs a little food." [My father] was sympathetic, and that was his great crime, because at that time you weren't allowed to help—that was in '77.

When the 1979 war began, we were already here [in San Ramón]. I was just starting first grade—at 12 years old, because the situation in the village... There were classes, but you couldn't study. Here, against all the odds, my mother managed to enrol me in first grade. I was embarrassed and ashamed, because I saw so many children younger than me, and I looked at them and they were in higher grades. It hurt me, but I said, if I don't do it now, I'll never be able to—I'll never know anything, I'll not even be able to sign my name.

When I was about 15, I began to work with the popular organisations of the time. Later, they formed the militias, which I also joined, because I saw the need to defend the country. So I took part from time to time, when they needed me. I was still a girl then. [It was] not until I was 19 that I met my partner, and we're still together now.

I continued my work, because he was also "organised". We didn't stop working until the end, when we [Sandinistas] lost the elections [in 1990]. But I will always be with the *Frente*—it's been my party since I was young, and I'm not thinking of going back.

Women in the militia

Within the militias, they were nearly all men, and they put us [women] there [doing political work] because they saw that we could, as they say, boss around a squadron of men or a company. But the leaders almost never sent us [women] out—we wanted to, but they didn't use us like that. Many [women] told us they wanted to join up, but they couldn't because their husbands were jealous, or sometimes it was the father or the mother. Because of this, there were hardly any women. I had no problem [with my husband] because, as I told you, since we were both "organised", we understood each other well. Anyway, even before I got together with him, I was already working and he knew I had to continue.

For me, it was good, because the male comrades respected us, .and we them. If a male comrade failed to respect a woman he was punished, and women were also punished for their mistakes. At the time we were participating it was very strict. Later, after we left, we heard it had become one big mess, with men abusing women... When we were there, there was none of that.

I see [my political work] as something very important, because even if we were afraid, we had to be at the front, we had to be in the thick of things. I see it as good, I mean important, that women participated and not just men. What we had was the will. Women weren't in the army at the time, but we had the will and we knew that we were defending our country, not some other country, but our country.

Disintegration

Lately, we have not really been working in earnest, because there've been so many problems in terms of unity and everything. There's been a lot of trouble too in the municipality, and because of this I've withdrawn from everything—except from the party. It's not like it was before, when we were 100% involved. It made us happy. Now, everything has changed. Everything is different.

[When the Sandinistas lost the elections] we thought that it

Sandinista women demanding their rights
Paul Smith/Panos Pictures

was going to go from bad to worse. If there was *machismo* before, now it would be worse—and also crime. Why will *machismo* be worse? Because there won't be any laws to protect women, so men will be able to go from one woman to the other, leaving children scattered here and there. [During the war, in the 1980s], maybe there wasn't less [*machismo*] but they were fighting to get rid of it. They weren't successful, but it's clear they paid attention to women, we had support, I mean they treated women as equals. Not any more.

We [women] should organise more, agree between us that if, for example, I see my husband doing something wrong and I keep quiet, then I am helping to increase the *machismo* and not solving anything... not for me as a woman, or for the rest of my *compañeras* who have to suffer men getting them pregnant, then leaving them... And the children don't even know who their fathers are when they are born.

So I think that we women must watch out for this and not just go so fast with a man, without knowing him. But there are women who are very open and they've hardly talked to the man when they're already saying "Yes." We women also make our mistakes.

Guillermina   NIC 18

Guillermina is 50, a widow who participated first in the Sandinista guerrilla movement, and then, after the victory, joined their army.

Before the war I worked at home, baking, butchering pigs. I made trousers, shirts... I can't remember very well, but it was quite a while before the triumph (Sandinista victory). We started hearing people talk about how we'd be able to survive [and] the things the government was doing. The Church gave courses on organisation: they made us aware of the role we would play once we were organised. We started holding meetings in people's houses.

"We are all your children"

[My son] died in the war of liberation. After that I went to a camp. I met up with some young men I knew, who had been with my son and they told me all about his death. I took my girls and left them with my sisters. I was heartbroken having to leave [my daughters] behind. But how could I stay? [The National Guard] were certain to kill me—I'd already received threats. The young women [in the camp] would say to me, "Look, mother, we and all the *compañeros* here are your children. Don't worry, we're going to fight."

I wasn't able to continue with them, because my foot was fractured [but] I kept working until the liberation. Although I couldn't take up arms and move around, I became a cook making panfuls of food and tortillas. We couldn't let the people who were on the barricades go hungry.

I had problems with my family, not with my daughters, because they were little, but my brothers didn't agree with me. They'd tell me off... My son had already died and that's what encouraged me to fight even more. And not just for my son, but for so many who were killed so that their families could live better. They didn't sever relations with me, but they didn't approve. In other words, they didn't agree [with what I was doing], but they always helped me out with food and things—perhaps against their will.

[My husband] didn't get involved in anything. I don't know why he didn't reproach me, but he didn't for things like that. What he'd say was that he didn't like the [National] Guard because they'd killed his brother years ago, but he didn't know that I was already very involved. When he realised, he took off. He left to escape from the war, because he had his oxen. He valued his oxen more than anything, and his cart. He went to the mountains.

In the army

After the triumph, I joined up again, this time armed and in uniform. It wasn't that they needed my work [in the army], but more that they put me in to help me out, so that I'd get my little salary. I deserved it, they said, because I'd fought and my son had been killed, and so I stayed in the army for five years.

I worked at the military hospital [for three years]. I made sheets, mosquito nets, pyjamas. I became fond of the work and the comradeship and [enjoyed] the fact that any morsel of food belonged to everyone. When I left, I became the head of the neighbourhood militias, but that was voluntary so I started baking again. I joined a bakers' cooperative.

Betrayal

By the time it was all coming to an end in 1989 things were no longer so good. The Sandinista leaders felt different. Because of our dedication, we hadn't noticed all those sleepless nights... [But then] all of us, men and women, began to see that it wasn't good to be working like an animal. Can you imagine, after two loads of baking and going out into the busy streets and then to get up to do guard duty...

We thought things would be different, not like the way we used to live during Somoza's time. And in fact we ended up worse. Those of us who worked hard were never asked, "What do you need?" They divided up what we'd worked for among themselves and they forgot about those of us who had fought and sacrificed our sons. Because there are a lot of us mothers of heroes and martyrs who, I'm not ashamed to say, wander around hoping that someone will give us a pound of rice to eat.

I've talked to many women and they don't want to organise themselves because they say it does them no good to kill themselves so that others can live well. It's very difficult to win people back and persuade them to organise. People don't want anything to do with it anymore because [those at the top] don't even visit the neighbourhoods now to see how people are doing, to find out if they're ill or hungry.

I don't think there's any possibility of peace. [Not] when the government doesn't keep its promises that everyone who hands in their rifles will be given land and bank loans. It turns out that if they give you land, they don't give you a loan. What can people do with land and no money to work it?

It was a trick.

María   NIC 15

María, 54, coordinates cultural activities for the Committee of Mothers of Heroes and Martyrs of the Revolution, in Matagalpa. Two of her sons have died fighting.

My son joined the struggle in 1974. Those are times that will always be remembered. They took to the streets to fight for a free and sovereign country, which many never got to see. The struggle began during the Somoza dictatorship, which was a difficult era for [our children] and us mothers. What were we supposed to do? We had to support them, because it was the only way to end the unjust assassinations of so many boys, students, farmers, everyone.

What was happening was so awful and that's why we supported our sons and continue to do so. It is very hard remembering those times of struggle... because sometimes, you felt you were going to die. You never knew, when they took to the streets to protest against the massacres, if they would come home alive. Your stomach would tremble, not knowing if those shots would signal your worst nightmare—your son dead in the middle of the street, or thrown in some vacant lot. Sometimes they hid the bodies. It was bitter, horrible. It's hard to remember those times, but we must.

"A safe-house"

I lived in Jinotega and had five children. Our house was a safe-house, where they'd come—five, six, seven, eight boys—almost every day. They were comrades of our sons and it was a just fight, in which we also played our part. We women had a place, a place in history, because we fought from the beginning. They can never ignore us.

We made bandannas there on my sewing machine, which I keep as a piece of history. I've never wanted to sell it. We made a ton of red and black bandannas on that machine. Many of the rebels came through my house and slept there after being in the mountains. So, we got involved in all of this too—spreading Sandinista propaganda, so people would know who they were and support them. It was a struggle for change, that was why we fought. The problem is that there was a change, but there were also mistakes. But it was a wonderful fight because those who fought and died did not die in vain, they taught us how to fight for our rights, how to defend ourselves, to have a decent job, housing... Sometimes people say that so many died, but the truth is they aren't dead, because as long as we keep fighting they never die.

You have to look at things realistically. Under the Somoza

dictatorship, we never would have fought for jobs, never would have gone on strike, because, well, they would just massacre everybody. But we have learnt how to speak out, and this is what the heroes and martyrs taught us. We women used to be marginalised, and they would like to marginalise us again. But it's not going to happen, because we know how to fight [now].

We have learnt to speak out; this is what the heroes and martyrs taught us

On the front line

I personally lived through the war on the front line, as they say. I used to go to the mountains a lot with a cultural brigade trying to boost the morale of the boys (soldiers). We lived through the war, saw many *compañeros* die every day. Every time I saw one of them fall, it was a blow to me. It was like it was my son [all over] again.

I also worked with the Soldiers Support Commission and took part in the programme to aid the dead and wounded. I had to go to the morgue when there were seven or eight dead... to see the pieces of those boys, with their throats slit, with no fingernails, with no eyes. It was awful—so many children who could have grown up to be something, were left there, destroyed. Since then, I've had heart troubles, because I can't help remembering... and to remember is to live through it [again]. It's horrible.

Economic imperatives... for women

[When the men went off to war], everyone joined in the production. Don't forget it, we went to pick coffee, to plant... everyone. If not, we would have died of hunger. So, many women planted little communal gardens in their communities. And many women took over their husband's job—some even drove tractors. [And now], because of the real economic crisis, people have had to tighten their belts, as we say. We were hoping it would be better, but it is actually worse.

As mothers, we never fooled ourselves that things would be better [after the victory of UNO]. Obviously, we didn't say so, because people weren't going to believe us. They said that we'd have dollars, that we'd have this and that. We listened to them and told ourselves how deluded they were. After just one month, they started seeing a change; after two months, forget it! At the end of three months they were already firing workers.

When the first strikes started, [people] realised they weren't going to be eating meat, that they weren't going to have dollars. The problem is that even beans have become expensive—and without beans, we cannot eat. You don't need glasses to see what's before your eyes.

A foreign visitor asked us a question: do you think the *Frente* can win? And we couldn't say for sure if they could—only God knows that—but what we can tell the whole world is that, despite the fact that we buried 15, 20 *compañeros* a day, there was work, there was plenty of money. Even if the notes were worthless, nobody was hungry. Sure we waited in line, because they had to distribute the food equally... Not now. You look in the stores and there is a mountain of stuff, but in the markets the food rots. And why does the food rot? Because the people don't have any work. People aren't blind. The same people who voted for [a change] are the same people who don't have anything.

"Wars don't end"

We knew that wars really don't end. Still, we thought that perhaps there wouldn't be so many deaths, that with disarmament we would see some peace. The problem is that we still don't have peace. At the time, one only thought about that sacred moment—thank God, they're disarming! But what happened? People are still going around armed and killing people. So, people can't go into the country to work, because they're still afraid of being killed.

There are people who are very angry that [the government] hasn't met all its promises to those who fought, so people take up arms to put pressure on them. Sometimes they say that if that woman [President Chamorro] doesn't comply, we'll kidnap so-and-so to see if she does. Maybe if they met all their promises, the war wouldn't still be going on. [It's not] the same kind of war as before, but it's [still] dangerous in the country, and as long as they don't come up with what they promised, it's going to continue like this.

Women's revolution

Women's great liberation came with the [Sandinista] victory. Many of us had joined [the struggle]... even if the men didn't like it. I lost my husband nine, 10 years ago because of this. I went with my dance troupe. I always loved culture and after the victory I dedicated myself to the festivals. I went to the mountains, to where the troops were, to bring a little happiness to the boys. Once my husband said to me, "The revolution or me?" And I told him, "The revolution! My sons died for this, and I'm sticking with it."

What often happens is that a husband doesn't want the woman to be out: he wants his wife at home. They think that women's liberation is all about being "loose"—but it was to give us the right to education, to better ourselves and be equal with men in terms of work. If you are able to perform a job, then you should be allowed to. This is what I understand by women's liberation—not what they think. [And] the liberation was a success, because today women are better educated, have more access to culture...

We cannot support this hatred for another mother

Culture: "no colour, no party"

I've learnt masses about our culture that I didn't know before. I used to dance in school, but I didn't know about our cultural roots, none of that. You used to dance, just to dance, because it was fun and good exercise. I knew nothing about folklore. I learned about it after the revolution, when we began to form the Centres for Popular Culture. We went about historically rescuing our cultural roots, our customs, our peoples' traditions. That is where I truly learned what Nicaraguan culture was, and that is why I keep on developing it, because it is so big and beautiful... it doesn't have any colour, or party. It doesn't have politics, because it is of the people and for the people. Everyone can take part. That's the most marvellous thing about it.

The cultural project exists [now], but we still haven't found financing. The Committee of Mothers has provided some costumes and other little things, so we can perform. I have a great desire to do this, because it's a job with young people, getting them to avoid drugs and alcohol, [or] getting into trouble because of [so much] unemployment. They are all students, all young, but run the risk of ruining their lives. It's an important job we're doing, what with all the crime and corruption now, the prostitution... young girls without work.

Reconciliation

A mother is never responsible for what her child does. If a child wants to join one side, each to his own. Everyone is free to think whatever he wants. There are mothers who don't even know where their sons died, where they were captured, who took them. But they feel the same pain that we feel of having lost their dearest possession—their son—whether he was with the *Frente* or the **Resistance**. One gives birth with pain and raises them with love. We are all mothers. As the Christians that we are, we cannot support this hatred for another mother. We must give them our hands and help those who have most hurt us. We cannot hold on to these hatreds if we want a dignified peace and if we want reconciliation.

Vicenta   NIC 4

After the Sandinista victory, Vicenta, 23, was kidnapped twice by the Contras—accused of informing on a Contra leader murdered near her home. She left her job as a teacher for fear of being kidnapped again.

I was giving classes. It was almost **19th July** and I was going to do something with my students—make a **piñata**. It was going to be a celebration... But what a scare I had! I was in mid-conversation with my mother and [some of] the girls when I heard a loud bang on the door: "Open up, please." I ran to my room and locked it. They went on knocking and my father asked if he should open the door. And the others said no, it must be the Contras. But then they opened the door and the first thing they said was, "Where's the teacher? The school teacher?"

"You're coming with us," they said and one of them, who was masked, grabbed me and started to push me out. But I said, "No. I can't go like this. Give me time to dress." My mother began to beg and my father told them to take him instead, that he was a man and I was just—as if they didn't know—a young girl, just 18. But they said, "No. It's her we want." They pushed me outside and took me [away]. Then they went back to my room to get my clothes—a pair of trousers and a shirt—and made me dress in front of them.

Interrogation

They took me to the woods and began to interrogate me. At that time, one of them had been killed in front of [a neighbour's] house. He was a Contra leader and they said it was my fault, that I had gone to inform. It was a lie. I worked with a teacher and he had gone to give the information, but they said it was me—they had seen me at [that] house. They had me from eight in the morning and they didn't let me go until two or three in the afternoon. They told me that if I said anything [about my arrest] they would take me to one of their leaders who liked young girls like me... and they would give me to him... and worse.

When they took me [the second time] I was terrified. My mother was a wreck. They told her to give them I don't know how many *rosquillas* (pastries) so that I'd have some food. My mother baked to sell—that was her business. They said if she gave them the *rosquillas* they would let me go. She made a ton of *rosquillas* and gave them to them. They told me how delicious they were. I thought they were probably going to kill me and use the same *rosquillas* for my wake.

Caught between two sides

They let me go the next day, around midnight. Meanwhile, the Sandinistas had already investigated the fact that I had been kidnapped and since my mother kept quiet and didn't tell them anything, they took her prisoner for eight days and kept her incommunicado—they didn't let anybody see her.

I continued to give classes, but I was frightened, afraid that any day the same thing could recur because they told me that if I kept giving classes... [They said] that there was no need for the children to know how to read so that teachers could lead them astray. At that time the books had a lot about Sandino in them and it was my duty to teach about him to the children.

It disturbed me a lot. Although I went on teaching, I did so in fear. I no longer went to school with the same enthusiasm. Later on I resigned, because I was afraid. They said that wherever there was a teacher, there were the seeds of *Sandinismo*, and that they would set fire to our homes—and us. I thought that because of me, my family would suffer—and my mother did. They had her there for eight days, just on water. She said she had to sleep standing up and that if she sat down they'd start saying rude things to her. They made her pee in a boot in front of all the men. There were only two women, and all the rest were men.

[The Sandinistas] arrested my mother when they found out she'd made *rosquillas* [for the Contras]. They said [she] was baking for them... that she was killing pigs and cows, and who knows what else, so that they could eat. That was a lie.

I didn't feel any affiliation for either side. My job was to give classes. I taught what they told me to and didn't feel anything—neither for the Sandinistas, nor the others. Obviously, at this time I was among Sandinistas, but I didn't believe in either side.

Elections

What happens sometimes [is that] the man supports one party and the woman the other. This happened during the elections [in 1990]: my husband, having been in the army, was going to vote for the Sandinistas, and I wasn't. I felt I had to vote for UNO, so that my brothers, who were in Costa Rica, could come home. So we argued because he said I had to vote for his side, and I said I was going to vote for who I liked. He voted and I didn't—in order not to fight or argue and have problems with him.

Now, I am fighting to get my job back. There are several children who have told me that if I come back they will go back to school. But it's not the same. If I hadn't quit back then, I would still

My husband is a working man, he is not a man of war

be giving classes, because I was a good teacher... but I was too much of a coward.

Anonymous   NIC 2

This 47-year-old woman talks of the difficulties of being a woman alone.

With the start of the war, as a woman, it affected me very much, because I had to take on responsibilities which I really wasn't used to. Because it was always [my husband] who had taken care of the house and dealt with anything that had to be dealt with, in every situation.

Harassment

[The Sandinistas] began to insist he join the army. But [my husband] is a working man, he is not a man of war. We avoided [conscription] as long as we could, but it soon became impossible... If they came looking for us at the *finca* (farm), we would go into town, and if they came for us in town, we would head for the *finca*. But in 1982 they killed my husband's cousin. Some of the Sandinistas came and killed him. They also grabbed [the cousin's] father and took him off to State Security. The women were running all over the place, not knowing where it was safe to hide. The house was bullet-ridden.

Afterwards, they went on harassing us, maybe because we were a very close family and what happened to the others was the same as it happening to us. After the murder, they dragged another cousin off to prison and held him for six months. We went to visit him and, I guess this is the same with every family, because he was a relative, it was even more distressing. My children, especially, had problems with it. Every time we went, things were more difficult at home.

Then my husband had to escape. He said he wasn't capable of killing anyone—it was something he'd never been taught and his conscience wasn't capable of. So he tried to escape through the mountains, with another cousin, not knowing where they were going, with no idea what kind of luck they'd have. He said goodbye to the children and us here. It was like our life was being uprooted, part of my life had been destroyed. How was I going to bring up my children in a country at war?

The husband is captured and imprisoned in San Carlos; the cousin is killed.

When I reached San Carlos I spent four days fighting to see him.

He'd been accused of being a Contra. My whole life was dark and there was no one to say, "I will help you." Meanwhile, I had to think about home, where there was combat after combat and where I'd left my children alone. I was there for four days. Every day I felt I was dying. I lost a lot of weight.

I felt like my soul wanted to fly out of my mouth at the horror

Religious strength

I went on praying to God to ask what I should do so I could get to see him, and the Lord answered my prayers. I don't know how I managed to get where he was, but when I found him he was bad, very bad. The bullets in his shoulder were infected and psychologically he was destroyed. I felt ever more alone and unprotected—having to take responsibility in such a hard situation was very difficult for me. But I did get to see him and I told him to pray, that we would pray every day for him and that God would get him out of there.

No buses [went to the jail], only a military bus. And, this is something that my husband doesn't even know: in the night, the soldier who gave us a ride tried to rape me. It was a nightmare to think how what had happened to me might have repercussions on my children, my husband and me. I thought I was going crazy.

I went again the next night and the following day I was able to see [my husband]. I walked back to San Miguelito from San Carlos on foot [approximately 40 kms]. I did the whole thing alone and felt like it wasn't me walking, because I felt like my soul wanted to fly out of my mouth at the horror. I thought that if anyone found me they would rape me, or kill me. [But] Christ went with me. He was the only one to help me.

Torture

When I got home, my children thought I was bringing their father. And when they saw me alone, the girl flew at me in a rage—and I just died. I told them I didn't know if we would ever see him again, because the day after I'd visited him, they were going to transfer him to State Security. He told me he no longer had the strength to live, because the tortures were so great. The only thing that could help him survive was the love we had.

I wouldn't want what happened to me to happen to anybody, because it is something that destroys the spirit and the soul, totally, there is no comparison. To talk about it is hard for me, because it all comes back at once... all that terror, that horror.

Anonymous   NIC 5

This 34-year-old woman was a fighter in the National Resistance Army.

The first one to join the **Resistance** was my brother. Then they started hassling my family, particularly me, because I'd started mixing with people from the Resistance, bringing them medicines, clothes and things. State Security began sending anonymous notes to my house threatening my family—and me. I started working as a messenger for the Resistance. I'd give them information about people from Security, because I was practically inside what we called the Sandinista Party... everybody thought I was a Sandinista. When they found out I wasn't, I had no other choice but to join the military wing of the Resistance. I joined on my birthday, the very day I turned 18.

I was much more mature than the other [women who joined], so they sent me to study. I still hadn't had sexual relations with anyone, because they respected you there. If you wanted to have sex with someone, there was no problem, but they respected the woman's decision. After three years, I began to get involved with a leader known as "the Cat". We got married on a trip to Honduras... and returned to the mountains with higher rank.

She becomes pregnant and her husband is wounded; they are both sent to recuperate in Costa Rica.

In Costa Rica we continued to work with the Resistance. Some foreign members [of the Resistance] took us to a hotel where there was everything, arms and all that. They gave us a car. Later, we had serious problems with an American over the way they manipulated us with arms, food and everything to do with the military side and [about] how this man was pocketing all the aid that came from abroad.

Another man, who lived in the States, was working with another organisation from the US. He had his ways... I wouldn't exactly call him Communist, but he was one of those people who likes to do exactly what they say he should, even if he sees they are making mistakes. We had serious problems with this man, so we returned to civilian life.

We met a soldier in Costa Rica to whom we are very grateful. This man took us to a farm where we were to live. [By this time], I had practically retired [from the Resistance]. My husband continued in the organisation—we never demobilised. We returned to Nicaragua as a repatriated family.

Disarmament

From the moment they talked about disarming, I thought about what would happen—it's turned out almost exactly as I thought. If I hadn't disarmed, everybody would have known that I was with the Resistance. But here, very few people know. Sure, the people I worked with, the people who saw me... many foreigners from various countries know, because I lived with them.

We were taught that you must not kill... Spiritually you feel very bad

[We've had problems] in both the economic and the political sense. Allegedly, the people who went abroad to live didn't fight for their county—that's what some said—or they were *Somocistas* (followers of Somoza) who had to flee. But nobody knows what other people do for their country or their families.

The legacy of war

In economic terms, I'd say [the war] has had a very strong [impact]. Before, in the time of Somoza, I remember how poor everybody was, but they weren't hungry. They had their three meals a day, and if you worked for the government you didn't do too bad. But now, if you work for the government you make very little, not even enough to support a family—even if both spouses work. So, I'd say the economic situation is pretty critical.

[There's] also the spiritual [impact], because remember, we were brought up as Catholics and taught that you must not kill or lie or do a lot of things—all of which we did. Spiritually you can feel very bad, like God doesn't care for you or like you don't follow His path. And even though they say that if you repent you will enter the Kingdom of Heaven, I don't think so... if you are stained, there is no way to clean yourself.

I think that, up to a certain point, yes, God has forgiveness. I'm not sure, but I think that this fight wasn't about killing or robbing, but so that there would be democracy in Nicaragua, which there wasn't, and so that there would be respect for human rights, which is something that pleases God. But this is something you can only find out directly from God, or from someone with much more spiritual understanding.

In the psychological sense, I think that all Nicaraguans have been affected by the traumas of death, fear, shock... I don't think this has just damaged a minority, but all Nicaraguans, especially those who took full part in the war.

Rosaura   NIC 14

Rosaura, 44, lost a son in combat and her husband was left severely injured. She talks of the need for reconciliation between mothers of those who have died.

They came to tell me at about five in the afternoon. His death was very cruel and I don't really like to talk about it... because it is so very painful. I was left with a daughter of his, who's now seven. His girlfriend was very young. Five months after his death she brought me the baby girl. Since then I've been her mother.

Heroes and martyrs

It was after [his] death that I started feeling really sad. I didn't know what to do. There was a woman who did some work in the neighbourhood and she said, "Let's organise a committee." I began going to the meetings and started to feel better. There is a priest there, who helps a lot. So when we feel really down, he helps us, gives advice, holds mass... it's been really nice.

From the time I joined the Committee [of Mothers of Heroes and Martyrs of the Revolution], I've felt that I've changed. When I joined, there weren't as many mothers as there are now. We have five or six hundred mothers, just here in Matagalpa. But back then, there were only a few. Still, we were growing and delegations [from abroad] started to come and we would tell our stories. So they started sending us donations and starting projects.

There are also mothers who have come from the mountain region, from even further away than where I come from, and older women with even greater problems, some whose whole families were murdered. There are mothers who have lost five children, their husband, son-in-law, everyone... there are a lot like that.

I've received a lot of support from the Committee, both emotionally and economically. I don't receive a stipend from my son's death—they just give [to] his wife. So I have to work, find something to do... sometimes I wash, sometimes I iron. Doña Esperanza gives me clothing to sell. We earn one or two *pesos* per piece of clothing, and many of us mothers live this way.

A mother's peace

I feel protected by the Committee, whereas there are other mothers... I'm thinking about the mothers of boys in the Contra and there are many of them and they are not organised, so they have no help. [At first] I almost didn't want to talk to them because... at times, you feel afraid or remember your sons. I sometimes thought it could be this woman's son who killed my boy, and I'd feel bad.

We've got to help each other... as mothers... as women

If there is going to be peace there will be reconciliation. Obviously you are going to feel as if you should hate this other mother. But Father Arnaldo has made us understand that if I am a mother, and she is a mother, then the death of her son must hurt her too. Now, I can speak calmly with these women, obviously not with the same trust as with mothers of the **Frente**. It is different, but now we are beginning to feel for them too, especially as we see that no one is supporting them.

Last year we hosted the national annual meeting [of the Committee]: 250 mothers came from all over the country. We spent three days cooking to have enough food for everybody. We tried to cook the best meals possible and have it ready on time. [The mothers of Contra fighters] were really pleased and thanked us for treating them so well. What's more, one mother told me she didn't have anywhere to stay, so I let her sleep here in my house. I said even if it had been bad between us before, that she should feel comfortable here, and so she stayed.

I think this unity helps us a lot as women. We've got to help each other... as mothers... as women.

Jenny   NIC 23

As a mother of two Sandinista soldiers, Jenny (42) supported the war effort.

I'd say [relationships between men and women] probably did change during the war. Do you know why? Because the revolution brought many things that we women didn't know about before. And one of them was the demand for equal rights—something that men will never accept, because *machismo* is so ingrained in them. Why are there so many women's organisations now? It's precisely because of that. Before, I never used to hear women complain when their husbands mistreated them. And it was unusual to hear the police ask, "Why did you mistreat her?" Not any more. Now there are many laws, but it's also because women were more united and have started to demand their rights.

But men won't accept it—because it's what they say that counts. What do they think? That women want to be libertines, that they [just] want to do as they wish? It's not a question of what we want, but what we consider fair. This is what we're demanding. If you're with your husband and he shows up at three or four in

The person who doesn't have aspirations is like the living dead

the morning, we women have the right to say, "Look here, boy, there's nothing to eat here and you're working and I think you've been wasting our money and your children are going hungry."

However, these things were never said before. I saw it with my mother. Her husband would come home and give her whatever [money] he felt like and sometimes he'd arrive really drunk. And my mother would stay with him and find some way to feed us. Since the [revolutionary] process, I've seen how women have changed.

I think what we need to do here is to educate men and make them more aware. Make them understand that women are human beings just like them, that we have the same feelings, but perhaps greater, because we experience the deepest and greatest feelings as mothers. They're fathers, but remember that our feelings are deeper because we carry our children in our wombs. They just put them there. But not all [women] have that feeling, because there are many who get rid of them, who have abortions.

I'm not against abortion. I'm in favour of abortion, because why should you bring a child to suffer here. Maybe you got pregnant after being raped, whether by your husband or in the street, because, as they say, there's not just street rape, there's also rape by husbands. Imagine, that's one of the rights that we must claim.

Promises of peace

I think there should be peace, but other countries shouldn't meddle in our affairs. As Nicaraguans, we're capable of resolving these problems. I'm not saying that I'm a Sandinista or a Contra at the moment. At the moment I'm neutral.

I haven't seen a reconciliation process, not in any sense. On the contrary. As soon as one group calms down, others rise up. We're in the same situation, in the same conditions. With one difference: there's no military service.

My aspirations, in the first place, are for peace in Nicaragua. If there's war, there's no future. Secondly, I'd like to find some way of improving myself as a woman. I feel I have the ability to study, I think women should never say I'm too old to do this or that. We women must always go forwards, forwards. Why should we go backwards, we're not crabs! Look, whether it's a man or a woman, the person who doesn't have aspirations is like the living dead. No, I say, you have to die fighting for something, learning something, finding ways of improving yourself. In all these aspects we women have to take the initiative. There's *machismo* out there, and the more ignorant women are, then the worse men's *machismo* is towards them.

Anonymous   **NIC 17**

This 26-year-old student became involved in political activities through her husband's position in the FSLN.

The war left a lot of casualties, in terms of relationships

He was [involved in logistics] in Nueva Guinea. So we married in 1985 and moved there. At first, [my involvement] came out of the responsibility of being his wife. Back then, I felt afraid of what I was doing—but I had to chip in as his wife. Then later, sure, I overcame the fear and did the work with a passion to participate.

At first, he was participating as a paid member of the support commission, but later, things began getting difficult. They drafted him into the army. From then on I could no longer count on his salary, and it fell on me to take over all the work at home. I remember that they gave him a stipend of 40 *córdobas* and he would come home to give it to me ashamed... but he always went back with some of it in his pack, because I wasn't going to let him give me all 40 *córdobas* and go back with nothing.

No time for tenderness

I'd say [our] relationship was more of friendship than of a couple, because there was no time for us to spend in the tenderness of a couple. Obviously, after the war ended, we got over that. We returned to our normal roles of parents, our normal role as a couple. But truly, during the time of war it is hard to be a couple— it was a time just to take care of ourselves, to share the negative experience that we were going through to help each other forget about it.

"Like a match being struck"

Now that the war is behind us—and I hope it never returns—I realise that the war left a lot of casualties, in terms of relationships. I married a calm and responsible man, and while he is still responsible, he is no longer calm. He is a person more given to violence than to tranquility, if I'm not around to calm him down. He's like a match being struck. I think this is something that the war left with a lot of men and women. They learned how to be *macho*. This wasn't a good education: one learned with kicks and blows and, at times, they transfer these kicks and these blows to their relationships and partners. And even if sometimes they don't give the kick, or the punch, they give the blow with their vocabulary and their actions.

Women who had never had any work experience were forced to work by the war. It forced us women to run our own houses

The government must change its view of women

without the men. The war had two sides and there were as many women suffering over their husbands in the army as women suffering over men who were with the Contras.

About 60% of the women continued with their [new] roles, for two reasons: one is that they realised that they were not just an object in the home, that [they were] not just mothers, not just wives serving their husband's food, taking care of the house... but that they could feel much more productive, participating in the community in other ways. Of course, the remaining percentage didn't want to. Or perhaps it wasn't because they didn't want to, but because they were used to being submissive, and would prefer to continue with the division of labour that is normal in Nicaraguan homes. I think that Nicaraguan society changed a lot with the war, because some woke up, while others preferred to continue in their normal roles.

The role of women

There is a great coverage of the needs of women, but I think it only goes so far. It's only talk... that we women have needs, that we must protect our rights, but in reality, it is in the hands of the government, and they don't do anything. All they do is listen to the media, which covers the problems of women, but does nothing to resolve them. I've heard, for example, that there are various support houses for women, but I don't know of any where the support is totally free. They are services that cost some 400 or 500 *córdobas*: if a woman is beaten by her husband or partner, she might prefer to keep quiet because she doesn't have the 200 or 300 for a meeting with the lawyer. And all these situations prevent women from advancing.

If a woman is fired from her job or mistreated because she is pregnant... [they should make laws] that create [better] conditions for women who are single mothers, or married with children, or want to study. They should create programmes [so] that women won't have to leave their children alone, or leave their jobs at a certain time to study. First the government must begin to change its view of women, because that is where the advancement of Nicaraguan society should begin.

Women and reconciliation

Women have had a lot to do with the work of reconciliation. Many women tried to convince their husbands to return to a peaceful life. Mothers tried to get their sons to come home from the war... and they've finally succeeded. Nicaraguan society had reached a point where we believed that everything could be solved through arms. Reconciliation was not solely the work of the government, but also of families trying to convince and encourage the man to realise that his presence was necessary in the home, that he really should help the woman, because the woman had assumed the role of mother, wife and husband. It began with the smallest step, which was to convince the man of the house, convince the son, the uncle, the cousin, that violence was not the solution. I think this was the greatest task accomplished.

Reconciliation began with the smallest step...

Nohemi   NIC 1

Nohemi, 33, was a messenger for the National Resistance Army but spent much of the conflict in exile in Honduras. She talks here of her return to Nicaragua after the elections in 1990.

They gave us aid for about six months, then they cut it off. We have the plots of land that they gave us, but it's been almost two years and they haven't given us the titles. Yesterday this guy came. He said there'd be a big fair on 16th March—that's when we have the patron saint's day in the village—and that they'd give out the titles then. That's what we're hoping for. Because without titles you can't get loans, and the lands that they are giving out are only good for cattle, not for crops.

[My husband] was going to go [to Costa Rica]. He's a cabinet-maker—but there are very few jobs. But they said they'd give out the titles in February, so I said, "Don't go", because they have to give it to him personally. He's got his passport, but he can't go because of [the titles], he's waiting on this.

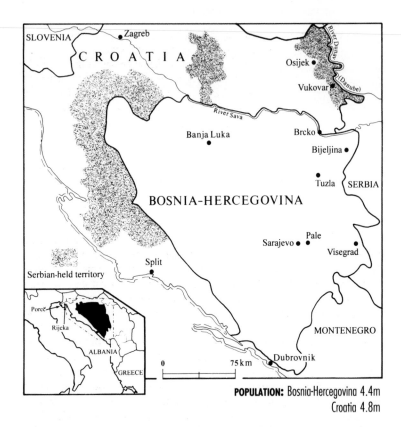

SLOVENIA • Zagreb

C R O A T I A

Osijek •

Vukovar •

River Sava

Banja Luka •

Brcko •

Bijeljina •

Tuzla (SERBIA

BOSNIA-HERCEGOVINA

Pale
Sarajevo • •

Visegrad •

Split

Serbian-held territory

Poreč

Rijeka

MONTENEGRO

ALBANIA

GREECE

0   75 km   Dubrovnik •

River Dunav

(Danube)

POPULATION: Bosnia-Hercegovina 4.4m
Croatia 4.8m

925 Croatian kingdom, joined to Hungary in 11th century **14th century** Bosnian kingdom **1389-1526** Ottoman conquest of the Balkans **1878** Independent kingdom of Serbia **1912-1913** Balkan wars **1918** First Yugoslav state **1941** Invasion by Axis powers; independent state of Croatia under Axis auspices **1941-45** Anti-fascist Partisan/Communist resistance, led by Tito **1945** Defeat of Axis powers; establishment of second Yugoslavia **1974** New constitution gives republics effective sovereignty and right to secede **1980** Tito dies **1990** Multi-party elections in Slovenia, Croatia and Bosnia; referendum for independence in Slovenia **1991** Collective presidency fails to resolve secession crisis; anti-Milošević demonstrations in Belgrade put down by army; referendum for independence in Croatia; Croatia and Slovenia declare independence; Serbian war against Croatia; UN arms embargo **1992** Serbian-Croatian ceasefire; Bosnian referendum for independence; Bosnian people reject EC plan for partition of Bosnia; war in Bosnia

— CROATIA AND BOSNIA —

The war in former Yugoslavia, which broke out in 1991, has caused an estimated 250,000 deaths and 3 million refugees.

In Yugoslavia down the centuries three civilisations pressed against each other—European Christendom, Eastern Orthodox Christendom, and then the Islamic Ottoman empire. The formation of the monarchy of Yugoslavia in 1918, after the collapse of the Ottoman and Hapsburg empires, brought together several peoples, many ethnically related but shaped into "nations" by their separate histories. The Serbs, Croats, Muslim Bosnians, and Montenegrins speak variations of the same Slavonic language; Slovenes, Macedonians, and the smaller numbers of Hungarians and Albanians speak their own languages.

The first Yugoslav state disintegrated at the start of World War Two. Out of the ensuing war—in which atrocities were perpetrated whose memory adds fuel to the present conflict—a new united Yugoslavia was created in 1943 by the Communist party under Tito. It was a republic of eight federal units: these coincided with historic national boundaries, but as many as a quarter of both Serbs and Croatians lived outside their nations' borders.

Tito's one-party, one-leader communist state discouraged "ethnic" identification, and maintained an ethnic balance within the state's structures. Peaceful co-existence was the norm, and Yugoslav identity was promoted, helped by economic success. Tito died in 1980, and was succeeded by a collective presidency. With the loss of his strong hold, suppressed differences began to resurface. In the later 1980s, deterioration of the state-run economy fuelled dissatisfaction and demands for decentralisation; in the absence of any tradition of political parties, it was easy for elites, nervous of losing power in the post-communist era, to inflame and manipulate nationalist emotions to win support.

Slobodan Milošević, who became president of Serbia in 1987, was ambitious to gain control over the whole of Yugoslavia, and willing to use Serbian nationalist emotions to do this. In 1989, in an attempt to gain a majority in the collective presidency, he abolished the autonomy of the two smallest federal units, Vojvodina and Kosovo, and infiltrated the Montenegrin authorities to secure the Montenegrin vote. The consitutional crisis which his ambitions created fuelled widespread unrest: nationalism to match that of Milošević was gaining ground in Slovenia and Croatia, and elections in these two republics in 1990 declared for independence.

The 600,000 Serbs living in Croatia feared for their future as a minority in an ethnically-based state (with reason) and violently opposed secession; this was a pretext for Milošević to start war in June 1991. The Yugoslav People's Army (JNA—by then effectively a Serbian army) was willing to concede victory to Slovenia within 10 days. In Croatia, on the other hand, Serbia's aim was to establish Serbian-populated territories—in effect, to expand the existing boundaries of Serbia. The Serbs occupied one third of Croatian territory. This occupation, monitored by UN forces from January 1992, was marked by "ethnic cleansing", heavy bombardment and seige of towns by the JNA and atrocities by both sides. The new states of Slovenia, Croatia, and Bosnia were recognised by the international community during 1992.

In the 1991 elections, Bosnia-Hercegovina (usually abbreviated to BiH or Bosnia)—made up of a population 44% Bosnian Muslim, 34% Serb and 17% Croatian—voted in three national parties, who formed a tri-national government. Bosnia's President Izetbegović sought UN military deployment, in an attempt to maintain the state's cohesion against the separatist nationalist pressures which were being supported politically and militarily by the Serbian and Croatian state leaders. Their aim was the division of Bosnia into separate ethnically homogenous parts. War erupted in Bosnia in May 1992, resulting in more atrocities including systematic rape, physical destruction, seiges and displacement of civilians of all nationalities, in all directions. None of the international diplomatic attempts to end the war have been accepted by all parties. Serbs gained control of 70% of the country, Croatians 20%, and both groups were still in possession of these gains at the time of writing. Bosnians and those Serbs and Croats who still believe in a multi-ethnic state are squeezed into enclaves, and though they are a numerous and motivated force their efforts to resist have been limited by the international arms embargo introduced in 1992.

Interview collection was coordinated by Dr Neala Schönwald and testimonies gathered by Dr Helena Nakić-Alfirević of the Medical Centre for Human Rights, Zagreb, and Halim Djurković, Melita Talić, and Nadja from the Association of Bosnian Women. Additional testimonies were collected by Nina Pečnik of the NGO Suncokret, which works with the refugee community of Zagreb. With the exception of Katarina, all interviewees are Croatian or Bosnian refugees.

Katarina   CRO 7

Katarina is director of the Centre for Peace, Nonviolence and Human Rights in Osijek, Croatia.

I [maintained] a distance from the period we lived in, having understood quite early on the discrepancy between what was proclaimed, the ideas of socialism and communism, and the way we actually lived.

Non-violent action for peace

I experienced the beginning of the war as a very painful [process of] consciousness-raising. For me, it was like [receiving] personal news about my own responsibility, since my passivity had probably contributed to the fact that today we have a society like this one. It was a painful experience. Then I quickly started working for peace—without any previous knowledge of NGOs or pacifism... actually [I was] ignorant in terms of politics and social engagement.

I joined some mothers who were on their way to **Belgrade**. It was one of my first [experiences of] non-violent action and a profound one. The mothers, who called themselves the "Bulwark of Love", were going to Belgrade to protest and to demand their children back. Their sons were serving compulsory military service in the Federal Yugoslav Army (JNA). The action had started when the so-called war in Slovenia broke out. These mothers were laughed at for their request, so the initial movement was destroyed. But it inspired mothers in Croatia, Bosnia-Hercegovina and Macedonia. [They wanted] to make sure their sons did military service in their respective republics. This was a revolutionary idea which would have ruined JNA's plan and prevented this awful war.

Sabotage

I don't know exactly how many were there, maybe around 3,000 women. Since I was not a directly interested party—because I was not a mother of a child who was or could be drafted—and since I was not an organiser, I was able to observe what was happening. I saw carefully planned attempts to undermine the whole action, ranging from obstruction to stirring up discontent among women. It was probably done by the military secret service or **KOS**. In the end, these women were completely broken. For example, we spent three to four days in a big military barracks out of town. Women were dragged there and not allowed to meet other women who were waiting for them in the centre of Belgrade. Not a single piece of information could get through. But the *agents provocateurs* were let in and they spoke in favour of the Federal Army. The microphone was switched off and 2,000 women had to hold a gathering while the music was turned on full blast. Then some internal disagreement erupted between Macedonian women and some others, and so on, and so on. Anyway, when we got out of there, it was no longer a united movement. At the end, handsome young men were let in and told us they liked being in the army, asking us why we had come and saying that if their mothers had come, they would have been terribly disappointed. It was then I realised what a horribly powerful machine the Federal Army was, that it had a terrible strength apart from weapons. It [waged] a sophisticated psychological war.

On the other hand, pro-Croatian propaganda had already started in Croatia. The women came back disappointed, destroyed, having achieved nothing. But they were welcomed by the media as heroes who had to be given a new direction to benefit Croatia. The movement ended up [getting involved] with some propaganda activities by mothers in Western Europe. In this way the mothers probably contributed to faster recognition of Croatia, but their movement had completely lost its original purpose.

The need for a clear goal

I also joined the convoy for **Dubrovnik** in November 1991. This was also a significant experience which helped me to realise how important it is to know what the goal is and to work on it. A non-violent action cannot be spontaneous. It can start spontaneously but it must build up a vision. [It requires] all your energy and constant work. It gives you direction and clarity in vague situations, and helps you to know what has to be done. It's amazing how quickly the main idea can be lost when the goal is not clear.

This convoy sailing from Rijeka to Dubrovnik brought together many artists and public figures but also a lot of ordinary people [including] elderly women. [But] it was like an assembly of lunatics who were heading somewhere but nobody knew where or why. I was thinking of going back because I came from Osijek, which was under siege and being shelled constantly. I was concerned about my children. This trip seemed like exposing myself to unnecessary perils, as if I had not had enough troubles already. But in the end I decided it was good that I was there and I went on. A large number of small boats joined the convoy. [These people] could have got hurt in a storm, or killed or injured if the Yugoslav Navy had attacked. It was an impressive picture—a huge ferry boat and all those little boats with brave people on board. The arrival in Dubrovnik seemed like a kiss [of life] to a dead city.

We must not wait for peace in order to do something

[In Dubrovnik there] was total apathy, the citizens even had a negative attitude towards the people that arrived. They were saying: "You will leave in the same way as you have come, and we shall have to stay here." [The action] helped revive the citizens' spirits and also maintain sea access to Dubrovnik. It turned into a prolonged non-violent action which helped Dubrovnik to survive not only physically, but also spiritually—the spirit of the town has been preserved. But I could also see how easily the entire action could be turned into private, personal interests. People all went on that trip out of goodwill, but [when] you see 10,000 people in Split welcoming you, you just cannot resist. You fall into the power trap.

So I learnt how extremely important is to work on the vision. We have to think it through seriously. We must not wait for peace in order to do something. Dubrovnik was without electricity, the hospitals could not function and someone had the idea that ship engines could be used as power units. The creative response means not accepting the war passively, but to trick it.

Osijek under siege

The horror was all over the city. I worked in Civil Defence, in public shelters. When I returned from Dubrovnik I decided that something had to be done in these shelters, not so much just as a response to the war, but also as a creation of peace in different circumstances. I don't know how to explain this. Our peace activists started [saying things like]: "Don't forget to water your plants", "Don't forget to talk to your family", "When you come home from your work as a peace activist, don't forget to take a hot bath." If you forget to do [these everyday things], it may happen that you lose [a sense of] your real life and you'll be only fighting for peace.

Fear emptied the city in snatches

I started organising playrooms, reading rooms, hairdressers' shops and holy mass in the shelters. I was pleasantly surprised when I realised that all these things were already there, in their early stages. For example, we wanted to help teachers who lived in shelters to lead a more normal life, so we decided to organise schools, and then we found out that lessons were already going on in six shelters. Nurses also started doing their job in shelters, people started organising themselves.

Facing the fear

When the war started, the first phase I had to go through was facing the fear. I knew I had to face it, look at it and not run away from it or repress it. I had a terrible fear of physical suffering, killing and disability which lasted one week. I looked at my fear prayerfully, without asking protection from God. I wished that whatever it was I had to go through, I could go through with Him. I was working hard on my fear and then it was no longer a problem for me to stay in Osijek.

This fear emptied the city in snatches and those who remained built an incredibly solid community of resistance and solidarity. When heavy shellings stopped and people started coming back, those who remained and went through terrible situations found themselves frustrated because they could not cope with the loss of that solidarity. A kind of veteran syndrome... People who used to leave the city at weekends to visit their families were not able to feel the same solidarity with their families or relatives and they would come back to their real community in their beseiged city.

At the beginning of the war, intellectuals in Osijek started thinking about what could be done for peace, against the war. Two of us got involved in peace activities. We had to recognise that we could not deal with the war, we could not stop it or change its course. But this did not make our responsibility any the less. What we wanted to do was to work on building up civil society and becoming a kind of a messenger to the authorities, pointing out the needs of the whole community.

Breaking the spiral of hatred

We got in touch with people from the anti-war campaign in Zagreb, they gave us addresses of people from abroad who then brought to us certain skills and knowledge and, most importantly, their moral support. We had to find out how to show our resistance towards the violence. It was not only the violence imposed on us from outside, it was also spreading among us, within our community—in response to this external violence. We wanted to break this spiral of hatred, revenge, fear...

First we overcame our fear and then we started working to abolish the division of people caused by violence. We refused to be nationalistic in orientation, although it seemed quite logical that priority had to be given to the defence of the nation when the nation was attacked. So we focused on defending basic human, universal values and in doing this we were opening ourselves out to all those who accepted these values. We were experiencing a sort of reconciliation process with people of other nationalities.

Once this process is started it logically leads you to perceive a person as an individual, even when he or she belongs to the nation that started the aggression against yours. It is not that you "give" this person all the rights you have, or that you "treat" her or him as your equal: you are equal.

In this way we were building a non-violent community which was growing rapidly. Within a year we had 30 active members and over 30 supporters. All our activities today are oriented towards creating the community in an alternative way. For example, the coordinators of many projects for displaced persons are Serbs and they, displaced persons themselves, are working with displaced persons who are mainly Croats. It required a lot of hard work to convince the authorities and local administration to admit these people as coordinators. But we just had to go through all that. Also, teachers who are Serbs and cannot get a job are working in our children's projects. A Serbian nurse who lost her hospital job is running our women's support project.

Marica   CRO 3

Marica, 30, lived in an underground shelter for three months while Vukovar was bombed.

There were hundreds of us, from the building and surrounding [streets]. Every day JNA planes bombed the city. Occasionally, we went out of the shelter to see what was going on outside. After a few days most of the stores were closed and the last time I bought food was at the end of September. Besides bombs and shells, you could die from the snipers. You couldn't leave the shelter without hearing the bullets whistling.

We had food, only we lacked bread. We cooked on a gas stove. We had no electricity. At the beginning we had water, brought to us in cisterns. We had to boil it to avoid infectious diseases. Later, they didn't come any more and we had to go to the River Danube or collect rainwater. But the rainwater wasn't drinkable because the *chetniks* kept using war gases and blister gases. When we had soap, we washed our clothes but later there was no soap.

In the shelter we were all united and helped each other. [Then] a man came—later we discovered he was a Serb—to spy on us. This building used to be a post office, so information could be sent [out from it]. We watched that man. We didn't want him to send certain messages. As time passed, it became more and more unbearable in the shelter. Autumn was approaching and it was growing colder. We went out in pairs to collect firewood.

"How would you feel?"

[After the fall of Vukovar, the Serbs] started to take away our people, threatening us with machine-guns. They took us to a barracks where we were imprisoned for 10 days. I was raped there.

They ordered me to take off my clothes. I refused [but] they threatened me with a knife. One by one, they raped me on the floor. There were always two men always holding me down. When the fifth came, I asked him: "How would you feel if someone treated your mother, sister or daughter like this?" He hesitated, as if he had lost the desire, and opened the door. He asked the others if there was anyone else nearby who would like to do it too. There was nobody, so they left.

Hopes of healing

Of course I want to go back. I love my town, because it's a very special town. I love the people that I grew up with. I left everything in Vukovar. I know I would often be reminded [of having been raped] but the love towards my town is stronger and it would be possible to overcome it. Besides, I have two kids. I think that taking care of them could help me not to think about it. We can rebuild the town. We can do it, if only we can get back.

The blame [for the mass rapes] can be equally placed on individuals and on the politics in general. I think it was the will of individuals, but also the strategy of Serbian politics to perform "ethnic cleansing" of the non-Serbian population in Croatia.

Some [women] can talk about [their ordeal] while others find it hard. The reasons are numerous and I can understand them. For women who were mothers and who, up till then, lived in harmonious families, it is hard to stand because of their hurt husbands and because of their children. And young, unmarried girls try to hide it because they hope to have a family in the future.

Although our people are very conservative, these [raped]

women are accepted and understood. [The scale of] rape in this war has been so massive that it ceased to be a taboo. And, besides rape, other very serious crimes happened... massacres, torture. The most important thing for women is to be well accepted in their families. Unfortunately, I know of some cases of women who got pregnant after being raped and were imprisoned until it was too late to perform an abortion. They had to give birth to those poor babies. Their husbands' reactions varied. Most of [the women] gave away the child for adoption and continued to live within the family. But a few of the husbands didn't want to accept them after [what had happened].

The scale of rape in this war has been so massive that it ceased to be a taboo

Eva   CRO 8

Eva is from Ilok, a Croatian village near the border with Serbia, now under Serb control. She lives in a centre for displaced people in Zagreb.

The hardest thing [when war broke out] was the fear and the panic. We thought only about escaping. There was nowhere to go except to jump into the Danube. When we finally escaped and when our buses crossed the Croatian border, there were people waiting for us. The politicians spoke to us, and we were given hot tea and sandwiches. It was a great relief.

They told us we would be back home in two weeks, so we didn't see the tragedy that was happening. When we realised, my husband cried. Nobody told me anything. I was asking a lot—anyone who came. The situation here [Zagreb] was very hard. [There was] the struggle to survive—I had to find a job—and [the anxiety] about my mother.

Death of parents

Just this year we [learnt] what happened. My parents were killed in front of their house. The so-called "White Eagles" (**chetniks**) demanded that all the bodies collected were to be taken to their camp. I still don't know where they are buried. There are several mass graves around the village.

It was the anniversary of their death some days ago. Only recently were they pronounced dead officially. Witnesses were hard to find. Some of them were in another part of the country. The man who had collected my parents' dead bodies was in a village near Virovitica. I feel better [now that I know what happened], but it is very hard. I would rather they had died in a shell explosion.

We did not think we were leaving for ever

I recall the last holiday we celebrated with my parents. My mother was crying, almost as if she knew we were together for the last time. A kind of fear was present in the midst of the celebrations after the Croatian Democratic Union won the elections in our villages. They should not have celebrated in the way they did. Those barbecued oxen and loud parties were perhaps excessive. Our hearts were full of joy and we were in ecstasy. Freedom had come at last, we could sing out our songs. But we had strange feelings of suspicion and fear. After the Yugoslav Federal Army attacked the police station in Ilok, the men began to keep guard. My husband, too.

Attack on Croatia

Then the attack happened. The tanks were on the roads, the aeroplanes in the sky. We were gathering the last crops in the fields and gardens. There were so many tomatoes, onions, potatoes and beans, it was indescribable. It has to be that way, I believe, when evil or war is coming. We saw the aeroplanes attacking Vukovar while we worked in the fields. The explosions were so loud as the bombs fell. The horror was already present. But we [kept on] working. I was cooking tomatoes—there were 100 litres of tomato juice in bottles—and storing the potatoes and beans. We planned to send some of it to Vukovar to help people.

[When we were forced to flee] we did not think we were leaving for ever, so I took only a few things with me, including something to remind me of life in Ilok. Winter was coming so I took boots and coats, and a few vests and shirts. Among all the embroideries, I chose the last ones my mother had made—I couldn't leave them there.

They checked us all with detectors in case were carrying weapons, the women and children separately from the men. We stood in a long queue from seven in the morning till four in the afternoon. They checked about 12,000 people.

Adjustment and loss

My husband worked at Savric (a furniture factory) from the first day we came [to Zagreb]. The children went to school with the others. I was working too, we did everything we could to survive. We got this room by chance. It was not designed for [a family].

The children? They became used to the circumstances bit by bit. My son has his friends, fellow pupils from the school in Ilok. Now they go out in the evenings together. My youngest daughter has adjusted to the new way of life, too, and she goes to secondary school. They have adjusted, they're not destroyed. They didn't

suffer as much as I did. My elder daughter says to me, "I had my *I don't*
childhood. When I see these children in the collective centre, I am *know how*
happy to remember my childhood. I still [remember and] feel the *to forget*
joy of playing in my own yard, while these poor children will never
know that feeling."

The pressure of history

The worst thing for me is that I carry that pressure from my
childhood. My father went through all these things, and I
remember it from my childhood. He was a boy of 14 when [the
chetnik militia] killed his father, in 1944. They killed his father, who
wasn't guilty of anything, just because he was a member of
Matica. My grandfather was 34. There was the so-called National
Committee, mostly Serbs, in the village and they put my
grandfather on the [black] list, just as today's committee put my
father on their list. Can you imagine how I feel?

My parents didn't bring me up [to feel] hatred. I had a Serbian
boyfriend, who was nice. Then my father heard about it and
shouted and railed against it. He said, "I've already given them
enough of my blood." I couldn't even think about seeing the boy
after that. It was the first time I learned about that hatred. I felt it.
There is no need to tell my children about it, they know it
themselves. Relationships between the two nations are impossible,
too much harm was done. My father had to forgive the people he
was living among, and he surely did. The men who killed his father
were around him. He had to wrap the blanket around his father's
dead body when he was a young boy. And now it's happening all
over again.

Now when these changes came, I remembered the events [of
my childhood] and thought I should say something about them for
the newspapers. My father used to [talk about] the Second World
War and what [Serbians] did to Croatians at that time. They used
to throw people from the Serbian church tower on to the palisade,
so that they were impaled. He told a journalist the names of the
people involved and the truth about those events. Everything he
talked about was Croatian, and denying [one's Croatian identity]
was the greatest crime for him. They found him guilty of being an
ustasha. What happened to him keeps me brave, so when they talk
about forgiving... All our homes were there, my parents' home
[was there]. I cannot imagine us there again. Just suppose all these
horrible things happened again. I don't know how to forget. I
simply cannot forgive and forget.

We used to live together with our neighbours as well as the

"The pressure of history": for some generations, war seems an endless cycle
Marc French/Panos Pictures

people in Vukovar. You should hear Croatians speaking about sharing their last pieces of dry bread with their Serbian neighbours when they were hiding in the shelters. When Vukovar fell to the enemy, all the Serbian people forgot the suffering and began to denounce their Croatian neighbours. If Zagreb fell—dear God, don't let it happen—the same thing would happen, I am sure.

Not one of them showed a bit of solidarity towards us. Why? I mean those Serbians who are still living in Ilok. They haven't felt the need to say we've been treated unjustly. Even the people who are living in our homes now do not feel uncomfortable.

The displaced: "Our relationships are terrible"

[In the centre] we are not close at all. Some of our relatives are here... my husband's brother with his wife. I prefer being alone. My husband says it would be better for me to talk with people. It's somehow too much for me. People are greedy, wanting material things and just money. We were very close once, living in the same neighbourhood, having coffee together every day, meeting in the yard. But this life is different. Some of my neighbours are also here, but our relationships are terrible. Everybody is so selfish. Maybe it's the normal behaviour in a situation like ours.

How can we live together again when we argue about using the kitchen? There is so much rowing and swearing about a packet of flour or sugar from the humanitarian aid [agency]. They shout: "All you do is steal and rob. This man gets everything all the time, and you don't give me anything!" All the things given to us now cannot be compared with our property at home. I can't lose anything [more] now. Fights about a litre of oil!

How would my father have stood this? When I remember his great affection towards his cows, I think he wouldn't have been able to bear this kind of life here. I would be happy if only they had died naturally, if only they had not suffered so much. He used to drink rather a lot, he had brandy and wine of his own. He could not live this way. In the end, this was the way God wanted.

A better life?

[Change] will only be possible when the generation which did all these things to us dies out and the new young generation comes— like it happened in Germany. Deep in my soul I believe it is going to happen some day.

I would like to work in the garden, as I used to at home. We have some relatives here in Zagreb. They have gardens and I went there with my husband. But the earth is not as fertile as ours. Anyway, it was good for me.

When I worked at the Ministry, it was an enormous change for me. The hardest thing was to come and go at the exact time. I used to work in the wide open fields and there was no one around, it was quiet. We had a close bond with the earth. Now I have to work so much that I can't even do any embroidery.

It's hard to get along with other (local) women at work. You

Change will only be possible when the generation which did this dies out

Friends were shooting at us... people with whom I have shared sadness and happiness should hear some of their conversations. They dream of clothes, making plans, going to the seaside, and then I feel so miserable. One of them asked me whether I would like to buy an apartment in Zagreb. She knew my husband had gone to Germany. She said it was rather cheap—"only" 70,000 **marks** for 60 square metres—and very fine.

Anonymous   BOS 5

This 43-year-old refugee is from Sarajevo.

The war was going on in Croatia. We all were witnesses to the terrors inflicted on Vukovar. We felt disgust at the massive killings. We hated to see **Dubrovnik** destroyed. We heard about the brutalities in Bijeljina and Visegrad [in Bosnia]. The war had started in our country. We asked ourselves in astonishment: "What's going on? Why?" We heard stories that Sarajevo would be attacked, and that Bosnia-Hercegovina would be attacked once it had been recognised internationally.

We, the inhabitants of Sarajevo, didn't believe it. I mean, why Sarajevo, [where] Eastern and Western culture [had] melted into one? It's a beautiful town in a valley, surrounded by mountains covered with leafy forests. Scented meadows in summer... mountain streams. Now, these mountains have become a nest of evil.

"The soul hurts"

I would like to say something about my so-called colleagues, about my so-called friends. After the first attacks on Sarajevo, [Serbs] left the town and went to **Pale**, to Banja Luka [a Serb-controlled town] and elsewhere... My friends were shooting at me, at us. Do you know the feeling when the soul hurts? It grieves me to the very heart. I suffered deeply because of that. A lot of them really were my good friends, people who used to help me, with whom I have shared both sadness and happiness. I lost them for ever, in the most unacceptable way. I went through the biggest human dilemma.

Fearless kids

The sound of shells and explosions drove us crazy, as well as the sound of the multi-rocket-launchers. But the sound of machine-guns which went on 24 hours a day and the whistle of those single bullet shots was terrifying.

Can you believe it that the kids were more calm than the adults? My son, who was nine at that time, didn't show any fear at all.

Whenever I panicked and pushed him into some doorway, he would calm me down: "Didn't you hear that the shell flew over this building? It will fall elsewhere". And that's how it was. In the moments of lull we would go out. Children would collect pieces of bombs and shells and used bullets. My son had a collection—he was sad when I didn't let him take it with him when we escaped from Sarajevo.

I cannot enjoy the smell of flowers any more

[My husband and son] were at home [while I was at work]. I was sick with fear, wondering whether I would find them alive when I came home. They were wondering if I would ever come home. I was very frightened all the time. I felt permanent pain and cramp in my stomach. Whenever I got home I started to cry. My nerves would break down.

We used to gather around one small radio, listening to the news and waiting for a miracle. We thought it was a nightmare and that we would wake up. But the dead bodies, wounded and crippled people, were real. And the killers were our former friends and neighbours.

Leaving Sarajevo

Although I knew it was the only way to save my son's life, it was terrible to leave behind my beloved town, husband, friends and to go with one bag into the unknown. The convoy brought us to Split. I was in a state of shock. It was a nice peaceful day. No shelling, no bombing. The stores were full of food and clothes. I saw fruit and vegetables...

In May 1993 I came back to Zagreb. Then I regulated our refugee status. I felt a panic about the future. I couldn't eat, couldn't sleep at night for thinking what to do. It was another kind of living hell. I got sick and it lasted for a month.

I am just floating through life. The days pass, one after another. The months pass and I don't even notice the change of seasons. I cannot enjoy the smell of flowers any more.

[My son] likes Zagreb. He has become very independent. He goes to school and is an excellent student. With me he could easily bear another adventure into the unknown. He could go around the world. He is learning foreign languages "just in case", he says, "I might need them". He is a very intelligent boy who had the strength to help me, comfort me and encourage me in the moments of crises. Without his support I don't know if I would be alive today. He is the meaning of my life, the only bright spot in it. Because of him I have to endure, and give him as much as I can. I have to fight for his happiness in the future.

Anonymous   BOS 6

This Muslim refugee, whose family, like many others, intermarried with Croats and Serbs, now finds her relatives have scattered throughout Europe and the Middle East.

We were very ambitious. I was a professor of chemistry. Just after we had opened the [first] pharmacy, I said on the local TV that we were planning to cover the whole area of northeastern Bosnia with a chain of pharmacy shops.

We were all convinced that [war] wouldn't happen in Bosnia. Muslims, Croats and Serbs mixed—both in marriage and in everyday life. They lived in the same buildings, led the same lives.

"We felt an evil silence"

On the first day of **Bajram**, the TV reported that Serbian soldiers had entered Bijeljina. A girl was raped in a mosque, in the presence of her grandfather. The people praying in [another] mosque were slaughtered. Events became more and more terrifying.

My husband proposed that we go immediately to our [home] town. On the road we saw long lines of vehicles, waiting to cross the River Sava and escape to Croatia. A large and magnificent bridge had fallen, its iron structure sticking out of the water, like a wounded beast. We heard stories about the bridge being mined and then struck by lightening [which] activated the mines. Nobody believes that story. We know that the destruction of the bridge was to stop the army from Tuzla crossing the river and entering Croatia. People seem to be very confused by these events.

All the way to our town we felt an evil silence. We passed deserted villages. There was no one to be seen, not even chickens in the yards. We met a lot of buses on the road and read the destinations: Frankfurt, Munich... all German towns.

In our town we witnessed a few peaceful rallies against the war in Bosnia. On the TV our president, Izetbegović, kept repeating: "The war in Bosnia is not possible!" That evening I was alone at home. The phone rang. It was my friend from Bijeljina. She was crying: "Run away, as soon as possible! All the things you've heard about the events in Bijeljina are a hundred times worse!"

Flight

The TV was showing horrible images from Bijeljina and killings of civilians in Sarajevo. My daughter and I packed. We planned to go to Belgrade (capital of Serbia) to my husband's cousins. Their grandmother was Serbian and we hoped that this would save us.

We still didn't know who was the aggressor in Bosnia. When we were about to leave my daughter cried, saying she didn't want to leave her father because they would "kill him like the men on TV". My husband cried as well, so we decided to stay. Two days later we decided to go by bus to Ljubljana (capital of Slovenia). Our business partner was living there and he had invited us to stay.

It wasn't safe to drive a car. Anybody could stop you, take your car, rob you or kill you. My husband decided [we should] go by bus. At the bus station there was a large crowd. The bus couldn't leave because a line of army vehicles was passing by. I looked at the soldiers. I was thinking, thinking and watching. They were not young, but older and bearded, with weapons around their shoulders and necks. Some of them raised three fingers high in the air. This was the well-known Serbian sign.

That was the first time I felt really frightened of that army. My husband and I are intellectuals, middle-aged. Now I ask myself: "How could we be so naive? Couldn't we have foreseen that something bad could happen to us, too? How come the example from Croatia didn't tell us anything?" With one suitcase and a 1,000 *marks* we left town. Oh, my God! We thought we'd be back in a week! We thought everything would calm down. We didn't believe that the war would go on and on.

Refugee status

My parents, sisters and their families, as well as other inhabitants of Posavina who were not obliged to join the BiH army, were evacuated overnight to the Croatian side of the river. The Croatians cordially accepted refugees because they had been in the same situation. They knew how it felt to be in a war. All the men stayed to defend [their] area. They were not organised. Only a few men had pistols or hunting rifles.

The status of a "refugee" is given automatically when you cross the River Sava and enter Croatia. We were given a refugee file-card with personal data. My younger sister told me that as soon as they arrived in Croatia, her little son got a high fever. They took him to a doctor. The doctor shook his head because he was concerned about the convulsions which the child was suffering from. He wrote [the diagnosis] down on a card and that's when my sister saw for the first time the word "refugee" next to her name. She took it hard, almost harder than the child's illness.

In the house where we were placed we met two girls who had escaped from Sarajevo. They told us about the horrors in the town. They used to do "night duty" in their flat, keeping water boiling on

I lost my homeland and my personality

the stove because this was the only "weapon" they possessed. It was just in case *chetniks* broke in.

Our Slovenian friend warned us not to answer the phone because his business partners didn't like hearing any language except Slovenian or another "European language". Naturally, they didn't think that our language was European, too. That was the first shock. Afterwards, we were informed that we had to report, as foreign citizens, to the Centre for Social Work. There we received an official document for refugees. They explained to us our status, rights, and how to get humanitarian help. That's the moment when I became aware of my loss. I lost my homeland and my personality. In return, I gained a doubtful future and a lot of misery about Bosnia. It was so big it couldn't fit into my heart.

During the summer my whole family stayed in Poreč. My husband, daughter and I went to Germany. [My husband's] brother is a doctor, a rich man. My husband wanted to discuss the future of our numerous family because most of them were still in Bosnia. His brother left home a long time ago and he couldn't or wouldn't understand the burden [of anxiety]. So we returned to Poreč a few days later. The family grew even bigger. Another brother-in-law came with two daughters. His wife, a Serbian, stayed with her mother in Belgrade. Their son joined the BiH Army and doesn't want to hear about his mother.

We "celebrated" New Year's Eve in Zagreb in the house of my brother-in-law, [the one] who lives in Germany. There were 18 members of his family staying there, mainly coming from Brcko, one of the first towns to be occupied. That evening only the children seemed to be happy. I remember the words of a Russian writer: "All happy families look alike, but each unhappy family is unhappy in its own way". I remembered the celebration the year before. We were in Egypt, in Cairo. We didn't imagine that the next year we would be refugees. My previous life now seems a distant past.

Mothers lost and gained

One day I had a phone call from my town in Bosnia. It was the mother of a soldier who had had an operation on his head here in Zagreb. She called me because she didn't know anyone [else] in Zagreb. She asked me to visit him and help him. So, I went there and met a lot of young people from Bosnia—wounded, invalids. My new friend had been wounded in the head. His memories are weak, they've faded away. I visit him often, get drugs for him, bring him coffee and cakes. His mother calls me from time to time.

Once she said: "You know, when you come back, you will have a *We lived in* second mother here!" My eyes fill with tears when I remember *constant fear* that many people have lost their mothers while I have gained another one.

Rabija   BOS 1

A 25-year-old Bosnian Muslim, Rabija now lives in a Zagreb refugee camp.

I learned to write first in Cyrillic script and not until three years later in Roman script. In the fourth grade of elementary school, we Muslims were forced to learn Russian although nobody wanted it. Non-Serbian kids who had problems with learning were treated as if they were retarded, expelled from everyday tuition and put in "special" classes. When the war was declared, first in Croatia, then in Bosnia-Hercegovina, the situation rapidly became tense. Muslim and Croatian kids went to school frightened and came back in tears because they were threatened by Serbian children, and even by Serbian teachers. Some Muslim kids were beaten all over. Little by little, the kids started to drop out of classes. Employed adults were dismissed on a massive scale, [many] without being given their salary. Serbian neighbours constantly threatened to burn our houses, mosques... to kill us all. We lived in constant fear.

"A living hell"

The attack [on our village] began with houses being set on fire, starting from the outskirts [and moving] towards the centre. People were running in all directions. We were looking through the window and saw clouds of thick, black smoke. The heat was unbearable, but we sat helplessly inside the house, awaiting the worst. It was senseless trying to run away because the living hell was everywhere.

I saw tanks near the house. The soldiers were wearing masks, uniforms, boots, cockades. They were armed, hundreds of them, crawling in all directions. My mother-in-law asked me what was happening. I looked at her without saying a word and took the baby in my arms. **Chetniks** were drinking, smashing bottles, battering on doors, firing machine-guns, breaking into houses. I heard them singing songs. I remember one in particular—I have heard it a hundred times since: "Who is saying, who is lying: Serbia is small? It is not, it is not. We made war three times before. We shall make it again and defeat them all."

They were shouting: "Is anybody in the house?" We did not

They raped us, always in groups, all night long dare respond. They shouted again, demanding the men in the house. I went out and stood at the door but did not say that my father-in-law was inside. I saw another group of *chetniks* on the road. They were dragging an old man, a neighbour. He could hardly walk or breathe. They were forcing him to walk faster and kept kicking him, beating him with gun barrels and sticks on the head and on the body. Then the old man fell. The soldiers lost patience and fired at him. I turned my head. I could not watch. He was left lying on the road. I started to walk towards him but two *chetniks* held me back. They stepped inside [our house]. We were ordered to hand over all our jewellery and money. They left with my father-in-law.

They stopped in front of the next-door house and took the neighbour out. Both men had to lie down. For about half an hour five *chetniks* beat them all over. They were laughing and, in between the kicks, "offering" them cigarettes. Then they ordered them to move on. About 15 minutes later we saw our neighbour coming back with a *chetnik*. In front of his house, the poor man was ordered to kneel down and they shot him in the head. We heard screams from the house. His wife and daughters buried him in the garden. Three days later we heard that my father-in-law had been killed. Some acquaintances had buried his body in the forest and brought us his ID card covered in blood. I still keep it.

[Later] when I ended up in the camp at Trnopolje I heard from a boy who knew my husband that he had seen three dead bodies, in the woods next to the brook, beaten and disfigured. He thought one of them might have been my husband, but he wasn't sure.

"No strength to talk about it"

I was raped almost every day, by groups. And many other girls and women were raped in that house. We were imprisoned, we couldn't go out. There was never enough food. I was always hungry, I could not feed my baby. They even forbade us to drink water and, besides that, the summer heat was unbearable.

They came almost every evening, sometimes at night. They boozed all night long, singing, celebrating the "victory" and then, dead drunk, used to take us one by one into the next room or sometimes into one of the empty houses in the vicinity. They raped us, always in groups, all night long. Always the same ones, 10 of them or so. When I was forced to go, I left my baby with my mother-in-law. She watched helplessly as they dragged me off. The hardest thing for me was the fact that she knew about it all.

We've never talked about it. Besides that, she is suffering

anyway because she doesn't know if her son, my husband, is alive. *We've never* We are wondering if is true that he was killed. It is hard to live with *talked* her. We went through hell together but the worst thing is that *about it* neither of us has enough strength to talk about it. [It's] as if this situation makes me feel guilty for all the bad things that have happened to us. I presume that to some extent she feels pity for me, but also that her sorrow over the son she has lost is far stronger. She will never understand my situation, all I've lived through and what I'm feeling now. We don't talk much [at all]. She mainly looks after my child. My sister-in-law, who also lives with us in the refugee camp, experienced the same [ordeal] though she wasn't with us. I think she is able to understand me better although I rarely talk with her about it.

Sabina   BOS 2

Sabina, 24, is from Bosnia but is now in a refugee camp in Zagreb.

About 4,000 people lived in [my village], mostly Muslims, a smaller number of Serbs and even fewer Croats. Around our village there were a few Serbian villages. Relationships between us were good. We associated with each other, celebrated holidays together, often married each other. There was no evidence of misunderstandings or hate.

It was obvious that Serbs had always been more involved in political [and public] life, especially in state services, while male Muslims and Croats were often forced to take temporary work in foreign countries because they couldn't find jobs here. Nobody ever spoke about it. [It was as] if everyone was aware of it but no one dared to expose it in public.

The outbreak of war

The situation changed rapidly when Croatia went to war. We all knew that the war would reach us, too, but nobody foresaw its magnitude. I remember, when the fighting was going on in Croatia, the **chetniks** were coming in their uniforms and walking around the village saying they were going to "free Croatia from its enemies". They were looting there and their wives came to resell the stolen goods. Nobody wanted to buy [the plunder] because we knew where it came from.

On 22 May 1992, the *chetniks'* infantry, tanks and army carriers reached our village. They broke into houses in groups. They all wore masks, army uniforms, army boots, cockades on their heads.

Nobody was allowed to talk, move, cry, not even mourn

Males between 14 and 16 were killed instantly. Kids were asked about their older brothers and fathers and they were beaten. I saw them pulling one young man, they made him imitate a sheep. They struck him and then killed him. I saw how they tortured a group of four men and then showered them with bullets.

"I wanted to be dead"

Two *chetniks* forced my younger sister [aged 17] to enter the house, took her to the basement and raped her. I could only listen to her screams. Then they went to the neighbour's house, and came back after 30 minutes, this time with a girl from the neighbourhood [aged 14] and one from another village. They ordered me, my sister and those two girls to go to the basement with them and three men took turns to rape us. When I tried to fight them, one man slashed my lower leg. You can see the scar. Two men held me down while the third raped me. And then they swapped over. I don't know how long they were doing it because I almost fainted. I don't want to talk about it any more.

When they were done with me, it was my sister's turn. She had watched what they did to me but I was told to leave. It was even harder listening [to the screams] because I couldn't help. For the first time in my life I wanted to be dead.

In the evening the *chetniks* left the village. We went out of the house. Everywhere, around the houses, in the yards, in the gardens, on the fields, on the road, there were dead bodies. I knew them all. They were my relatives, cousins, friends, neighbours, acquaintances. I felt the ground moving under me. It was summer... strong heat. The smell of blood filled the place.

For five days the *chetniks* forbade us to bury the bodies. After that it took us, the survivors, two days to bury them. They were stinking, worms were crawling over them and flies buzzing around them. On 29 June the *chetniks* came again. They ordered us to leave our homes.

"Destroying the soul of a nation"

About 300 of us ended up in the concentration camp called Trnopolje. Thousands of people were already there. Women and children were separated from the men. The living conditions were terrible. During the day [things] seemed to be calm but at night we heard shooting. And they used to take dozens of young girls and women, and rape them all night long. They were killing kids and adults with electric shocks. Nobody was allowed to talk, move, cry, not even mourn over somebody. I was surrounded by blank faces, faces like masks.

I have no explanation for [the massive incidence of rape]. I don't know why. [But] I think it was planned in advance and intended to destroy the soul of a nation. At first, talking [about it] gave me some relief. But, as time passes by, I feel less and less like talking. I think it would be the best for me to try to forget it all... well, as much as I can. I know that is going to be very hard. Life goes on, I am still very young and I have to think about my future.

Anonymous   BOS 9

A Bosnian refugee whose husband went missing in 1992.

The children were asking for their father, getting up at night and crying. Everyone was crying. I was living in a classroom with 45 people—women, children, the wounded. My younger daughter used to want to open the door, saying that her dad was coming to us. The older one made drawings of him, bending her head over the paper, hiding it from me. I just cried and cried. The advice given by women who had been through the same experience did not help me. It seemed that they bore it more easily, or it only appeared like that to me. They were telling me that I must fight, that I must be strong, that I was not the only one who had experienced this. But in vain. They did not calm me down.

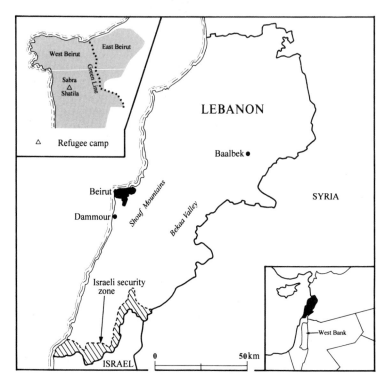

△ Refugee camp

HUMAN DEVELOPMENT INDEX (UNDP): 103 (medium)
POPULATION: 3.5m (plus 400,000 Palestinians)
FEMALE LITERACY: 71%
FEMALE LIFE EXPECTANCY: 70.1 years

1920 French mandate for Lebanon and Syria **1926** Creation of Lebanese Republic **1943** Independence **1948** Establishment of Israel; influx of Palestinian refugees to Lebanon **1958** First Civil War **1967** Israel occupies Palestinian West Bank; more refugees to Lebanon **1969** Cairo agreement gives PLO rights of operation in Lebanon **1970** Influx of Palestinian refugees from Jordan **1975** Second Civil War begins **1978** Israeli invasion **1982** Israeli invasion; assassination of President Gemayel; massacres in Sabra and Shatila camps **1985** Israeli withdrawal to "security zone"; Camp Wars begin **1986-88** Fighting among former allies on both sides **1988** Third Israeli invasion; presidential elections cancelled; rival governments set up in East and West Beirut **1989** Aoun's "Liberation War"; Taif peace accord ratified **1990** Renewed inter-Christian war; release of some foreign hostages; reunification of Beirut; new Syrian-backed Government of National Unity **1991** Lebanon-Syria treaty; more foreign hostages released **1992** General elections

⟿ LEBANON ⟿

Lebanon contains 17 religious groups, the largest being Shi'a Muslims, Sunni Muslims, and Maronite Christians. Also politically significant are the Druze (the Druze faith is an early offshoot from Islam). Lebanon was a province of the Ottoman empire; after World War One the state was established under French mandate within its present borders, and the Maronites had privileged status. Independence in 1943 was based on a National Pact to share power among the religious communities according to population figures from a 1932 census, which showed Christians to be a slight majority. The president was to be a Maronite, the prime minister a Sunni, the speaker of parliament a Shi'ite. Subsequent population growth removed the Christian majority, while skewed economic development gave the greatest benefits of the thriving economy to urban elites, creating severe tensions.

Another destabilising factor was the presence of Palestinians expelled from Israel in 1948 and 1967 and from Jordan in 1970, who may now number 400,000. A 1969 agreement gave the PLO authority over the refugee camps and some areas of the south, which became the base of PLO operations until 1982, and targets of Israeli attack.

Civil war broke out in 1975, going through several stages and changing alliances between political/religious groups. It was sustained and intensified by the involvement of foreign powers—particularly Israel, Syria and the US—and Cold War tensions. Some 80% of the population was never actively involved, though everyone was affected by insecurity, physical damage and the collapse of the economy. Government power, revenue and services collapsed, and at times militias ruled large areas of the country. Between 1975 and 1991, at least 150,000 were killed, up to 600,000 emigrated (especially men), and 20-30% of the population were displaced within the country, often several times.

The first phase saw the Christian Lebanese Front defend the status quo against a more progressive National Movement, which was joined by the Palestinians. Some 50,000 mostly non-combatants died in savage sectarian killing, and Beirut was divided into Christian East and Muslim West—separated by the "Green Line". In 1976 the president asked Syria to intervene—the start of a continuing armed Syrian presence—but intermittent fighting continued. Israel invaded the south in 1978, displacing 250,000 people to Beirut.

Israel's 1981 attacks and 1982 invasion aimed to destroy the PLO and reduce the power of Syria. After fierce resistance in the streets of Beirut, the PLO was eventually evacuated, under international protection— which failed to prevent the massacre of civilian Palestinians in Sabra and Shatila refugee camps by Israeli-backed Christian militias.

The next few years saw continual struggles, often between former allies. Shi'ite Amal militia fought the Palestinians from 1985-87 in the "Camp Wars"; a Government of National Unity was established in 1984, but its plan to deconfessionalise the political system fell victim to a coup within the Christian Lebanese Forces; former Muslim/leftist allies fought in West Beirut. When Parliament failed to elect a new president in 1988, the crisis deepened with two rival governments being set up, one Christian in East Beirut under General Aoun, one Sunni in West Beirut. Fighting between them erupted in 1989.

The same year, the Lebanese parliament met in Taif, Saudi Arabia, and accepted an Arab League peace plan. But Aoun, leading a populist Christian movement opposed to Syrian interference, rejected the plan, and fought fiercely against another Christian faction within East Beirut, with some of the heaviest damage and loss of life of the entire war. Syrian forces attacked him in October 1990, and Aoun fled to France. Since then Lebanon has experienced relative peace—under a strong Syrian military presence. Most of the militias are disarmed, the first parliamentary elections for 20 years were held in 1992, and efforts to reconstruct the country are under way. In the south Israel's continued occupation of a "security zone" is resisted by the Shi'ite Hizbollah militias, provoking retaliatory attacks, often affecting civilians. For Palestinian refugees, the future looks bleak: the current Israeli/Palestinian peace plan includes no plans for them, and they are still denied Lebanese citizenship and the right to integrate into Lebanese society.

In Lebanon's male-dominated society, women played little part in the politics which caused the war, and few participated in fighting or in military support roles. Insecurity may have increased families' closeness and protectiveness towards women; but women had to sustain their families in very difficult conditions, often moving into the workforce for the first time, and were active in many NGOs supplying the services that government was failing to provide: education, medical, relief and welfare.

Interviews were collected by Ramla Khalidi, Mirvat Abou Khalil, Kitty Warnock and members of the Rassemblement Démocratique des Femmes Libanaises, with the cooperation of the Middle East Council of Churches and the Association Najdeh.

Wadad   LEB 16

Wadad is Chair of the Committee of Families of the Kidnapped.

I consider that all Lebanese participated in the war. Not only those who carried arms. Even the person who sat at home, in his heart was happy for one side and shunning the other.

While I was growing up I knew that I belonged to a country which belongs to a group of Arab countries; I have drunk Arabism since I was a little girl. In [our] area were both Muslims and Christians and we were good friends. Then [hatred] grew... For me to come and kidnap you because I am a Muslim and you are a Christian, without you having committed any crime, I used to find it strange; and when it happened [to me] I refused to believe it.

Unfortunately, everything we learned in books about the country's glory and its 17 different sects, and that it's the Switzerland of the Middle East—we memorised these things as though they were the national anthem. In the end we became disgusted with them, the sea and the mountains and the **cedar**, and wished they didn't exist so that we could live in a normal place.

For the sake of the cedar we butchered each other: "Who loves the cedar most?" Nobody said, "If we love the country we should stay united to take care of it."

During the war I was partial to one side, and used to help in social things, cleaning-up campaigns, first aid. I had small children and I was afraid. Adnan my husband was more active, especially during the Israeli invasion. This I consider to be very different from the civil war. Any citizen who contributed with a drop of blood, or a loaf of bread, to [the stand] against Israel, can be proud. Adnan was not a soldier. He supported the people who stayed in Beirut, ensuring that there was flour for bakeries, fuel and petrol for the hospitals, water.

The people **The kidnapping**
who were
kidnapped [My husband] was kidnapped in 1982. Two men came to the door.
have names They showed us official cards, and said the enquiry had to do with
a car accident. [I was surprised.] Every day a hundred people were
butchered or shot—at this moment, this was important? But
Adnan said, "Don't worry."

The five minutes after which they said he would return became
I don't know how many days [before] I comprehended what had
happened. I began to check up with the authorities immediately,
[but] all my efforts came to nothing. They said, "Poor Wadad,
many have complained before you." But... I wanted to know who
these others were.

The birth of the Committee

One day I had an idea. There are many private radio stations, so I
put a short notice on the air to the families of the kidnapped,
calling on them to meet. Maybe someone would come, and instead
of being alone I would be more effective with two or three others.
I was surprised at the numbers who turned up, hundreds. Most of
us were women, because at the time there was a state of
emergency or something and [men] were being rounded up from
each and every way. We decided to go to the prime minister. We
hadn't planned, we took the steps as we went along.

Of course the soldiers did not let us reach the PM's office. [The
women] began chanting and screaming, and finally [the guards]
said, "Five of you can go in." We argued about the five. We all
wanted to go. Each one wants to ask about her husband or son or
daughter. The yelling began, and 10 or 15 who were able to fight
their way through got to the jeep.

We hadn't prepared anything. We saw the prime minister and
told him the situation. Some were crying, some talking, some
cursing. Every one of us showed her grief in some way. Of course
he told us he would do his best, but we decided to continue this
work; and eventually we founded the Committee.

The first thing in my head was that the people who were
kidnapped have names. We started to make lists. [We have] the
names of 2,111 people, certainly not the complete number. In the
first two years we were active almost every day, and used all means
to demand our relatives—demonstrations, meetings, sit-ins. There
was not one political or religious official we did not meet.

We put a lot of pressure on the government, and they set up a
committee, to defuse the issue. We fought hard to be in this
Committee, and after a while the government included us—but it

was useless. [It] included those who were accused of ordering the kidnappings. Of course they put snags in the work so we reached no result whatsoever, in 12 years.

Personal versus collective interests

Once our Committee [of the Families of the Kidnapped] was formed, I no longer asked about Adnan's case individually. I began to consider that [would be] a selfishness or betrayal [of the] cause. I was trying to stop some of the families [who] would ask about their relatives individually. One woman, Umm Nabil, [who] had a primary role in all our actions, was ashamed to tell us that she was asking after her two kidnapped sons. [One of the political parties] was taking money to return her children. We didn't know the story until Umm Nabil was killed. She was not rich. [The "negotiator"] would tell her to bring him such and such an amount. Her family had created a kind of fund, so she took from this fund and borrowed, until all hope was lost that he could take any more money from her—then he killed her. We did a poster for Umm Nabil.

Every now and then we do a re-evaluation of the "troops" to rejuvenate them. We have to remind them that this issue would not have moved but for [them]. We should continue to make demands; 12 years are no small thing when even the taxi fare for [a woman] to come to a meeting is a problem, and she has to leave her children with the neighbour, without cooking for them.

The distress of uncertainty

If someone is killed, it's easier than kidnapping where you don't know if he's dead or alive. You don't know how to deal with yourself. And what do you tell children—do you give them hope that [their] father may come back? We used to reach a point where we just wanted to know. Even if there are only remains, we want the bones, something tangible.

Last year our Committee wrote a memorandum to the government: "OK, now there's a government and a rule of law and you're speaking of reconstruction and peace, this must be part of it, this is a phenomenon that reaches thousands of citizens. Don't you want to include them in the peace process?" We reminded the government that now there are no excuses, we want a real investigation. "We're not asking that you bring the dead from their place of burial. We want to know if any are still alive. If so, release them. And if there is no trace, announce their death. So that we and our children get out of this cycle, and know what to do."

Some people's daily lives hang by the recognition of the death.

Some people's daily lives hang by the recognition of death

One woman has her husband's taxi, that he used to support the family. She won't drive a public car herself, so she tried to sell it to feed her children. She can't, because it's in her husband's name, and her husband is kidnapped.

The need for compensation

We want to remove the traces of the war and forget the past, but you can't guarantee that this will be accepted by children who grew up without a father. And there are things that are impossible to change by talk alone. For many people, it's not a matter of helping them psychologically—the child who could not go to school because the family's breadwinner was kidnapped, or who can't eat properly, or whose mother can't take him to the doctor.

The government didn't answer [our memorandum] with even a little interest. They could do financial and moral things to ease the worries of the family, and make people feel that they belong to this country, and have lost something important. Give them health care, [free] schooling, books. An employee who was kidnapped— give his salary for 10 years and after 10 years and a day, say: "We're sorry, we searched for this person but couldn't find him. We want to inform you that he's passed away and we have to stop his salary; take his pension." None of this was done.

"Punishing an innocent with an innocent"

Maybe [the women of the kidnapped] became more aware, increasing their empathy. They don't have a religious or sectarian bias: Umm Ali sits with Umm George and Odette sits with Fatima. This problem united them and I consider them some of the few in this society who have a very open perspective and a wide lens. They became aware of something called human rights. They did not resort to counter-kidnapping, something they were being pressured to do by political forces who tried to use the issue of the kidnapped to play with. We determined that this wouldn't happen through the families of the kidnapped because we understand the meaning of kidnapping. To kidnap someone just because he's a Christian—and the person who kidnapped my husband belongs to a Christian militia—I would be punishing an innocent with an innocent. Counter-kidnapping did not enter the dictionary of the kidnapped families—they were more aware than the leaders.

"A qualitative transition"

The wife of a kidnapped man goes through several phases: in the first phase, I see her as I used to see myself. She lost everything when she lost her husband, the one she leaned on. With weakness and collapsing and crying, she forgets things, or she dreams strange dreams which seem real. She might say, "I saw him, he put money in my pocket," for example, and she'd wake up and find money. She is forced to stand on her own feet, and search for work, to raise her children. This is an important transition because she is part of this society that used to consider that the woman's place is in the home only. She began to see herself as being important, that she has a role to play. Some of the women until today work in secret, because the narrow society in which they live considers that work is shameful for a woman.

Also she has developed a national awareness. If she hears the news, for example that two party leaders—who have destroyed the country by shelling and killing and kidnapping—are now reconciled and embracing each other, she comments on it: "Who are they kidding?" Before, such things did not concern her and she thought everything being said and done is correct. Now she can analyse and deduce and differentiate between things, and is attached to the word justice. [She knows] that [she] has rights and is going to continue demanding. This is a qualitative transition.

I am like them, though I used to work even when Adnan was here. But when the catastrophe happened there was a thin line between being "poor Wadad" like my family and neighbours and friends wanted, and deciding to stand on my feet. It was the presence of my sons that helped me. I was able to change the perception of society through my actions, to a degree that they began to deal with me as though I was different from other humans. [They think] that I am so strong, that if I am startled or afraid, or if I wanted to leave a meeting early to come and see my kids, these were seen as things that I shouldn't be doing.

Impact of her activism on her own family

This issue [of the kidnapped] touches me so directly, that I consider it is a duty. I became embroiled at the expense of my sons, but I don't regret it. Despite [what it cost] my nerves, my work and my children, I don't think the decision is in my hands to take a back seat.

[When] Adnan was kidnapped, Ziad was six and Ghassan three. I used to wake up and leave to search for Adnan and I would come back late. Their grandparents took care of them. I hadn't told the children what had happened, but there was something abnormal in the air. I told them after a while. It was not easy. Despite their love for Adnan, they took a stand, wanting me with them and being afraid for me. "Don't do this any more, or you too will be

Sometimes the children worry like adults

kidnapped." I was trying my utmost to lessen the negative effects, but with a child talk doesn't do everything. I couldn't free myself to cuddle them and take them away from this environment.

I'm sure despite themselves they hold a grudge against me, this I read in their eyes. They would beg me, "Mom, please don't go to the demonstration." It's not because Adnan does not concern them, on the contrary it's because this has hurt them so much, it's taken away their father and then for many years when they needed me I was not always there for them. Despite myself I hurt them. They don't want to try me but there is an accusation. I'm forgiven, but there is still something which hurts.

With all my feelings of guilt and what I've done against them, when I put the emotional suffering aside, I can see there have also been positive developments for Ziad and Ghassan. They are more mature than children their age. There is an awareness about issues in the country, and beliefs which I did not have to make them read or memorise. They are against oppression, they feel with others, they listen to others, they try to help. But this has a negative side: sometimes they worry like adults.

This doesn't apply to all the children of the kidnapped. Ziad and Ghassan continued to go to school, but there are children who were forced on to the streets, to sell chewing gum. They have been marginalised, and some may have the feeling that they need to avenge the crime. I can't rule out that my children might also stray, but until now they appear sound.

Personal and public responsibility

That the files of the kidnapped are still open, I hold the government responsible. I lack trust in my government so long as it has not done its minimum duty towards me as a citizen. I hold a grudge against the kidnappers, but of course I wouldn't go and blow them up. First I don't have the means to do that, but I consider that there is a government that is responsible for me. It contains me and the kidnapper, the victim and the criminal, so I ask of the government who knows who the criminal is, if it doesn't want to punish him or kill him, at least put his evil away from me. Why should I continue to be a victim and why should he no longer be a criminal? If I continue to make my demands, why should I be turned into criminal and he is rewarded?

My motives were initially personal but they became general. Like everyone who was exposed to the war in all its ugliness, I feel I have a responsibility to ensure that war does not break out again. I can't stand aside, I can't accept that "Wadad's husband was kidnapped and she's following up the story". Of course. But this is not separate from belonging to a country and the reconstruction of a country where so many norms fell apart after 17 years of war. Every citizen has a role, every real citizen who wants to see a nation instead of 17 sects.

What prevents the same thing happening again if there is another outbreak? The history should be written, and why shouldn't these things be known and recorded with accuracy? If we deny it, we are distorting and lying about our history.

What prevents the same thing happening again?

"A booby-trapped peace"

The damage is done, what's happened to the country in victims and ruins and twisting of minds. But the more dangerous thing that I fear is that we're building for a new war. People are happy that the shelling has stopped, but we fear the future.

Are we trying—as Wadad, as the government—to rebuild the mentality or the institutions in a new way, not like the old ones which fuelled the war? Under the name of peace and reconstruction confessionalism still has a major role in the country. In jobs, anything, there is a quota between the sects. If I'm a Christian and I want to be employed there should be a Muslim counterpart. This is one of the more serious issues and it's taking root.

This is a booby-trapped peace. It's not enough that I see beautiful skyscrapers, and a highway extending from the sea to the Gulf, and bridges and tunnels and cellular phones. In the end if I only rebuild the stone and sand and steel, if I don't rebuild the people first... The reform of people is much more important because eventually they'll be the ones who will fix and rebuild the country. This citizen who is really a citizen will hesitate a hundred times before he breaks a traffic signal or vandalises a building.

They tell us we should be thankful we have electricity [for] I don't know how many hours, and telephones, and the roads don't have as many potholes. But we're paying taxes, and electricity bills, and paying to allow our cars on the road. So this is a minimum [the government] should provide me. Why should I feel obliged to them? Let me feel that I am a human with my dignity and my rights, before they build buildings that my eyesight can't reach the top of. Before that they should be constructing houses for the thousands of refugees.

I hope there
will never be
peace. I hope
for total
destruction

Umm Hamad   LEB 2

Umm Hamad means "Mother of Hamad", and is the respectful form of
address for married women in Arab countries—Hamad was her eldest son.
A Palestinian, she has been a refugee in Lebanon since 1948. At present she
lives in Shatila camp in south Beirut.

I was eight years old when I left my birthplace Haifa, and we ran
because of our enemies, the Zionists, who are calling for peace. But
I hope there will never be peace. I hope for total destruction for
them and for us. My sister was planning to get married. [When we
ran] she took a few of the costumes she had made, so these clothes
meant for a bride became covers to protect the children on the
road. The Zionists are so happy and taking advantage of everything
that is rightfully ours, while we are still passing through hardships.

What is there for us Palestinians in Lebanon to hope for? Our
future is not in Lebanon. Even sitting under a tree at home in
Palestine is better than to be here and to be called a refugee. We
have offered the things that were most precious to our hearts, and
we did so in order to get something in return, but we find we are
still refugees—what does this mean? These peace talks are not for
our benefit; we feel cheated by those compromises of the
Gaza/Jericho agreement. But it's out of our hands, we cannot do
anything. Allah takes care of everybody. Our future is very shaky,
we don't know what is going to happen to us.

Sometimes we feel that we want to settle, just sit and live, but even
then obstacles are put in front of us. In Jordan, Palestinians have civil
and legal rights, and in Syria, but in Lebanon we have none of that.

"Mother of the three martyrs"

My mother is Lebanese, but I don't love my Lebanese relatives,
because of the '85 **Camp War**. They are Shi'ites, I don't want
anything to do with them. My heart cannot bear the idea of mixing
with them, especially after losing my sons.

This house was destroyed in 1982; then in '85, and in '87. In '82
we left Shatila and went to central Beirut during the Israeli
invasion, then we came back and were welcomed by the
massacre. I lost my sister-in-law in the massacre, and my three
sons in the Camp Wars. I have six daughters. We lost the boys and
kept the girls. The girls are more tender and caring and helpful
than the boys. What my daughters have done for me cannot be
compared with what the sons did, may God be my witness.

My youngest daughter went on a mission against the Israelis in
1988, after she lost her three brothers and her home. She was

captured and held prisoner in the south of Lebanon. At first girls *My daughter's* from the Hizbollah used to bring me news, but now it's been two *letter would* years since I heard anything. She was 17. One day she was having *make rocks cry* a lesson in Islam at home. She asked the Sheikh, "Is a suicide mission a sin?" I didn't think at the time that she meant herself. One day she went to school and never came back. She took off her jewellery and left it for me with a letter. This letter would make rocks cry. She wrote, "To my mother, the mother of the three martyrs: Look what the Zionists are doing to us. Remember our people in Tel az-Zaatar, remember the massacre. So when you hear what I have done, please have a smile on your face. It is not the one who loses his mother and father who is an orphan, but the one who loses his country."

Everyone had to become strong in those years, fear became a weak notion. She was put in **Khiyam prison** which shows she was strong and did not give in. I wish I were with her.

The massacre

We had come back after the Israeli invasion, and we stayed in one small room. My daughter saw from the window one of her neighbours killed, so she ran and told us, "They are killing us, there is a massacre." We ran down to a shelter. Then a neighbour came and said, "Whoever can, get on your feet and run for your life, because they are killing us here." So we left the shelter, and ran barefoot to the mosque.

The mosque was so crowded, we all piled in. There was no way out. When we could escape we went and hid in the shelter of [a big] building next to the camp. Next to [it] they were calling through loudspeakers, "Surrender and you will be saved." But how could they expect us to surrender, when we had already seen dead bodies?

We fled [again] to the Gaza hospital. They wouldn't let us in because it was already too crowded—we were lucky because just a few hours later the **Kataeb** arrived and took all the people in there.

I had grabbed about 30 kids from the camp with us. This army and I left the hospital, and walked to the Barbir area where we found an Israeli tank. There were so many people with us now, so many people fleeing, it was like a demonstration. I was carrying my baby granddaughter, and I was waving a white cloth. I threw myself on the tank because they were blocking the way and we needed to pass, and I didn't care because I was going to die anyway and I might as well confront them.

The officer came and talked to us, but I couldn't talk clearly. I

Identifying the dead: Shatila camp massacre
Micha Bar'Am/Magnum

was in a panic and saying a hundred words at once, so the officer told the translator to slow down so he could understand. I said, "Can't you see, there is a massacre." "Take us to it." I said, "On top of everything else I have to ride with you?" Finally they opened the road, and so many people, as many as the hairs on my head, surged through. They were trying to hide anywhere, but all the residents in that area were afraid and the doors were shut in our face.

The minute the massacre was over, the first women to go back in were me and my neighbour. No journalists, nobody dared go in. My sister-in-law went to get milk for her son, she disappeared, we don't know what happened to her. Alleys were covered with bodies, piled on top of each other like sardines in a tin, everywhere. They had taken all the people who had come out of the shelter; they were not shot but hit by a **balta**—you could tell, their heads were smashed in. The sun was hot that day, and they were so swollen that their clothes didn't fit them any more. At that point I lost all my senses. I went into a house and it seemed so quiet, I saw bodies under the bed, a family of five who had all been killed. There were reporters coming in. I grabbed one by the hair and showed him this house.

They had entered the house of my mother-in-law [but] didn't kill her. She was about 80, with her neighbour who was equally old, and her deaf husband. They found them crouching in the corner hiding. They said, "Who is with you?" She said, "I am here, and my neighbour." Then they heard the old man coughing upstairs. "Who is that?" "He can't hear you, it's her husband." They said, "Aren't you scared being here by yourself?" "Yes dear, but I am too old to move." "We are going to raze the house, aren't you scared? Leave the house." She said, "Where are we going to go? Just to sit outside in the streets?" And they left them. They probably thought they would die anyway because they had no food. That's how we found them, all in the room.

Aside from rifles, I'm also trained on tanks

Ahlam   LEB 5

Ahlam is a young Druze woman who participated as a fighter during the war.

In the beginning I was the only woman and then a few friends joined. We started helping in the clinic, then we began to feel that the men needed help, maybe to refill cartridges—if we can help more, then why not? We would not say, "We want to fight": that is forbidden. We would say, "We'll take the training." So we do the training, then there's a short trip, then... you know, slowly. By that time I was married. My husband said, "You must learn if you want to go with us. If you don't, if I always have to be scared about you, then I will want you to stay at home." I had no children, and I wanted to help them, so I started training. Aside from rifles, I'm also trained on tanks. I was the only woman, and I came third in the training course, that was very nice.

We were enthusiastic and happy during the war, not because we were killing people, but because we were at ease, we knew we were keeping a danger away. My tank was mine, I was responsible for it, like my own car, and I was fighting for our land and helping our brothers.

In the beginning everybody would ask how a woman or a girl could do this? Then the idea began to sink in and they began accepting it. Later my family, because of my achievement, were showing off that I did this or that.

One who believes in something goes on. If I don't die maybe my honour would die, and [for] one whose honour is insulted, maybe

We did not choose war, war came to us

death is better. If I had a daughter I would have her do the same. Even my son now, I am teaching him that I am happy I did what I did. I regret very much that I was not photographed and I have no pictures. Human nature is forgetful, but I will tell my son what happened. We will live with [Christians], but the new generation should know what happened so that it doesn't happen again: [the Christians] did this to us, they planned to kick us out of our homes, and we will not forget.

We could not avoid the war. We woke up one day to find the Lebanese Forces at our doorstep, firing at our house. We could not leave. Where is there any room to avoid war? We did not choose war, war came to us.

Intisar   LEB 7

28-year-old Intisar is a Sunni Muslim and lives in Baalbek.

I encouraged armed men to make war—not for the sake of fighting but because of our shortage of basic needs. We lack water and electricity, and it is women who have to deal with these problems. I requested all men to give women their support. In my opinion, the purpose of war was to cancel religious extremism, to have equality in our society, and to eliminate religious discrimination in work.

Changing view of the war

I was 11 years old when the war started. Like every Lebanese child, I was frightened. My house was attacked many times by armed men. Even now this makes me feel insecure.

At first, I was very enthusiastic for the war. But after all these years, I am convinced that the only result was the destruction of our country and the displacement of its inhabitants. In 1972, one of my brothers was killed in a battle in South Lebanon, and my second brother was killed in Beirut. We feel that we lost precious people for nothing. Now we are disgusted with this war.

I don't think the war is finished for good yet, because we have still not got our rights as Lebanese citizens. War remains the only solution for hopeless poor people to ensure their needs. This civil war was not Christians against Muslims, but war for equality in rights for all the citizens. We request our government to establish new and free schools, public hospitals, to fulfil plans to create work for people, and to meet our needs so that we feel secure.

Marie   LEB 11

47-year-old Marie is an academic. She stayed in the United States from 1977 to 1985, after her father was kidnapped and killed early in the civil war. She is a Christian, but lives in West Beirut.

Sometimes it was very exciting, living through shelling and surviving, living with life and death—you had a great rush of adrenalin. There was a time when the only people in our apartment building were us and an old neighbour, everyone else had left. We were determined not to leave, not to be driven out by the Syrians. We often huddled in the kitchen. My daughter says it was exciting for her too. She remembers being at home together under the shelling, making puppet plays. We were in a state of suspended animation. All you think about is survival.

You collapse with exhaustion after the excitement. I was depressed for nine months after the war ended. I had made a decision not to be frightened. I was much less nervous than my husband, for instance. I don't know what that cost me psychologically, I am still paying for it probably.

"War is what happens afterwards"

In some ways war is easier for women. Whatever the situation, even in shelters, they are busy, looking after the children, managing the house. Men meanwhile have lost their role, if they cannot go out to work. When we were here, with relatives who had taken refuge with us from East Beirut, I wouldn't let anyone touch the dishes, for instance. We had very little water, and washing up with little water is difficult, but I was determined to keep control of everything. When we didn't have any bread, and there wasn't any electricity for the oven, I found a recipe for making bread in a frying pan; that seemed a very exciting achievement.

War is a different experience for different people—I would not be saying this if I was trapped in one room with a disabled husband. The real experience of war is not the shelling, those are just moments, though they are the ones you see on TV. War is what happens afterwards, the years of suffering hopelessly with a disabled husband and no money, or struggling to rebuild when all your property has been destroyed.

Women's power

I can understand how people kill. I never believe anyone who says "I could never kill anyone". There were times when I would have shot people if I'd had a gun. I don't think women are any different

Women my age have the power to intimidate young men

from men in that way. There were times of collective madness, when people were misled by all sorts of propaganda.

Women my age have a power we do not use nearly enough— the power to intimidate young men, because we are like their mothers. If we look them in the eye and challenge them, as if they were our sons... How can we do this if we dye our hair and try to look young? We lose the authority, without ever actually being taken for younger than we are. And this is something younger women cannot do. How many women of 20 can look a man in the eye? You have to know a lot about sex to be able to do it, and if she did, he would take it as a sexual invitation.

Men wouldn't rape Lebanese women, they are too much protected by their community. But towards the end of the war, one heard of a lot of rape of Sri Lankan women, I suppose because they are alone and vulnerable [working as domestic servants in Lebanon].

The war came at just the wrong time for women's liberation. With the war, people's only security was with their family and their community—it reinforced the old structures and control. But perhaps things will open up again now. Now 50% of the students in universities are women. During the war women were at home with nothing much to do except study. Their standards are very high.

Jeanette   LEB 15

Jeanette, an ex-teacher, was displaced to Beirut. She wonders where she will go when the displaced are obliged to move back to their home areas as part of the reconstruction process.

I had three houses and I lost everything. I had a house in Dammour [which] I bought myself—I used to teach and I saved and bought the house, before I got married. In the summers I took the children [there] for the three months.We left Dammour in 1975. Suddenly the war broke out [and] the Syrians took Dammour. We stayed 12 days under bombardment, one couldn't get out. When they had taken the town, **Chamoun** said, "It is finished, the roads are open, go where you like." More than 5,000 people went up to Debiye. We watched our own house burn on our way up. We brought nothing from Dammour, everything was burnt.

The house [in Debiye] was my husband's. There were 45 [refugees]. We put them on the floor everywhere, with cushions. They had to eat. In the mountains we had provisions, flour, wheat. I called a woman there to make bread and she made 40 flat loaves for breakfast. They left one by one, after 20, 25 days.

Jeanette stays in the mountains for four years, but spends the winters in Jiyye so her daughter can attend school. Israeli attacks from the sea eventually force the family to move again, to the house of a doctor friend in Beirut.

The war came at just the wrong time for women's liberation

My daughter is married, just this year. She is expecting a baby. We haven't got anything to give, a bit of linen and clothes for the baby. I am happy that she is married, because she is my only child. It was because of us that she waited so long before marrying. She has known him for a long time. He is a neighbour, a Muslim, so at first we didn't want it. He is very good, he has a house, which his uncle gave him. Before she married I told her, you must make sure that everything in the house belongs to you, so he did it in her name—so if he ever leaves her, she will stay in the house and it will be him who goes outside—he accepted that. We are all under Allah. She has no problem with his family. When she has her baby... he likes Christians, and if she has a boy he is going to call him Joe. He is very nice, religions are the same to him. He will baptise his children. He will not talk about it in front of his relatives, because they might talk and people would make trouble for him. It is just between her and him. Why talk about it? He doesn't pray or anything, he blasphemes the mosque and the church the same!

I would like to go back to one of the places I have lived, but the houses are demolished. At Debiye, it still has a roof but it's in need of repair. We haven't any money to repair it, nor to rebuild the house at Dammour. And now, where I am, the doctor has returned, and he wants his house back. I have told him, "I can't go. Do you want us to sit on the road?" But he has the right, it is his house.

I don't feel anything towards the people who destroyed my homes, because the whole of Lebanon is demolished. Christians, Muslims, Druze, everybody has been killed. There are people much worse off than us, with little children.

Laure   LEB 1

Laure is a lawyer, a grandmother, active in the Lebanese Association for Human Rights and a founder member of the Movement for Non-Violence.

Women are absent from power—from politics, from unions, even from important NGOs. They were not among those who decided on the war. Well, if they had been in the centres of power, what would they have decided? One mustn't make optimistic assumptions.

There is a passivity in women. Women's organisations don't seek power, they do social work, in the traditional sense of the word; so they were not at all prepared to make militant decisions themselves, or to confront the decisions made by others. They were a bit isolated, and their objectives, alas, were still fairly traditional. They took care of orphans, shelter, first aid—always the traditional roles of women. It is to the credit of Lebanese women that they did not take part in the war, and now they have certainly worked hard to heal the ills the war created, and have made many sacrifices. But if they didn't participate in the war, they didn't on the whole oppose it either; they didn't make a strong movement against the war.

Women don't think in terms of being citizens, they think of their role in the family. They certainly protected their families. I am the mother of five children, I know what mothers in Lebanon had to suffer, feeding their children, cooking without water, electricity, or gas. How could you even boil eggs, if you were lucky enough to have any? This touched women more than men, it was they who were in charge of caring for the family.

"Peace is for everybody"

At the beginning, all the actions against the war were taken by women. But I didn't want women to be doing things in isolation, so as not to marginalise women even more. Peace is for everybody. So it was a women's movement, but we were always calling on men as well. Above all we insisted on including all religions; nothing was done without representatives from all the confessions.

The fact that we were women did help us. There is still in this oriental society a concept of honour, which protects women a little. I and my husband were kidnapped twice, near the demarcation line, as we were coming out of meetings. We thought our end was approaching, and they said to me, "You get into the car." But I could say to a militia man, "I am from Beirut, Beirut is for both of us, I am your sister, your mother..." and he would say, "OK." It was because I was a woman that I could have this discussion. I am sure that a man would not have been able to. He couldn't touch me or push me.

There was a manifesto of Lebanese intellectuals for a united Lebanon, and it was very largely women. There were four or five men who signed with us. Perhaps women were able to move about, they dared give their opinion, we were less watched perhaps—but in this particular group, we certainly showed more courage.

Women "against the current"

Let us talk about initiatives women took in working against the war. In 1975, in the name of the National Council of Lebanese Women, we took apart some barricades... just a symbolic action. Then I called a meeting of lawyers. We were all in our lawyers' robes, so as you can imagine the papers got hold of this straight away. We made a manifesto: non-use of violence, dialogue, the rule of law...

Perhaps we have only been tools of war, but very active tools

A committee [that later become the Movement for Non-Violence] tried in 1984 to hold a big demonstration on the demarcation line, Muslims and Christians. That day the bombardment was terrible. Certain members of this committee were afraid, and if anyone telephoned me to ask "What are we doing?" I would say, "I am going, but you must do what you like." We were very few the next day, and in front of the TV cameras, we announced that this march would not happen, because it was a big responsibility. But we said to ourselves, we will replace this march by a collection of signatures on a Peace Charter.

We went from door to door, to collect signatures: "We the Lebanese proclaim peace among ourselves." It was important to talk about peace and unity and the responsibility of the Lebanese. People talk as if it was not our fault, they blame the Israelis, the Palestinians, the Americans, the Syrians... I always tell them, "These wars that we have, we have carried them out. Perhaps we have only been tools, but very active tools. Other countries do have interests here, but in the end it is we who killed one another."

This argument was not well-received. The militias did not like it on either side, nor higher level politicians. We were going against the current. We continued to cross the line, as if nothing was happening, from one side to the other, so we were badly received—"Where do you come from?" "From Beirut." "Which Beirut?" But for me there is only one Beirut, and that was hard for people to accept.

The Movement for Non-Violence, with the National Association for the Handicapped, did a famous March for Peace and Human Rights. It was to show that we refused the division of the country. We crossed Lebanon, three days from the north to the south, Christian, Muslim, and Druze areas. The roads were full of militias, the army, everybody, but nobody touched us because we had a group of 54 handicapped people—50 wheelchairs, four blind people. We were about 100. When we telephoned the army at the beginning, they tried to dissuade us, saying, "We can't take this responsibility." We said, "It's not your responsibility, it's ours." We were trembling for the people we were leading.

The militias were shocked but I don't know if it had any effect on them. They were so indoctrinated... they probably took us for fools.

Another time we made a big poster of "United Lebanon" and covered the demarcation line with it. We had organised a big demonstration with people from all the parties of Lebanon. At six o'clock in the morning we were there, all the women... but the television, and the movements who were supposed to come, didn't come. So we women set ourselves to sticking up the posters [but] we didn't have any paste because we hadn't been expecting to do this. A few taxi drivers who saw this strange sight got out and said, "I am coming to help you." It was very moving. At about 11 o'clock the general of the army calls me: "Madame, are you responsible for this?" "Yes." He said, "You are asked to come over to this side of the line." I said, "No, our witness doesn't have any importance unless we are on the line." "I am ordering you." I said, "You cannot give me an order, I am a citizen and these are citizens with me." "It is your responsibility then."

Non-violence as action

Non-violence is not very well understood as a strategy for action. It is not just pacifism. We held two information seminars, but you see how much we were against the current, we couldn't find a place to hold them. Nobody wanted to host a seminar on non-violence, for fear of being attacked.

When we made a logo for the Movement, the artist didn't understand that non-violence is a force, and he did a dove with a heart—then happily someone had the idea of a strong hand, a fist.

People feel that it was "other people's war", and they say the government is responsible for the peace. But it is us, the citizens. We were responsible for the war, we are responsible for the peace. What are we doing? How are we educating our children for peace? Recently someone wanted to interview my grandchildren, some little Christians. He said to Ziad who is eight, "Do you have friends who are Muslims?" Ziad said, "I have never asked them." "Why not?" Ziad said, "They are just like me, we play together, we go to school together." Ziad was frightened: "I don't know who is Christian and who is Muslim." Joseph and I are Catholics but we gave our children Arab names which do not show their religious identity. We tried at the beginning of the war to get many people to name their children with these names.

We must give education in the family, and in schools. It sounds a bit like a slogan of UNESCO: it is in the heads of men that war is made, and it is in the spirit of men that peace must be created.

As women, it's all very well to say we are outside power, but if we wish to be partners, we must be partners in the construction as well. We are not going to be given things, we have to make them, we have to participate, as agents and as beneficiaries. We have the power of NGOs, that is a great power, and the power of civil society, which we can develop.

The Lebanese Association for Human Rights has achieved quite a lot for women—against the violence that women suffer, not just women who are beaten, but the violence of the laws, and of ignorance. It is against illiteracy, and customs that are against women. We drew up a strategy for action to inform women of their rights: "Know your rights in order to exercise and promote them." Women must not just be victims, they must exercise their rights and help to formulate and modify the laws, because we are in a democratic regime where citizens have a role in the creation of laws. We did a series of guides called "Know your rights". We treat the problems of women as the problems of human beings. Our second guide will be called "I am a citizen": as a citizen, what do I have to know? What is the legislative power, the executive power, what are NGOs, what is non-violence?

It's in the head that war is made; it's in the spirit the peace must be created

← GLOSSARY →

LIBERIA

kobo	Nigerian currency. 100 *kobo* = one *naira*
8,000 *naira*	at the time, about US$150 on the black market
Octopus	NPLF codename for their second major campaign, 1992-93, when they attacked ECOMOG and Monrovia

SOMALILAND

"brothers' wars"	the bloody confrontations of early 1992 between different militias of the Isaaq clan
faataha	the first verse from the Qur'an
qat	a mildly narcotic leaf widely chewed in Somaliland, mainly by men
shilling	2,800 shillings = US$1 (1995)
tabeleh	after the war between the government and SNM intensified in 1985, *tabeleh* committees were established to monitor movement in residential districts. Families would be questioned about any "guests" (especially men). The objective was to discourage information passing between the SNM and civilians

TIGRAY (ETHIOPIA)

birr	1 *birr* = 15-20 US cents (1995)
EPRP	Ethiopian People's Revolutionary Party: another opposition group which, like the TPLF, had its origins in the student-led opposition to Haile Selassie in the early 1970s. The TPLF emerged as the stronger movement, but not without conflict
February's light	refers to the launching of the TPLF's armed struggle against the Derg, on 18 February 1975
Front	TPLF
injera	a flat bread made from a local grain, *teff*, or from sorghum
quintal	a measure equivalent to 100 lbs
wearing trousers	female TPLF fighters were generally the first women wearing trousers that rural people had ever seen

UGANDA

Cilil	a rebel group, literally meaning "go and get them"
Holy Spirit/*Lakwena*	a movement among the Acholi against
Kony	Museveni's NRM from 1986. The leader, Alice, was believed possessed by a holy spirit, "Lakwena", who spoke through her. Alice was succeeded by Joseph Kony, leader of the

	Lord's Resistance Army. Followers of both movements were mostly disaffected ex-soldiers
panga	broad, heavy knife used as a tool or weapon
posho	beans and corn mash
RC	refers to elected member of Resistance Council, the administrative system set up by the NRM. Every council has one woman member. RCs were seen by rebels as representing the government and by the army as protecting rebels
salt	at this time, salt was in such short supply, people valued it more than clothes or soap

INDIA

Babri Masjid	the mosque pulled down by Hindu fundamentalists in 1992, provoking extensive communal rioting. It was said to have been built on the birthplace of the Hindu god Rama
babus	literally, upper-class gentleman, but here middle-class people generally, and specifically the relief workers
granthi	Sikh religious teacher and community leader
gurdwara	Sikh place of worship and community centre
house	the Indian government set up housing for those widows whose homes were destroyed. The extent to which the flats were given outright or were meant to be paid for remains a cause of anxiety for some women
Jinnah	the founder of Pakistan
kafila	a caravan of refugees that was escorted across the new national borders by the military
lakh	100,000 *rupees*
Rajiv Gandhi	Indira Gandhi's son, who became prime minister and was assassinated in 1991. It was widely believed in India that his assassin, a young Tamil woman, had been raped by the Indian Peace-Keeping Force in Sri Lanka. It was also felt by many that he and his party bore responsibility for the 1984 riots
rakhee	a thread which Hindu and Sikh girls tie on to a brother or cousin's wrist to signify bonds of mutual love and protection, at an annual festival called Raksha Bandhan
rupees	31 *rupees* = US$1 (1995)
Sultanpuri	area of Delhi where the anti-Sikh rioting was particularly severe
thava	flat, circular iron griddle used for cooking

12th day	the 12th or 13th day ceremony for the dead is common ritual for Hindu and Sikh families
Urdu	one of the primary languages of South Asian Muslims

SRI LANKA

Ayurvedic	classical Indian medical system
Burgher	descendents of Dutch colonists
rupees	49 *rupees* = US$1 (1995)

VIETNAM

Agent orange	Chemical defoliant used by the Americans to deny the Vietcong cover. It contained dioxin, a highly toxic substance with devastating effects on humans, including illness and genetic damage, affecting their future children
Cu Chi	this area was famous for its wartime labyrinth of underground tunnels and its role in the 1960s in facilitating Vietcong control of a large rural area only 30 km from Saigon (Ho Chi Minh City)
heroic villages	honour given to villages and communes which played an important part during the war against the South
re-education camps	forced labour camps for people who had ties with the US/South Vietnamese regime
social activities	social activism or social work
strategic hamlets	fortified encampments built to house people relocated from Communist-controlled areas
thankful house	house given by a village to a family that has made an unusual sacrifice during the war
Uncle Ho	(1890-1969) First President of the Democratic Republic of Vietnam from 1945 until his death. Founder of the Indochina Communist Party, he led Vietnam first to independence from France and then in the struggle to reunify the country. Highly revered as the father of his country, he asked Vietnamese to address him simply as "Uncle Ho"

EL SALVADOR

compa	FMLN fighter
compañero/a	partner, companion or comrade
Frente	FMLN
guinda	collective escape during the war to escape army repression
LP-28	People's League of February 28th, a leading popular coalition linked to ERP

Martínez	General Martínez was dictator between 1931 and 1944 and played a major part in the 1932 massacre
Nuevo Gualcho	one of the repopulated communities, established in the main by returning refugees
operativo	armed forces' attack, targeting civilians, crops and livestock
Púchica	Salvadoran expression of surprise
return	organised mass repatriations of refugees
tatu	underground hiding place
zone	areas where the FMLN and the army were fighting for military and political control

NICARAGUA

compañero/a	partner, companion or comrade
córdoba	7.2 *córdobas* = US$1 (1995)
Frente	FSLN
19th July	anniversary of the triumph of the Sandinista Revolution (victory over Somoza)
piñata	large doll filled with sweets. At festivals, it is hung up high and battered open with sticks by blindfolded children, showering them with sweets
Resistance	National Resistance Army (Contras)

CROATIA AND BOSNIA

Bajram	a Muslim holiday
Belgrade	in 1992, during the Serbian-Croatian war, two women organised a rally in Belgrade for over 3,000 women from all over Yugoslavia
chetnik	member of World War II Serbian fascist militia. Used today for extreme Serb nationalists
Dubrovnik	an ancient Croatian town on the Adriatic, of great cultural significance
KOS	Yugoslav Counter Intelligence Service
mark	the German *mark* has informally become standard currency throughout former Yugoslavia. 1 *mark* = US$1.45 (1995)
Matica	state-sponsored organisation set up to preserve national, in this case Croatian, cultural and linguistic heritage
Pale	village above Sarajevo from which Serbs attacked, and still attack, Sarajevo
partisans	fighters against facism and for the re-establishment of Yugoslavia as an independent communist state during World War Two

ustasha	the fascist movement, supported by Mussolini, which established the Independent State of Croatia in 1941

LEBANON

balta	rock attached to a stick, used for killing animals
Camp War	the Shi'ite Amal movement, supported by the Lebanese army, attacked their former allies the Palestinians, fearing a resurgence of Palestinian power. Three refugee camps in particular—Shatila and Bourj al Barajneh in Beirut, and Rashidiyeh in the south—were heavily beseiged and bombarded
cedar	the cedar tree is the national symbol, and appears on the Lebanese flag. "Cedars of Lebanon" have been famous since biblical times, though few exist now
Chamoun	President Camille Chamoun, member of one of the principal Maronite Christian families
Kataeb	(Phalange) militia of a Maronite Christian party, headed by the Gemayel family and part of the Lebanese Forces
Khiyam Prison	prison in the Israeli-occupied strip of southern Lebanon, notorious for its harsh regime
massacre	in September 1982, over 1,000 Palestinian civilians in the refugee camps Sabra and Shatila in south Beirut, were killed by Israeli-backed Christian Lebanese Forces, in the aftermath of the Israeli invasion, PLO withdrawal, and assassination of President Beshir Gemayel

Figures used on the map pages are from a variety of sources, but predominantly the UNDP *Human Development Report 1994*, and the World Bank *Social Indicators of Development 1994*

— INDEX —

PANOS ORAL TESTIMONY

Panos Books publishes authoritative, challenging, accessible books offering new and seldom heard perspectives on sustainable development. It is the trading subsidiary of Panos London, an independent information organisation working internationally for development that is socially, environmentally, and economically sustainable.

Panos' Oral Testimony Programme seeks to explore and illustrate the potential of oral testimony in the development process and to gather, publish and amplify the views and experiences of local communities on specific development themes. The next book (1996) will contain testimonies from highland or mountain communities, speaking about the impact of development and the increasing rate of change—social, economic and environmental—in their lives.

PANOS BOOKS

**9 WHITE LION STREET
LONDON N1 9PD, UK**

**TEL (44) 171 278 1111
FAX (44) 171 278 0345**

LISTENING FOR A CHANGE
ORAL TESTIMONY AND DEVELOPMENT
Hugo Slim and Paul Thompson

Contributing editors: Olivia Bennett and Nigel Cross

Listening for a Change is a guide to collecting, using and interpreting oral testimony in the development process. With case-studies from all over the world, it explores the many different ways testimonies can be used, and gives practical guidelines on methods of collection, recording, transcription and translation. It also explores the limitations and ambiguities of oral evidence, as well as ethical issues.
Listening for a Change challenges everyone in the aid world to listen to the awkwardly individual voices of the people at the heart of development.

"Immensely fascinating, as it articulates very succinctly what many of us have felt strongly during our action-research experiences."
Sandhan, development NGO, Jaipur, India

"This book seems at the very least to signal changes in how NGOs might be thinking and working, and it is likely to be influential..."
Anthropology Today, UK, August 1994

AT THE DESERT'S EDGE
ORAL HISTORIES FROM THE SAHEL
Editors: Nigel Cross and Rhiannon Barker

This book explores the culture, history and environment of the Sahel through the memories of its people. "Sahel" is Arabic for the "edge" of the Sahara desert. The region is characterised by low rainfall and poor soils, yet some 60 million people manage to make a living from the land.

At the Desert's Edge draws on interviews conducted with hundreds of men and women from eight Sahelian countries, who have been living through a time of unprecedented social and environmental change. A fascinating blend of stories, anecdotes, information and opinion, it is also a moving testimony to the resilience and resourcefulness of the Sahelian people.

"...a joyful read for the well-informed public and the lay-man alike."
Normadic Peoples, 1992

"...insights come thick and fast...a truly fascinating jumble of ecological, agricultural, culinary or medical titbits embedded in strongly religious yet personalised value systems, and spiked with rich humour... a treat for the reader who wishes to be enlightened and entertained at the same time..."
Development Policy Review, UK, 1992

Panos' oral testimony books will be of interest to anyone working with communities in the collection and dissemination of first-hand testimony, but also policymakers, practitioners and students of social and economic development.

To order copies please send this form to Panos Books, 9 White Lion Street, London N1 9PD UK

Listening for a Change	£9.95/$14.95	No of copies	❑
At the Desert's Edge	£12.95/$19.95	No of copies	❑
Arms to fight, Arms to Protect	£10.95/$15.95	No of copies	❑

I would like a Panos Books Catalogue ❑

Name _____

Address _____

_____